John D. Edwards, JD, MALS
Editor

Emerging Solutions in Reference Services: Implications for Libraries in the New Millennium

Emerging Solutions in Reference Services: Implications for Libraries in the New Millennium has been co-published simultaneously as *Legal Reference Services Quarterly,* Volume 19, Numbers 1/2 2001.

Pre-publication
REVIEWS,
COMMENTARIES,
EVALUATIONS . . .

"*E merging Solutions in Reference Services: Implications for Libraries in the New Millennium* was a pleasure to review. A scan of the table of contents shows why. This is a book that seems well conceived from the outset. The topics are vital now and will continue to be discussed for the foreseeable future. It is well organized and well written; its strength lies, not in the originality of the concepts, but in the way they are assembled into a volume that is as useful as it is interesting, as compelling as it is versatile. I can see Professor Edwards' compilation being used as a text for a class or as a standard item for the reference office. It will certainly have a prominent place in my personal library."

Steven W. Lambson, JD, MLS
Senior Research
and Computer Services Librarian
University of Missouri-
Columbia Law Library

More pre-publication
REVIEWS, COMMENTARIES, EVALUATIONS . . .

"**J**ohn Edwards has done me a big favor. His *Emerging Solutions in Reference Services: Implications for Libraries in the New Millennium* presents the results of extensive research on many issues, research that I needed to do myself but have not had time for. He and his writers have helped me do my job. I am now pulling from these articles ideas that will enhance my performance and the library where I work. Any law librarian wishing to improve in the areas of legal research training at the reference desk, scripting library tours, accessing technology in the library, expanding reference services beyond the walls of the library, developing library policy, or staffing the reference desk will find help in this work–as will librarians who are struggling with the issues of the unauthorized practice of law or who are considering charging user fees. Although law librarians will benefit from a complete reading of *Emerging Solutions in Reference Services*, the abstracts and tables of contents for each article quickly guide the reader to particular desired information.

Thanks, John, I owe you one."

Gary Hill, JD
Deputy Director
Howard W. Hunter Law Library
Brigham Young University
Provo, Utah

"**P**rofessor John Edwards has assembled an experienced group of reference librarians to author the chapters in *Emerging Solutions in Reference Services: Implications for Libraries in the New Millennium*. The authors share practical insights in a manner designed to help meet today's challenges, whether the challenges be technological or traditional. Excellent chapters on technology are offered by James Duggan (Patrons and the PC), Robert Linz (Making Electronic Resources Available to Patrons), Beth Smith (Enhancing Reference Services Through Technology), and others. I found especially helpful the chapters in traditional topics authored by Jessie Cranford ("Library Police": Drafting and Implementing Enforceable Library Rules), Charles Condon (How to Avoid the Unauthorized Practice of Law at the Reference Desk: Improving Service Through Cross-Training and Other Programs).

The Haworth Information Press
An Imprint of The Haworth Press, Inc.

Emerging Solutions in Reference Services: Implications for Libraries in the New Millennium

Emerging Solutions in Reference Services: Implications for Libraries in the New Millennium has been co-published simultaneously as *Legal Reference Services Quarterly,* Volume 19, Numbers 1/2 2001.

The *Legal Reference Services Quarterly* Monographic "Separates"

Below is a list of "separates," which in serials librarianship means a special issue simultaneously published as a special journal issue or double-issue *and* as a "separate" hardbound monograph. (This is a format which we also call a "DocuSerial.")

"Separates" are published because specialized libraries or professionals may wish to purchase a specific thematic issue by itself in a format which can be separately cataloged and shelved, as opposed to purchasing the journal on an on-going basis. Faculty members may also more easily consider a "separate" for classroom adoption.

"Separates" are carefully classified separately with the major book jobbers so that the journal tie-in can be noted on new book order slips to avoid duplicate purchasing.

You may wish to visit Haworth's website at . . .

http://www.HaworthPress.com

. . . to search our online catalog for complete tables of contents of these separates and related publications.

You may also call 1-800-HAWORTH (outside US/Canada: 607-722-5857), or Fax 1-800-895-0582 (outside US/Canada: 607-771-0012), or e-mail at:

getinfo@haworthpressinc.com

Emerging Solutions in Reference Services: Implications for Libraries in the New Millennium, edited by John D. Edwards, JD, MALS (Vol. 19, No. 1/2, 2001). *"The authors provide practical advice on how to cope with everything from tight budgets to training needs to knife wielding patrons. I highly recommend that law school reference librarians purchase and read this outstanding work." (Bill Draper, BA, MS, JD, Reference Librarian and Lecturer, Biddle Law Library, University of Pennsylvania, Philadelphia)*

Law Librarians Abroad, edited by Janet Sinder, AB, JD, MS (Vol. 18, No. 3, 2000). *"A pure pleasure! Law librarians seeking information on how to find professional work abroad and useful advice on how to survive in a foreign land will be amply rewarded. Delightful." (Peter C. Schanck, JD, MLS, Law Library Director and Professor of Law, Marquette University Law Library, Milwaukee, Wisconsin)*

The Political Economy of Legal Information: The New Landscape, edited by Samuel E. Trosow (Vol. 17, No. 1/2, 1999). *Through this informative book you will gain new insights into such important issues as how industry consolidation will affect small legal publishers and the possibility that the law that governs public access to judicial opinions mandates citation reform.*

Symposium of Law Publishers, edited by Thomas A. Woxland, MLS, JD (Vol. 11, No. 3/4, 1991). *"Librarians involved in collection development would find the symposium useful as it provides an insider's view of the legal publishing industry." (Canadian Law Libraries)*

The Legal Bibliography: Tradition, Transitions, and Trends, edited by Scott B. Pagel, JD, MLS (Vol. 9, No. 1/2, 1989). *"An excellent introduction to major bibliographic titles and future concerns for the novice law librarian or student of legal librarianship. . . . A useful addition to the reference shelf of the private law or acquisitions librarian." (Legal Information Alert)*

Practical Approaches to Legal Research, edited by Kent C. Olson, JD, MLS, and Robert C. Berring, JD, MLS (Supp. #01, 1988). *"A long overdue book–a legal research manual for librarians. . . . A readable and entertaining text on locating and using law books. . . . Almost everything a law librarian needs to know about legal research is covered in this book." (Legal Information Alert)*

Emerging Solutions in Reference Services: Implications for Libraries in the New Millennium

John D. Edwards, JD, MALS
Editor

Emerging Solutions in Reference Services: Implications for Libraries in the New Millennium has been co-published simultaneously as *Legal Reference Services Quarterly,* Volume 19, Numbers 1/2 2001.

The Haworth Information Press
An Imprint of
The Haworth Press, Inc.
New York • London • Oxford

OCT 0 9 2002

Published by

The Haworth Information Press®, 10 Alice Street, Binghamton, NY 13904-1580 USA

The Haworth Information Press® is an imprint of the Haworth Press, Inc., 10 Alice Street, Binghamton, NY 13904-1580 USA.

Emerging Solutions in Reference Services: Implications for Libraries in the New Millennium has been co-published simultaneously as *Legal Reference Services Quarterly,* Volume 19, Numbers 1/2 2001.

The development, preparation, and publication of this work has been undertaken with great care. However, the publisher, employees, editors, and agents of The Haworth Press and all imprints of The Haworth Press, Inc., including The Haworth Medical Press and The Pharmaceutical Products Press, are not responsible for any errors contained herein or for consequences that may ensue from use of materials or information contained in this work. Opinions expressed by the author(s) are not necessarily those of The Haworth Press, Inc.

Cover design by Thomas J. Mayshock Jr.

Library of Congress Cataloging-in-Publication Data

Emerging solutions in reference services : implications for libraries in the new millennium / John D. Edwards, editor.
    p. cm.
    Co-published simultaneously as Legal reference services quarterly, v. 19, nos. 1/2 2001.
    Includes bibliographical references and index.
    ISBN 0-7890-1359-2 (alk. paper)–ISBN 0-7890-1360-6 (pbk : alk. paper)
    1. Reference services (Libraries)–United States. 2. Law libraries–Reference services–United States. I. Edwards, John (John Duncan), 1953- II. Legal reference services quarterly.

Z711 .E52 2001
025.5′2′0973–dc21

2001039147

Indexing, Abstracting & Website/Internet Coverage

This section provides you with a list of major indexing & abstracting services. That is to say, each service began covering this periodical during the year noted in the right column. Most Websites which are listed below have indicated that they will either post, disseminate, compile, archive, cite or alert their own Website users with research-based content from this work. (This list is as current as the copyright date of this publication.)

Abstracting, Website/Indexing Coverage ...... Year When Coverage Began

- *BUBL Information Service. An Internet-based Information Service for the UK higher education community*
  <URL: http://bubl.ac.uk/> **1994**

- *CNPIEC Reference Guide: Chinese National Directory of Foreign Periodicals* **1995**

- *Current Awareness Abstracts of Library & Information Management Literature, ASLIB (UK)* **1997**

- *Current Cites [Digital Libraries] [Electronic Publishing] [Multimedia & Hypermedia] [Networks & Networking] [General]* **1992**

- *Current Law Index* **1992**

- *FINDEX <www.publist.com>* **1999**

- *Hein's Legal Periodical Checklist: Index to Periodical Articles Pertaining to Law <www.wshein.com>* **1992**

- *IBZ International Bibliography of Periodical Literature* **1995**

- *Index Guide to College Journals (core list compiled by integrating 48 indexes frequently used to support undergraduate programs in small to medium sized libraries)* **1999**

(continued)

Special Bibliographic Notes related to special journal issues (separates) and indexing/abstracting:

- indexing/abstracting services in this list will also cover material in any "separate" that is co-published simultaneously with Haworth's special thematic journal issue or DocuSerial. Indexing/abstracting usually covers material at the article/chapter level.
- monographic co-editions are intended for either non-subscribers or libraries which intend to purchase a second copy for their circulating collections.
- monographic co-editions are reported to all jobbers/wholesalers/approval plans. The source journal is listed as the "series" to assist the prevention of duplicate purchasing in the same manner utilized for books-in-series.
- to facilitate user/access services all indexing/abstracting services are encouraged to utilize the co-indexing entry note indicated at the bottom of the first page of each article/chapter/contribution.
- this is intended to assist a library user of any reference tool (whether print, electronic, online, or CD-ROM) to locate the monographic version if the library has purchased this version but not a subscription to the source journal.
- individual articles/chapters in any Haworth publication are also available through the Haworth Document Delivery Service (HDDS).

ABOUT THE EDITOR

John D. Edwards, JD, MALS, is Professor of Law and Director of the Law Library at Drake University Law School. Professor Edwards also serves as Executive Director of Legal Research and Writing. For more than two decades as a practicing law librarian he has been teaching legal research to law students, legal assistants, and legal secretaries.

Professor Edwards is the author of numerous articles, which have appeared in the *Law Library Journal* and has written pieces for several monographic works as well. Professor Edwards has a JD from the University of Missouri at Kansas City, an MALS from the University of Missouri at Columbia, and a BA from Southeast Missouri State University. He is a member of the Missouri bar. His first professional position involved reference services, and his interest in the subject has grown since then.

Emerging Solutions in Reference Services: Implications for Libraries in the New Millennium

CONTENTS

Introduction–
Facing Library Problems:
Solutions for the Millennium

John D. Edwards

Librarians attempt to solve a variety of problems each day in the face of an increasingly complex workplace. The impetus for this work was to create a sourcebook for some of the key issues librarians must address. Questions posted to listservs often include the type of question this compendium will answer, such as "Has anyone ever dealt with ____ ?" A review of the topics covered here should indicate that the blank can be filled with one of a dozen different possible subjects. The issues covered in this compilation will provide librarians with a very practical guide for coping with rapidly changing technology and increasing demands for services.

The authors cover a range of topics dealing with the day-to-day issues facing librarians, including: technological competencies, problem patrons and security, reference responsibilities, web resources for teaching, reference desk instruction, library tours, electronic resources for patrons, technology in reference, drafting enforceable rules, avoid-

John D. Edwards is Director of the Law Library and Professor of Law at Drake University Law Library, Des Moines, IA 50311-4505 (E-mail: John.Edwards@ drake.edu). Professor Edwards also holds the titles of Executive Director of Legal Research and Writing and Director of Information Technology.

Special thanks for helping complete this work go to Associate Editor Beth Ann Edwards, Administrative Assistant Ruth Terrell, and Research Assistant Jill Beaird.

[Haworth co-indexing entry note]: "Introduction–Facing Library Problems: Solutions for the Millennium." Edwards, John D. Co-published simultaneously in *Legal Reference Services Quarterly* (The Haworth Information Press, an imprint of The Haworth Press, Inc.) Vol. 19, No. 1/2, 2001, pp. 1-4; and: *Emerging Solutions in Reference Services: Implications for Libraries in the New Millennium* (ed: John D. Edwards) The Haworth Information Press, an imprint of The Haworth Press, Inc., 2001, pp. 1-4. Single or multiple copies of this article are available for a fee from The Haworth Document Delivery Service [1-800-342-9678, 9:00 a.m. - 5:00 p.m. (EST). E-mail address: getinfo@haworthpressinc.com].

ing the unauthorized practice of law, fees for services, and cross-training of reference personnel.

Most librarians who have fielded patron queries about using computers or other technology may have questioned whether they have the level of expertise needed to help a patron with a computer problem. James Duggan addresses this issue by discussing the types of computer problems that a reference librarian should and should not attempt to solve. His guidelines for providing assistance will help librarians make that decision. He also reveals which basic skills should become part of the knowledge base for anyone at the reference desk and which ones should be left to the technical experts.

Donald Arndt addresses problem patrons and how to improve library security. Many of the unique issues in dealing with problem patrons are explored, along with what preventive measures and responses may prove most helpful. Specific techniques for dealing with difficult situations should provide librarians with more confidence should they ever be confronted with a difficult patron. Security of the overall facility and legal issues surrounding safety issues are discussed from the perspective of possible solutions. A list of additional sources on the topic is included as well.

Dealing with increasing demands for service and seemingly fewer hours in a day is the focus of Sandra Placzek's work. She reviews how the role of the reference librarian is evolving and suggests ways to cope with the stresses resulting from that evolution. Changes in user patterns and expectations impact how librarians do their work and those factors also are discussed. Time management and organizational techniques should help librarians see what methods might be most helpful in their libraries.

Developing a web site for training patrons to use Internet resources is an undertaking that may become increasingly common as libraries take advantage of the flexibility offered by the web. A web-based CLE program was produced to train attorneys to use Internet resources. W. David Gay and Jim Jackson describe what they did to develop the CLE program and their experiences in delivering the program at several locations throughout the state. Included are the URLs for the web sites they used and suggestions for those who are considering web-based instructional programs.

One of the challenges of delivering reference services is deciding how much information to give the patron. Some patrons only want the answer to their questions while others may benefit from having the librarian teach them how to use a resource to find the answer. Paul Arrigo discusses how to determine what would best meet the needs of the patron. Several tools for providing instruction at the reference desk are explained along with which methods may be most effective for particular types of questions. His guidelines for reference desk instruction should help librarians assess what is needed to meet patrons' needs.

Providing an effective library orientation may be a challenge for some libraries in light of the many electronic resources now available. Deborah Keene and Holliday Gordon explain the techniques academic and law firm libraries can use to give patrons basic information during an orientation tour. In addition to discussing the considerations for a traditional walk-around tour, the authors address the effectiveness of other types of orientation and training based on what they learned from their survey of law libraries.

As libraries provide more electronic resources, decisions must be made as to how those resources can be delivered most effectively. Robert Linz reviews the advantages and disadvantages of various technology options, including the Internet and CD-ROM, and describes what is necessary to create the optimal electronic environment. His design guidelines for web sites can be emulated by other libraries and facilitate patron access to electronic services.

The ways in which libraries are able to respond to reference questions have grown considerably in the past decade. Although the traditional face-to-face interaction may still be the most common method for delivering reference services, other means utilizing technology are becoming more widely accepted. Beth Smith reviews how technology can enhance reference services by giving patrons more opportunities to receive assistance, such as through e-mail, web forms, chat, videoconferencing, and remote application sharing. Her review includes identification of the key technology resources needed at today's reference desk and how technology can be integrated into reference services.

Meeting the challenge of drafting and implementing enforceable library rules is the focus of Jessie Cranford's article on "Library Police." Librarians may be able to avoid the "police" moniker in developing and enforcing rules if they follow some of the suggestions in the article, which examines existing rules, methods of enforcement, and implementation of new rules. Her survey of policies reveals how law libraries deal with various issues, including the continuing challenge for many libraries–food and drink.

The admonition given to every new law librarian is to avoid giving legal advice when a patron asks for assistance. Charles Condon describes the concerns that each librarian should address to reduce the risk that any action might be construed as the unauthorized practice of law. Strategies for dealing with patrons who come to the library or call seeking free legal advice are discussed in some detail. Training is a key issue, especially for well-meaning law students who may want to use their newly acquired skills of legal analysis and research to assist a confused patron.

As law library budgets become tighter, administrators seek ways to secure additional funds. One approach is to charge fees for library services. Kumar Percy explores the various fees libraries have implemented and the philosophical debate on free vs. fee services. The results of his survey indicate the range of fee options that libraries utilize, including charges for printing, copying, document delivery, reference services, borrowing privileges, and access. His tables and analysis provide a good overview of the array of factors libraries can consider.

Providing reference services sufficient to meet patron demands may be a challenge for some libraries. One option is to provide additional staff members with the opportunity to participate in reference functions. Margaret McDermott suggests how reference can be improved through cross-training and utilization of other library personnel. She also explores options beyond the traditional reference desk for providing those services, especially in light of today's technology.

From this collection of articles the reader should be able to find a number of strategies and suggestions to enhance services to patrons and improve the librarian's workplace. Notes are included following each article to provide additional sources that may be of interest. Contact information for each author is included so the reader can feel free to send an e-mail or otherwise engage the writer about the work. The purpose of this collection is to provide a practical resource for librarians to learn how other libraries and librarians have dealt with challenges they faced. The authors hope that *Emerging Solutions in Reference Services: Implications for Libraries in the New Millennium* provides librarians with some of the strategies and answers they need.

Patrons and the PC:
What Problems
Should Reference Librarians Solve?

James E. Duggan

SUMMARY. Reference librarians today face a variety of additional responsibilities and duties in the library setting due to the successful emergence of the personal computer. Computers have changed nearly every aspect of library operation, and while patrons have reaped many benefits, including newly available sources via the Internet and the ability to search the holdings of libraries across the world, reference librari-

---

James E. Duggan is Professor and Director of Information Technology at Southern Illinois University School of Law Library, 1150 Douglas Drive, Carbondale, IL 62901-6803 (E-mail: duggan@siu.edu).

[Haworth co-indexing entry note]: "Patrons and the PC: What Problems Should Reference Librarians Solve?" Duggan, James E. Co-published simultaneously in *Legal Reference Services Quarterly* (The Haworth Information Press, an imprint of The Haworth Press, Inc.) Vol. 19, No. 1/2, 2001 pp. 5-17; and: *Emerging Solutions in Reference Services: Implications for Libraries in the New Millennium* (ed: John D. Edwards) The Haworth Information Press, an imprint of The Haworth Press, Inc., 2001, pp. 5-17. Single or multiple copies of this article are available for a fee from The Haworth Document Delivery Service [1-800-342-9678, 9:00 a.m. - 5:00 p.m. (EST). E-mail address: getinfo@haworthpressinc.com].

ans have found that their jobs have changed dramatically as patrons expect increasingly complicated computer support. This article will provide some suggestions on which computer problems are suitable for a typical public services librarian to tackle, suggest a sample library policy on reference librarian computer support as a way to alert patrons about appropriate expectations, and offer guidance to those librarians on the front lines who face computer troubleshooting issues on a daily basis. *[Article copies available for a fee from The Haworth Document Delivery Service: 1-800-342-9678. E-mail address: <getinfo@haworthpressinc.com> Website: <http://www.HaworthPress.com> © 2001 by The Haworth Press, Inc. All rights reserved.]*

I. INTRODUCTION

Consider the Following Three Scenarios:

It is 9:50 a.m. on a mid-winter's morning at a busy reference desk. A second year law student rushes to the desk in a panic. The all-important moot court brief that the student worked on around the clock last night is due in ten minutes, and now the file will not open in Word Perfect. There is no lab monitor in sight, and the law student is near tears. What, if anything, can the reference librarian do?

An attorney browsing the web telephones the reference librarian on duty. After exchanging pleasantries, the attorney reveals the purpose of her call: after following a link from the library's web page to a tax web site, she has discovered that she needs a program called Adobe Acrobat in order to read the text of an IRS no-action letter. Can the librarian help her load the software plug-in?

The pro se patron has been happily searching the county law library's online catalog all afternoon, and steadily clicking on the print button whenever he pulls up something of interest. Unfortunately, after printing approximately 50 catalog records, he discovers that the print requests actually are routed to the networked public printer and the printer is jammed. He is concerned that he will lose several hours of work and looks to the nearest library employee (in this case, the reference librarian) for assistance. How should the librarian respond?

The answers to each of these scenarios will depend on a number of variables, including the librarian's willingness to help, past computer training, time available, and management policies. The bigger issue, however, is not whether librarians *can* help, but rather *should* they?

Does a reference librarian's service orientation extend beyond traditional library activities to helping patrons with computer-related problems? If so, which personal computer problems should the librarian attempt to solve? Or, will more harm than good be done by the well-meaning, but perhaps inadequately trained, librarian who tries to troubleshoot a computer without a better understanding of the possible consequences? What are the expectations of patrons, and how might they conflict with those of library co-workers and management?

This article provides some suggestions as to which computer problems are and are not suitable for the typical public services librarian to address, suggests a sample library policy on reference librarian computer support as a way to alert patrons about appropriate expectations, and offers guidance to those librarians on the front lines who must face on a daily basis that second-most[1] asked patron question, "Why won't this stupid printer work?"

II. THE CHANGING ROLE OF THE LIBRARIAN

Perhaps the greatest technological enhancement in libraries since the printing press, the personal computer has almost completely altered the way librarians perform their jobs. The Internet and web-based databases provide seemingly limitless sources in which reference librarians can search. Computerized union catalogs from around the world broaden the scope for interlibrary loans. Online vendors and bibliographic utilities enhance the work of the library's acquisitions, serials, and cataloging departments. But the personal computer has changed more than just the librarian's role. It has also changed the way library patrons utilize the library and interact with librarians.

Computers make it possible for savvy library patrons to search for information on their own, request materials via online catalogs, retrieve and review selected sources, and print and manipulate data, often without any librarian assistance. The advent of the library web page, complete with links to the online catalog and research sources, often means that the patron does not even need to be physically present in the library in order to do library research. And, just as patron questions at the reference desk previously centered on how to find legal information in the printed sources, now these same questions arise in the computer and online context.

The legal reference librarian today must be a master of many talents. The computer's incredible takeover of many library functions has meant that the librarian's traditional skills of knowing one's collection, conducting the patron interview and, ultimately, answering questions about how to find the law have been augmented by a variety of expected competencies in the operation and manipulation of computers. For some reference librarians, especially those who entered the field over ten years ago,[2] this has meant intensive on-the-job training while most newer librarians who grew up around personal computers take these additional responsibilities in stride.

III. BASIC COMPETENCIES

Most reference librarians today are presumed to have a basic understanding of computers in order to use them effectively on the job.[3] These "basic" skills include using: (a) a computer and word processing software in order to write documents required by the job (e.g., bibliographies, pathfinders and guides, and, for academic reference librarians facing tenure and/or continuing appointment, scholarly articles); (b) the library OPAC (online public access catalog) for finding in-house library materials and materials from other libraries; (c) CD-ROM databases (once extremely popular in the legal field, this format is gradually being replaced by online web products); (d) Web browsers in order to find materials via the Internet; (e) electronic mail (to send and respond to requests for materials and advice, as well as to subscribe to and read postings on professional listservs);[4] and (f) computer-assisted legal research services and printing.

These basic competencies can be summarized as follows:

General Computers: Properly starting and shutting down the computer; basic file management (including copying, renaming, moving and searching for files); minimizing and maximizing windows; running programs from a variety of methods (icons and menus); printing.

Word-Processing Software: Creating, saving, opening files; inserting, selecting, cutting, pasting and editing text; running spell check, thesaurus and other utilities; basic format options; pagination; footnotes/endnotes; headers/footers; search and replace; basic table and column management; printing documents; saving files as html and other formats (when using newer word processing applications).

Library OPAC: Basic searching by attribute as allowed by the OPAC, including subject, author, title, call number, etc.; limiting searches by selected attributes (e.g., limiting a search to a specific publisher); printing records; interpreting unfamiliar cataloging records for patrons.

CD-ROM Databases: Loading, searching, and closing the database from the CD-ROM if it is a stand-alone; running the database computer workstation if the CD-ROM is networked; having familiarity with and being able to teach basic operating software commands and features; printing documents.

Web Browsers: Loading and closing the web browser; accessing web sites by domain name/address; finding and using search engines; navigating back and forth through web sites visited during a session; creating and using bookmarks; printing documents.

Electronic Mail: Creating, saving, opening and retrieving e-mail; subscribing to and signing off electronic listservs; attaching, opening, and sending attached files; using spell check, filters, and multiple folders/mailboxes for those enhanced electronic mail packages; creating, editing, and using signature files; printing documents.

Computer-Assisted Legal Research: Loading and searching LEXIS and Westlaw databases; advising students and patrons how to correctly configure the CALR applications via proprietary software and the web; solving password problems (someone on the reference staff should be the primary contact with vendors for issuing, canceling, and troubleshooting passwords); and printing documents to the correct printer for LEXIS or Westlaw (which normally would be the stand-alone printer rather than the attached printer which might be accessed from home).

In their teaching role, librarians often are regarded as experts as they instruct patrons on how to use the various computer software applications, databases, and browsers. This teaching role requires reference librarians to stay on top of technology in order to do their jobs properly. Staying current on technology means mastering new forms of technology as they develop and keeping abreast of new ways of presenting and teaching information sources. Although reference librarians also must bring a healthy respect of the computer to the occupation, they should not be frightened of computers.[5] As with card catalogs and printed bibliographies, computers are merely tools that can be used to access materials. Utilizing these tools is simply part of the job.

IV. BEYOND THE BASICS:
THE REFERENCE LIBRARIAN DELIVERING
COMPUTER TECHNICAL SUPPORT

While much has changed with the advent of the personal computer in libraries, one thing has stayed the same: patrons just want help and could care less who provides it. And just as the patron's perception that everyone who works in a library–from the student worker at the front desk to the security guard out back–is a librarian, the proliferation of computers in the library means that librarians, especially the reference librarians, must be the computer experts. (*"Why else would they have all those computers if the librarians didn't know how to use them?"*)

This expectation of immediate assistance on the part of patrons is intensified when computer labs with multi-application terminals are installed either completely within the physical confines of the library or adjacent to library facilities. Even if labs have computer help desks and lab monitors, often the librarian as the de facto helpful person is called upon to assist. The presence of public workstations in the library engenders a reasonable demand on the part of patrons that the computers work, and if they do not, then someone (i.e., anyone working in a library is a "someone") should be able to fix them.

When should a reference librarian help with a computer-related problem? Unfortunately, there is no clear answer, as each problem should be examined on a case-by-case basis. Librarian computer training, staffing levels, job descriptions, time available, and management policies all must be considered in determining which approach to take. A quick review of each of these factors will help explain why there is no easy answer as to when a reference librarian should provide computer support.

Librarian Computer Training: Tinkering with an expensive piece of equipment is not a good idea, especially if the librarian has little or no computer experience, or if the equipment is the patron's personal computer. Reference librarians who have hardware and software expertise, such as those who are certified on various software applications[6] or whose job includes computer troubleshooting responsibilities,[7] are generally the ones that are best prepared for tackling computer problems, although librarians who have gained computer experience and knowledge on the job may have the necessary skills to address many problems.

Staffing Levels: A library with a sufficient number of full-time computer support personnel is a luxury for patrons in those libraries, and where these positions exist librarians should generally defer most if not all computer-related problems to the computer support staff. However, most libraries do not enjoy this level of staffing,[8] and must instead either utilize its reference staff as information technology support, disclaim all responsibility for computer problems (especially if located on patron-owned computers), or somehow strike a middle ground. For example, reference librarians might help with software application questions on library-owned computers, but they would not have the expertise to deal with hardware problems.

Job Descriptions: Most typical reference librarian job descriptions in the past have not included any kind of computer hardware or software support duties. Only the hybrid Computer/Reference Librarian description normally has addressed this issue and will generally only mention library computer equipment and not individual patron-owned PCs. Of course, reference librarians frequently perform many tasks not specifically mentioned in their job descriptions but which fall somewhat nebulously under the catch-all category of "other duties as assigned." However, there are important differences between turning a computer off to reset it and using a utility program to rebuild a damaged disk.

Time Available: This limitation is almost a given as busy reference staff members simply do not have the time to do more than the very basic computer troubleshooting, such as closing out and restarting the application program, restarting the computer, clearing a paper jam, changing the printer toner cartridge, or adding paper to the printer.

Management Policies: What expectations exist on the part of reference management? Library administration? The parent organization? Although there may be conflicts (e.g., law school or firm administrators may expect reference librarians to bend over backwards to help the tuition-paying student or high-billing attorney), managers of reference librarians should be consistent in creating and enforcing computer assistance policies and provide advanced training to all reference staff if they are expected to provide more than very basic computer help.

V. ADVANCED COMPETENCIES

If all of the factors above are satisfied (the library employs reference librarians with computer backgrounds or extensive computer training, places computer support in the job descriptions, has time available, and enjoys the support of management), what sort of advanced computer troubleshooting might reference librarians undertake?

1. *Software Installation.* Patrons browsing the Internet on library equipment frequently encounter the need to upgrade the web browsers or add software plug-ins to access certain types of Internet information. If library computer technicians are unavailable, reference librarians can assist in the software installation if they are familiar with the standard library browser configurations, Netscape or Internet Explorer requirements,[9] virus protection guidelines, and removing and replacing library security software if any is in use. Reference librarians also may guide the installation of programs, such as Adobe Acrobat,[10] by patrons on their own equipment over the telephone, provided librarians have a clear understanding of how the software installs, and the patrons are in a clearly delineated class (e.g., attorneys in the librarian's law firm or faculty at the librarian's law school).

2. *Upgrading CD-ROM Databases.* If the CD-ROM database is not networked, reference librarians may be asked to update access to CD-ROMs that have expired passwords or software. Librarians can do this quite easily if they can access the computer workstation's hard drive, such as by removing and ultimately replacing the library security software. Typically, the new CD-ROM will require the execution of a short update program which is often done through a program such as update.exe or by keying the library password when requested. Reference librarians also can do this with the networked CD-ROMs, provided they have the necessary security clearance and adequate training so that the CD-ROM tower setup is not changed.

3. *Employing Disk Utilities.* Because of the prevalence of word processing programs in libraries, reference librarians are often asked to fix files on disks that will not open. This typically means running a utility program, such as scan disk or Norton Disk Doctor,[11] to attempt

to repair or recover files on the disk. Inexperienced reference librarians should use these utility programs with extreme caution, however, as the utilities can frequently destroy needed data on the disks, and may result in a completely unusable disk.

4. *Using Virus Protection Programs.* Reference librarians should be familiar with virus protection programs, not only for their personal work, but also as necessary applications when patrons download programs and e-mail from the Internet onto library equipment. Although most computer workstations are configured to automatically run the virus protection utility every time a diskette is accessed or data is downloaded, the librarian may need to initiate a virus protection scan first, before attempting to restore data on a disk (see #3 above).

5. *Restarting Library OPACs.* All library public service personnel, including reference librarians, should have the authority and ability to restart a jammed library online public access catalog terminal. This may involve the widening of possible security breaches by assigning individual passwords for access to the OPAC networked menu, but will save patron frustration and wear and tear on overworked technical support personnel.

6. *Hardware Troubleshooting.* Computers freeze. Printers jam. Mice get dirty and refuse to budge. Computer monitor settings are reset by sticky-fingered patrons. Diskettes become stuck or broken in computer disk drives. Reference librarians frequently are called upon to fix all of these problems; they can realize great success if they remember to be gentle with easily breakable parts, reassemble everything in the correct order, and do not panic if initial efforts to repair the situation fail. One frequently used solution is to reset the computer if any unwanted changes occur either internally or externally. Resetting or rebooting the computer requires turning the computer off and then back on, which often solves the problem.

VI. DEVELOPING AND MAINTAINING COMPUTER SKILLS

Staying current on new technologies can be a challenge for any librarian, especially one who may spend many hours each week at the reference desk. Several options are outlined below which can help librarians develop and maintain computer skills.

In-House Training: Reference librarians should take advantage of any in-house computer training offered by their parent institution, both as a way to enhance their on-the-job skills and as a way to keep the job interesting, especially as the provision of reference services continues to grow towards an online environment-based system. Particularly helpful are courses that teach basic word-processing, database and spreadsheet applications, web browser and presentation software, and hardware troubleshooting.

Reference Materials: Each library should have a range of computer self-help manuals that can aid the librarian in identifying and correcting computer software problems. Basic questions often arise that can easily be solved by quick reference to a software manual, such as "How do I type the section symbol in Word?," "What is the URL for _____?," or "How can I get this spreadsheet to print?" Some libraries have established a separate working collection of manuals that are stored at the reference desk area, and include both basic (*Windows for Dummies* and similar titles)[12] and advanced works (any of the Que publications).[13]

Journals: Some libraries subscribe to a selection of popular computer magazines[14] and computer journals and newsletters more specific to the practice of law.[15] Many of these periodicals carry helpful articles of interest to reference librarians. The journals can either be routed to individual staff members or the computer service librarian may flag relevant articles and alert reference staff on a regular basis.

Listservs: As with journals and periodicals, electronic listservs such as Teknoids[16] and the AALL Computer Services SIS listserv[17] offer a wide variety of tips and tricks for configuring and solving computer and computer-related problems. The computer services librarian can either route selected postings or ask individual reference staff members to monitor selected lists and route tips when appropriate.

Conferences: Reference Staff members should take advantage of computer-related educational programs at national, regional, and local conferences. Examples of conferences with computer-related programming include those sponsored by the American Association of Law Libraries (AALL),[18] American Library Association (ALA),[19] Center for Computer-Assisted Legal Instruction (CALI),[20] Special Library Association (SLA),[21] and Computers in Libraries.[22]

VII. COMPUTER SUPPORT POLICY

Because the question of whether reference librarians should attempt to help or solve computer-related problems has no clear-cut answer, a policy should be developed that details which computer-related tasks reference librarians can assist with, and which ones they will not attempt. This policy should appear in the library handbook and web site and should be posted at the reference desk. Alerting patrons and staff to what the library considers reasonable expectations for the reference staff's computer problem-solving skills can help avoid many potential problems. The following sample policy helps address some of the key considerations.

Sample Policy

Computer Support by Reference Librarians

Although reference librarians are not specifically trained to provide computer support, they will, upon request and as time allows, provide assistance with database searching, web browsing, basic word processing and e-mail questions, and simple computer and printer troubleshooting on library equipment. Library employees are prohibited from working on any patron's personal computer equipment or diskettes.

This policy for legal reference staffs with basic computer backgrounds and training is less exacting than one for reference staffs who have advanced computer training, or for those libraries that aspire to provide higher levels of service to their patrons. Although libraries may provide whatever level computer support they decide is appropriate, patrons should be advised as to the limitations and to the potential for disaster should something go wrong. In all cases, libraries should strive to draw distinctions between library and patron-owned hardware and software. Library equipment must be maintained in good working order along with programs which require a minimum knowledge of how the application operates. Working on a patron-owned personal computer creates the possibility that an inadequately trained librarian might unintentionally delete important data with just a keystroke.

VIII. CONCLUSION

Due to the successful emergence of the personal computer during the past twenty years, reference librarians today face a variety of additional responsibilities and duties in the library setting. Computers have changed nearly every aspect of library operation, and while patrons have reaped many benefits, including newly available sources via the Internet and the ability to search the holdings of libraries across the world, reference librarians have found that their jobs have dramatically changed as patrons expect increasingly complicated computer support.

This article has examined basic and advanced computer competencies that might be expected of reference librarians by library management and patrons, and suggested a framework for providing limited computer support. A sample policy has been provided to give some guidance to reference staff as to what is and is not appropriate for computer support, and to alert patrons as to what they can expect in the way of help. No matter what level of support is offered, however, law library policies should specifically exclude hardware support of all patron-owned personal computers because of the potential for disaster.

NOTES

1. The most asked patron question is, of course, "Where is the restroom?"

2. *See* James E. Duggan, *My Life Has a Systems Error*, AALL SPECTRUM, Nov. 1997, at 24.

3. A quick review of all reference job postings on AALLNET, the homepage of the American Association of Law Libraries, <http://www.aallnet.org>, suggests that knowledge of computers and basic software packages is required. A growing number of positions also require experience with html and web page construction.

4. *See, e.g.*, law-lib, an electronic discussion group for law librarians hosted by the University of California-Davis at law-lib@ucdavis.edu with archives at <http://lawlibrary.ucdavis.edu/LAWLIB/lawlib.html/> and Stumpers, hosted by a Dominican University Graduate School of Library and Information Science student at STUMPERS-L@cuis.edu with archives at <http://www.cuis.edu/~stumpers/>.

5. *See* John Kupersmith, *Technostress and the Reference Librarian*, REFERENCE SERVICES REV., Summer 1992, at 7 <http://www.greatbasin.net/~jkup/tstr_ref.html>.

6. *E.g.*, Microsoft has a certification program for expert users of its applications and systems. *See Microsoft Training and Services Certification* (visited June 26, 2000) <http://www.microsoft.com/trainingandservices/default.asp?PageID=mcp>.

7. Many computer services librarians have reference responsibilities, and vice-versa.

8. A compilation of law school technology personnel is available from the computer staffing table maintained by Professor Ann Puckett, Law Library Director at the University of Georgia, at <http://www.lawsch.uga.edu/lawlib/stafcomp.html>.

9. *See* Netscape Communications, *Netscape Products* (visited June 26, 2000) <http://home.netscape.com/download/index.html>; Microsoft Corp., *Internet Explorer* (visited June 26, 2000) <http://www.microsoft.com/windows/ie/default.htm>.

10. *See* Adobe Systems Inc., *Adobe Acrobat Reader* (visited June 26, 2000) <http://www.adobe.com/products/acrobat/readermain.html>.

11. *See* Symantec Corp., *Norton Utilities Product Information* (visited June 26, 2000) <http://www.symantec.com/nu/index.html>.

12. For a list of technology titles from IDG Books, see <http://www.idgbooks. com/> or to review the "for Dummies" series, see <http://www.dummies.com/>.

13. For a list of Que publications for Microsoft Office products, see <http:// www.prenhall.com/cisapps/>.

14. *E.g.*, *PC World*, *Wired*, etc.

15. *E.g.*, *Law Office Computing*, *Internet Newsletter*, *WordPerfect for Lawyers*, etc.

16. Teknoids@listserv.law.cornell.edu. For subscribing information, see <http:// www3.law.cornell.edu/guest/info/TEKNOIDS>.

17. Cssis-l@aall.wuacc.edu. For subscribing information, see <http://www.aallnet. org/discuss/list_index_sis.asp>.

18. *See* <http://www.aallnet.org/prodev>.

19. *See* <http://www.ala.org/events>.

20. *See* <http://www.cali.org/>.

21. *See* <http://www.sla.org>.

22. *See* <http://www.infotoday.com/ci12000/default.htm>.

Problem Patrons and Library Security

Donald A. Arndt, Jr.

SUMMARY. Front-line library staff members often encounter "problem patrons"–those patrons who put others in fear for their own physical security, whether or not that fear is ultimately justified. This article

Donald A. Arndt, Jr. is Associate Director and Head of Public Services at the LaValley Law Library, University of Toledo, Toledo, OH 43606 (E-mail: darndt@utnet.utoledo.edu).

The author would like to thank his wife, Theresa Arndt, for her wise counsel, patient support, and invaluable assistance in the creation of this work.

[Haworth co-indexing entry note]: "Problem Patrons and Library Security." Arndt, Jr., Donald A. Co-published simultaneously in *Legal Reference Services Quarterly* (The Haworth Information Press, an imprint of The Haworth Press, Inc.) Vol. 19, No. 1/2, 2001, pp. 19-40; and: *Emerging Solutions in Reference Services: Implications for Libraries in the New Millennium* (ed: John D. Edwards) The Haworth Information Press, an imprint of The Haworth Press, Inc., 2001, pp. 19-40. Single or multiple copies of this article are available for a fee from The Haworth Document Delivery Service [1-800-342-9678, 9:00 a.m. - 5:00 p.m. (EST). E-mail address: getinfo@haworthpressinc.com].

19

identifies the risks and suggests some precautions, including: defusing anger at the service points through improved interpersonal communication techniques and staff training, drafting policies and procedures to help guide staff as they deal with incidents, and improving the security of library buildings. Legal issues surrounding library security also are examined. *[Article copies available for a fee from The Haworth Document Delivery Service: 1-800-342-9678. E-mail address: <getinfo@haworthpressinc. com> Website: <http://www.HaworthPress.com> © 2001 by The Haworth Press, Inc. All rights reserved.]*

I. INTRODUCTION

Front-line staff in law libraries open to the public often must deal with "problem patrons" who are perceived as a primary source of serious discomfort or disruption of routine service. While this definition could be applied to many library users, including the sleeping homeless person, the noisy unattended child, and the particularly demanding or obnoxious law clerk, this article focuses on a particular subset of problem patrons–those who threaten, harass, or put others in fear for their own physical security, whether or not that fear is ultimately justified. Although this group obviously includes the criminal element that comes into the library intending to steal, vandalize, or commit an assault, it also encompasses a diverse group who may not, at least initially, have that intent. They may be mentally ill, substance abusers, or someone simply having a really bad day.

Law libraries, by their very nature and purpose, are likely to attract those who are already a bit "on the edge." People come to law libraries for help in resolving disputes in which they are embroiled. Be it a messy divorce, a contractual problem, pending criminal charges, etc., the common denominator is usually a frustrating legal problem that has no easy answer. Thus, their fuse is already lit, and it may not take much to set them off. How public services personnel deal with them, and the preparations the library has made for problem situations, can make the difference in how these encounters are resolved. This article describes the problems that can occur and suggests certain precautionary preparations and approaches to help increase the chances that encounters with problem patrons are concluded successfully.

II. THE PROBLEMS LIBRARIANS FACE

A. Examples of Problem Behavior

The first step in preparing to meet challenges from patrons is to consider what problems can be expected. They often begin innocuously enough:

Patron A has been coming into the law library regularly for years, researching conspiracy cases. He is a little odd, and is frequently the subject of complaints from other patrons because he talks to himself in the stacks, but seems harmless enough. That perception changes one day when he pulls out a knife and starts angrily slashing computer printouts he found in a nearby trash can.

Patron B comes into the law school library for the first time that anyone can recall and almost immediately makes the circulation desk attendant feel physically threatened by his size and his demeanor. He wants answers to his legal problems, is not finding them easily, and is increasingly frustrated. He appears paranoid. He also was seen panhandling students for money to make photocopies and made at least one student feel threatened. Campus security is called. They, in turn, call the city police since a bulletin was issued to check on this individual's welfare after he reportedly threatened to blow up a municipal building elsewhere in town. The city police respond, question him and search him and his car for weapons, but finding none and having no reason to hold him since no actual crime has been committed, they leave. If he appeared angry before, now he seems fast approaching pure rage. Above all, he wants to know who called the cops on him.

Patron C is contesting a speeding ticket and has heard that the law school assigns students to represent people in court for free. When told that his is not the type of case the clinic accepts, he starts ranting about his infantry experience and how he might just have to pick up a gun again.

Patron D is an inmate. One evening a week, the local correctional facility brings certain inmates to the law school library so they can do legal research. These are not violent offenders, and they would not be granted the privilege of making this visit if they were not model citizens during incarceration. Patron D approaches the reference desk where the female librarian on duty is talking to a male colleague. The male librarian listens to the first minute of the reference interview before departing to take care of other work. As soon as he leaves, the inmate's conversation changes from legitimate research questions to lascivious comments.

Patron E is completely unfamiliar with legal research and needs a great deal of help from the reference librarian. His manner can best be described as creepy, and the librarian is worried because his research topic deals with stalking, but all in all the encounter is not too unusual. At one point, however, the patron begins punctuating his questions by putting his hand on the librarian's shoulder.

Examples of potential problem situations such as these are endless, and some of them from one librarian's personal experience may sound familiar. In just the last few years serious problems have plagued libraries of all types. In Utah, for example, on August 4, 1999, Brigham Young University's Harold B. Lee Library experienced a bomb scare;[1] on April 19, 1999, a 70-year-old gunman entered the genealogical library of the Church of Jesus Christ of Latter-Day Saints in Salt Lake City and calmly began firing, reloading, and firing again, leaving two dead and four wounded;[2] and on August 3, 1998, a man who was reported to be a regular user of the Salt Lake City Public Library committed suicide in the library while being sought by police in connection with an attempted kidnapping.[3]

By their nature, libraries have special security risks. Many academic libraries are open to the public. Law libraries often attract people who have a legal problem and may be upset or angry. If the library is also a federal government documents depository, completely barring the public to reduce security risks is not an option. In addition, libraries typically have open stack and study areas that are isolated. Long and sometimes around-the-clock hours of operation contribute further to security risks.[4]

B. Crime

The two major types of library crimes that involve victims (as opposed to so-called "victimless crimes" such as drug use or prostitution) can be classified as property crimes and criminal acts directed against persons. Literature on library security follows those divisions by focusing primarily on securing property (collections, equipment, computer networks, etc.) and dealing with creating and maintaining a safe environment for people. Studies indicate that both types of crime are serious problems for libraries.

One national study in the early 1980s on crime in libraries asked

1,700 libraries to report the most prevalent forms of crimes they encountered during a 12-month period. The incidence of crime reported by those libraries was: book theft–80-90%, theft of reference materials–60%, book mutilation–50%, indecent exposure–15-20%, incidents of assaults on patrons–7%, victims of arson–4%, and assault on a staff member–3%.[5]

A similar but smaller survey among Illinois public libraries in the summer of 1996 revealed these problems: book mutilation–62.5%, book theft–56%, threats or harassment of library staff or patrons–72%.[6] What the first study shows is that crimes against patrons and staff occur far less frequently than do library property crimes; however, they are widespread enough to merit concern. The second study seems to contradict this somewhat, showing that threats and harassment of individuals was the largest security problem in Illinois public libraries, at least during the 12 months preceding the survey. The apparent contradiction is illusory though, when one considers that the first survey framed the question of crimes against people in terms of actual assaults, while the second was more interested in threatening or harassing behavior,[7] which is more the focus of this article.

Emphasis is being given to threatening or harassing behavior because action is still possible at that stage of interaction to prevent it from escalating. Once an assault begins, the only action practicable is escape and calling the police. Librarians needing information on protection from crimes against property, rather than persons, should consult one of the many sources available in the library literature.[8]

C. Mental Illness

Mental illness is often central to the debate about library security. Patrons who seem to suffer from mental illness are a great cause of staff anxiety, in part due to a lack of understanding about the condition.[9] Twenty years ago libraries were not often faced with mentally ill visitors. The movement toward deinstitutionalization[10] has meant that persons with mental illnesses now commonly live and work in the community with varying levels of medical and social support. In many cases, untreated mental illness may lead to homelessness.[11] For those with access to medical care, drug therapy may provide a high degree of control over the illness, but symptoms may return if use of medication ceases.[12]

Most libraries have persons with mental illness as patrons, perhaps without the staff even realizing it. Medical experts estimate that one-third of all Americans will have a serious mental illness during their lifetime.[13] Of importance to librarians is the fact that the vast majority of those suffering from mental illness are not violent.[14]

Understanding something about the causes of mental illness is a first step toward developing an appropriate service attitude. Individuals with mental illness are suffering from a medical condition. If their behavior is not criminal or threatening, they should be treated with respect and compassion rather than fear and reproach.[15] Mental illness may be caused by genetic conditions, infection, brain injury, drug or alcohol abuse, and psychosocial factors such as stress or grief.[16] While many specific mental illnesses are associated with increased aggression, the library staff is not in a position to diagnose medical conditions. Focusing on specific behaviors or warning signs which can help assess the level of risk may be the appropriate response. Specific warning signs and responses are discussed in the context of interpersonal solutions later in this article.

III. SOLUTIONS

Advance planning, such as building security measures, often can prevent problems. Training can help prepare staff to respond appropriately during problem encounters. Part of that response is based on interpersonal skills that are the result of individual experience and training, and part has to do with steps that the library has taken to prepare for such events, such as having effective policies and procedures and staff training.

A. Assessing the Risk

Even after a great deal of public service experience, it is difficult to predict when or how problem situations will arise, or around which patrons one has to be especially cautious. The literature reveals at least one example where library security personnel in a major public library attempted to classify problem patrons into the broad categories of "dangerous," "harmless," and "who the heck knows?" and deal with them as classes.[17] Behaviors representative of the "dangerous" class include armed, sexually deviant, emotionally disturbed, predatory, combative, felonious, vandalizing, threatening, touching, paranoid, and drug-intoxicated, among others.[18]

While that particular library's guidelines call for a "very serious" response to such individuals, "[i]n the absence of on-site psychiatric evaluation of individuals, most such classifications become nothing more than impromptu judgment calls by untrained observers and will vary accordingly with the individual observer. The library staff member, however, does not always have the time and opportunity to analyze facts and render a measured judgment. Sometimes, an instant decision is both necessary and desirable."[19] The decision needed is that of separating the potential problems from the real problems and defusing the situation before a major incident erupts.[20] Although pigeonholing problem patrons may be useful for the purpose of determining whether a real problem exists, it is of doubtful usefulness in formulating a response. Each patron must be handled individually for the response to be effective.[21]

In a preventive approach, the first step in dealing with aggressive, violent, or criminal behavior is to assess areas of risk. Risk prevention assessment should address both building security and staff training. Staff development should include ongoing training in interpersonal communications skills for handling problem situations.[22] At the planning stage the library may contact security experts from within the institution, or hire a security consultant for a security audit.

B. Safer Library Buildings

The strategy for improving security of an existing building should begin with a security audit of both external and internal areas, perhaps by an outside security expert. Security methods, including alarm systems, written policies, emergency procedures, staff preparedness, ongoing training, and system maintenance, should be evaluated. Areas for improvement should be identified and a plan developed to implement the improvements.[23]

A checklist for assessing building security may be helpful in conducting such an assessment. One such checklist[24] includes the following items related to personal security issues:

Employee/Patron Security: (a) Exit/entrance controls, (b) Use of emergency exits, (c) Building design/surveillance, (d) Patrols or TV monitors, (e) Building access policy, (f) Staff ID badges, (g) Emergency telephones.

Key Policy and Building Security: (a) Procedures for issuing and reclaiming keys, (b) Periodic lock changes, (c) Silent alarms, (d) Parking lot security, (e) Adequate lighting, (f) Custodial services access, (g) Window and book-drop security.

Outside the building, parking and entrance areas should be well lighted. Landscaping should be pruned to eliminate potential hiding places for criminals. If possible, security phones should be installed in parking areas.[25] Security personnel at some institutions provide escort or shuttle service for those leaving buildings after dark. Staff and patrons should be encouraged to use those services, especially when leaving at closing time. Many libraries avoid scheduling staff to work alone.

The library building's interior layout should be reviewed to make sure staff members have at least one escape route and clear fields of vision from offices and work areas to help eliminate potential danger zones.[26] Sight lines can be increased by rearranging furniture and stacks. Lighting should be used to increase visibility. Isolated areas should be reduced or eliminated as much as possible; while private corners may seem desirable for study, they may increase the risk of personal assault.[27]

Because isolated areas can rarely be eliminated entirely, the following security strategies should be considered: personal alarms for staff working in remote stacks, "duress alarms" in areas such as women's restrooms, locking doors to staff-only areas at all times, alarms on fire-exit-only doors, locking upper floor restrooms during off-peak hours.[28] Metal detectors may be useful in high crime areas, but they require a great deal of on-site security support. Their usefulness must be weighed against their expense to maintain and the negative atmosphere they may create for patrons and staff.[29]

While retrofitting security systems into an existing library can be difficult, a new building or major renovation project affords an opportunity to incorporate security components at the design stage. Some designers and architects use a framework called Crime Prevention through Environmental Design (CPTED) to aid in integrating security and building design components.[30] CPTED has three basic strategies: (1) Natural access control reduces the opportunity for crime. An example is the use of secure "staff-only" restricted access areas. (2) Natural surveillance allows for monitoring of potential criminals. Examples include internal and external windows and clear lines of sight within the library. (3) Territorial reinforcement involves creation of clear boundaries which make prowlers more noticeable. Examples include fenced parking areas and guard desks or "sign-in" stations.

C. Policies and Procedures

While improved building security is an important preventative measure, it will not eliminate every problem. The library must have well conceived security policies and procedures in place for problem situations. Security policies should be simple and easy to explain, as should the procedures staff will be expected to follow in tense situations. There is no time for uncertainty when an incident occurs.[31] Emergency procedures should be kept on a clipboard or binder separate from other policy documents and easily accessible. When dealing with a potentially dangerous patron, having this clipboarded document in the staff member's hands has several advantages: first, it gives personnel something nonthreatening and inoffensive to do with their hands while holding it; second, it can be used as a shield to deflect an unexpected punch in case the patron suddenly becomes violent.[32]

A library security policy should begin with a statement of purpose, or mission statement, which clarifies the library's purpose and indicates that if a patron's behavior does not conform, the patron may be asked to leave. Next, the behavior policy should specifically delineate impermissible behavior.[33] The procedural section that follows lists the steps staff should take to deal with problem behavior. The policy document should specify appropriate and inappropriate uses of the library, as well as unacceptable patron behavior.

While each library has its own unique combination of setting, mission, clientele, staffing, and physical layout, the appropriate uses of facilities and materials in most libraries would include researching, reading, writing, attending programs, viewing exhibits, and similar tasks. Policies should list inappropriate uses, such as bathing, shaving, washing clothes, gambling, panhandling, and sleeping. Inappropriate behavior should be included as well, such as running, climbing, using abusive or obscene language, making threats or lewd suggestions, talking loudly on a cell phone, and eating or drinking items that are prohibited.[34]

Conducting a security audit is a good way to begin developing a security policy. The audit would identify security risks, assess the adequacy of existing unwritten policies and make recommendations for improvement, and formulate the core rules of behavior for the library.[35] The rules help with security because users are put on notice about acceptable and unacceptable conduct, and staff have the clear guidance needed to take action.

Staff members need to know the rules, why each rule exists so they can explain and answer questions, each staff member's role in enforcement, the roles of others, and how much discretion each staff member has in enforcing the rules and handling unusual circumstances. Rules should be specific as to behavior not allowed and should be publicly posted. The policy document can be developed into a detailed procedure manual with definitions of the conduct proscribed by the rules, as well as procedures for enforcement and complaint procedures for patrons affected by them.[36] The manual should provide directions for the staff and answer basic questions, such as how the staff is to interact with the public, who calls the police, how to evacuate the library, etc.[37]

D. Legal Considerations

1. Access

Policies must target specific behaviors rather than classes of people in order to be legally valid.[38] According to *Kreimer v. Bureau of Police*[39] and *Brinkmeier v. City of Freeport*,[40] access to public libraries is a limited First Amendment right to receive information; thus, the security policy's proscriptions on certain behaviors must be written and open for public review, carefully worded as specifically as possible, and limited in scope to patron conduct *inside* the library.

Policies should list specific conduct that would be disruptive or interfere with other patrons' use of the library. Procedures for patrons to appeal an expulsion should be detailed. The procedures do not have to be formal, but should allow a patron who questions the denial of access an opportunity to prove extenuating circumstances or request a reconsideration of the library's actions.[41]

2. Liability

Under premises liability law the library owes a duty to its users ("invitees") to keep the premises reasonably safe and to warn of defects, especially if the library knows, or should know, about a persistent problem, or in this case, a problem patron.[42] How can the risk of unsafe premises be minimized? Thomas Steele's article on *Managing Legal Liability*[43] suggests that risks can be minimized by: regular inspections of the premises by library staff; drafting quality library policies with periodic review by library managers; periodic inspections or spot reviews of specific problems or policies by nonlibrary experts like police, fire, medical, engineering, psychological and human resources experts; adequate reporting of problems; and adequate record-keeping.

Insurance is another option to consider. While most libraries are covered by insurance to some extent, they are usually included in collective policies owned by the parent institution or governmental body. At the very least, a library manager should ask the following questions of attorneys or insurance agents knowledgeable in these matters:

- What is the status of the state's sovereign immunity (for public libraries) or charitable immunity (for private libraries) doctrine with regard to libraries? Can either of these doctrines be relied upon to bar a lawsuit against the library or its employees?
- Does the state require insurance coverage of libraries? How does this affect the library's potential liability for injuries to patrons?
- Can the library restrict access under state law or local regulation as a way of minimizing risk? What steps must be followed to implement or enforce use policies?
- Is insurance required by the state adequate to cover potential liability?
- Can the agent make suggestions about arrangement of furniture and workspaces to alleviate otherwise isolated seating or workspaces which may be conducive to assault, accidents, etc.?
- Can the insurance agent provide on-the-job training programs to alert employees to potential security problems?[44]

E. Staff Training

Staff training, in conjunction with well-developed policies and procedures, is the key to prevention and control of problem encounters. For example, a man wielding a loaded .45 caliber automatic weapon and an antipersonnel bomb leaped onto the fiction desk at the Salt

Lake City Public Library on March 5, 1994, and began ordering patrons into a nearby conference room.[45] During the first critical minutes, staff remained calm, called police, conducted a sweep of the
building to implement the library's evacuation procedure, and reviewed building layout plans with police. After the incident Director J.
Dennis Day said, "Having staff who feel empowered and possess a
sense of ownership can make a difference. Because we give our staff a
strong background in handling emergency situations and because we
trust in their judgment to make critical decisions when needed, a lot of
things went right."[46]

Library staff members may not intrinsically have the skills necessary to handle difficult patron situations, nor do they usually learn
these skills in the course of their formal education.[47] An effective,
ongoing staff training program should consist of both in-service[48] and
more formal opportunities outside the library. Initial in-service training often can be completed in an hour or so and can help staff deal
with various situations, such as those posed by intoxicated or mentally
disturbed individuals.

Training helps staff understand what behavior to expect, how to
assess possible risks posed by disturbed patrons, and how to defuse
precarious situations. Training sessions should include ample time for
questions, discussion, and role-playing with the tone being as upbeat
and positive as possible. Good judgment in crisis situations comes
from lessons learned in real situations or practice exercises. Raising
staff comfort levels in role-playing situations, which enables them to
try different approaches, take risks, and learn from the experience, is
better than learning lessons in real-life confrontations. Above all, staff
must know they can trust supervisors to back them up, which can add
immeasurably to staff self-confidence. Training sessions also can be
used to brainstorm ideas for inclusion in policies and procedures since
staff deal with patron issues every day.

In addition to training, support should be provided after a staff
member has experienced a traumatic encounter with a difficult patron.
At a minimum, supervisors should allow the staff member to discuss
what happened, vent concerns, and express any feelings about the
incident.[49] Librarians should not hesitate to consult the wealth of print
resources and guides available for training and support.[50]

F. Interpersonal Solutions

When staff members are attentive to the patron, potential problem situations often can be resolved before they escalate. A staff member's perception sets the tone for any public service encounter so the focus should be on patron behavior rather than personalities. No one has much control over his or her basic personality traits;[51] some people just rub others the wrong way. A staff member may face a person who is angry, hostile, or aggressive. If the initial encounter is managed well to lessen the patron's anxiety, the aggravating factors can be overcome and communication begun. Good communication is essential to the successful resolution of problem encounters.

1. Content and Process of Communication

Communication consists of content (the message) and process (the context of the message, usually emotional). People tend to respond to nonverbal signals–the process of communication–with much more intensity than to the verbal message, especially when they are under stress. Nonverbal signals include body language, such as facial expressions, eye contact, postures, and hand movements, as well as the volume and tone of the voice.

Active listening should be employed to hear and respond to the meaning and feeling behind the other person's words.[52] Close attention should be given to nonverbal cues and their impact. The patrons can be put at ease if the librarian provides positive nonverbal cues and asks questions that help in understanding the patron's needs and intentions. Some of the following techniques may evoke positive responses from a distressed patron:

Show empathy. Try not to be judgmental of the patron's feelings. The emotions are real even if not based on reality.

Clarify messages. Ask reflective questions and use both silence and restatements.

Respect personal space. Stand at least two to three feet away from the person.

Be aware of body position. Squaring-off with an individual sends a message of challenge while standing at an angle to the side may be less likely to provoke.

Remember to breathe. Because physical and emotional responses are so interconnected, relaxing the body can be calming. Composed breathing and placing one's body in a relaxed, open posture can help soothe.

Permit verbal venting when possible. Allow the patron to release as much energy as possible in a verbal, nonthreatening way.

Set and enforce reasonable limits. Be clear and concise. Do not become involved in an argument over library policies, but do let the patron know that his or her behavior is unacceptable and will not produce the desired results.

Avoid overreacting. Remain calm, rational, and professional at all times. Librarians should know their own "hot buttons" and back off if they are pushed. A colleague could be asked to take over the interview while the initial library contact goes elsewhere.

Take the patron to a different part of the library. This allows for cooling off. More importantly, it takes the matter out of the public eye, where the patron may be either humiliated or excited by the attention received.

Use physical techniques only as a last resort. Employing physical techniques on an individual who is only acting out verbally can dramatically escalate the situation. The least restrictive method of intervention should be used.

Ignore challenge questions. Answering these questions often fuels a power struggle. Explanations appear defensive and justifications seem to be deflections of responsibility. Do not respond reflexively by repeating negative buzzwords or accusatory labels. Try to redirect the patron's attention to the issue at hand, and keep things moving in a positive direction.

Apologize for the patron's inconvenience. Even if the library is not at fault, it can make an irate person feel better.

Focus on the problem. Once the problem is understood, restate it clearly and concisely, but do not restate the solution offered by the patron. By separating needs from solutions, it becomes possible to identify many more alternatives. The more alternative solutions available, the better. Let the patron choose from among the possibilities to ensure that the solution is acceptable. Sometimes the patron finds no solution acceptable. It is still possible to minimize the patron's anger by stating that action will be taken, such as a memo to the director about the issue. Always explain the proposed action and check that the patron understands.

Prioritize the issues. If the patron has several concerns, deal with them one at a time. Whenever possible, start with a problem which is easily solved, or an error which can easily be addressed. This makes the library appear responsive and flexible, and encourages the patron to act accordingly.[53]

2. The First Minute

The first minute is the most important when dealing with an upset patron. By being as friendly and open as possible, the staff member can show that the patron is valued and that the staff is not defensive, which could increase a patron's anger or anxiety. A friendly, controlled approach may make it possible to deflect or defuse the initial anger, hostility, or overt aggression the patron is showing and deal with the underlying problem.

3. Anger, Aggression, and Hostility in Non-Threatening Situations

Although a problem patron may be angry, hostile, and/or aggressive,[54] this does not necessarily mean the patron is dangerously disturbed. If the staff believes an aggressive patron is not dangerous, being assertive might seem the proper course of action. Assertiveness may be effective when dealing with patrons who habitually combine aggression and anger as a control tactic. A polite but firm response is often the only way to handle the patron who is demonstrating anger-driven behavior that is only *verbal* in nature. In dealing with dangerous aggressiveness, however, where there is a clear threat of physical violence or injury, an assertive response would not be the correct approach because a more conciliatory demeanor is needed.[55]

4. Warning Signs of Violent, Dangerous Aggression

Indications that an individual is about to become violent include: pacing, clenching hands and teeth, signs of agitation, abusive language, loud and rapid speech, indications of drug or alcohol intoxication such as slurred speech and unsteadiness.[56] A staff member confronted by someone who threatens to become violent should consider the following techniques to help calm the patron: (1) Talk in a quiet tone of voice and give the person the sense that he or she is in control of him- or herself and the situation. (2) Give the person an "out"–a nonviolent way of easing out of the situation without losing self-esteem. If possible, provide a choice of "outs." (3) Give the person room–crowding a fearful, paranoid, or agitated person may increase the likelihood of violence. (4) Keep everything as quiet and calm as possible. Sometimes decreased stimulation helps alleviate a crisis.[57]

In dealing with a potentially violent patron, personal security of staff and other patrons is the priority. Leaving the area and/or calling the police may be necessary.[58]

G. Follow-Up

Encounters with problem patrons must be documented and communicated to all interested parties: law library staff, personnel who might also encounter this individual in the future such as law school staff, and perhaps campus security or local police so they can assess the situation. A confidential file on problem incidents will help track them and spot patterns. This documentation also will be invaluable when relating details to the police and may be used to justify decisions to bar repeat offenders from the library.

This record must only be used in the case of serious threats, however, and not as a way to track and intimidate certain patrons. The documentation should briefly record the details of the incident, including time, date, and exact location. The detail may depend on the seriousness and frequency of the offensive behavior and whether other patrons were victimized. Since the names of problem patrons often are not known, a complete description of the perpetrator is very important. As a minimum, this should include the patron's sex and race, general physical build, distinguishing physical characteristics such as tattoos or facial hair, clothing, and the behavior which caused the trouble.

While the staff member at the scene normally records this data, more in-depth analysis is usually done by a library administrator. This analysis should indicate such factors as any noted patterns of behavior, the seriousness of the incident, and what determination was made or action taken as a result. Also included are any special steps that should be taken and whether security should be called if the perpetrator appears or misbehaves again.[59]

IV. CONCLUSION

Security is becoming more important as libraries face the challenges presented by problem patrons. Violence is a fact of modern life and libraries are not immune. Risks can be lowered, however, by taking precautions such as: investing the time, energy and money in a comprehensive staff training program; drafting clear and concise policies and procedures to help staff deal with problem patrons; understanding the legal issues of access and liability as they apply to libraries; and creating a more secure physical environment in the library and its grounds. More detailed references on library security are available on the author's webpage.[60] A selective bibliography of additional resources is provided at the end of the notes.[61]

NOTES

1. Library Journal Digital, *Bomb Scare in Academic Library* (last modified Aug. 23, 1999) <http://www.ljdigital.com/articles/news/thisweek/19990823_5040.asp>.

2. Library Journal Digital, *Gunman Slays Two in Utah Library* (last modified Apr. 19, 1999) <http://www.ljdigital.com/articles/news/thisweek/p9517.asp>.

3. Library Journal Digital, *Fleeing Suspect Kills Self in Library* (last modified Aug. 17, 1998) <http://www.ljdigital.com/articles/news/thisweek/p9120.asp>.

4. *See* Daniel P. Keller, *Special Problems in the Library Setting*, 11 LIBR. ADMIN. & MGMT. 161, 162 (1997).

5. Evan St. Lifer, *How Safe Are Our Libraries?*, LIBR. J., Aug. 1994, at 35.

6. Michael Lorenzen, *Security in the Public Libraries of Illinois*, ILL. LIBR., Winter 1997, at 21.

7. *But cf.* David C. Duggar, *Security and Crime in Health Sciences Libraries in the Southern United States*, MED. REFERENCE SERVICES Q., Spring 1999, at 37. This study focused on threatening or harassing behavior, as opposed to actual physical violence, and appeared to show that property crimes are more prevalent (63%) than crimes against people (37%). *Id.*

8. *See, e.g.*, Richard W. Boss, *Security Technologies for Libraries: Policy Concerns and a Survey of Available Products*, 35 LIBR. TECH. REP. 271 (1999); James H. Billington, *Here Today, Here Tomorrow: The Imperative of Collections Security*, AM. LIBR., Aug. 1996, at 40; Gregor Trinkaus-Randall, *Library and Archival Security: Policies and Procedures to Protect Holdings from Theft and Damage*, 25(1) J. LIBR. ADMIN. 91 (1998). Another source of information on all types of library security issues is *Focus on Security: The Magazine of Library, Archive, and Museum Security*, published quarterly since 1994.

9. *See* Charles A. Salter & Jeffrey L. Salter, *Mentally Ill Patrons, in* PATRON BEHAVIOR IN LIBRARIES: A HANDBOOK OF POSITIVE APPROACHES TO NEGATIVE SITUATIONS 18-20 (Beth McNeil & Denise J. Johnson eds., 1996).

10. *See* Fay Zipkowitz, *"No One Wants to See Them": Meeting the Reference Needs of the Deinstitutionalized*, 31 REFERENCE LIBR. 53, 55 (1990).

11. *See* H. Richard Lamb, *Deinstitutionalization in the Nineties, in* TREATING THE HOMELESS MENTALLY ILL: A TASK FORCE REPORT OF THE AMERICAN PSYCHIATRIC ASSOCIATION 41 (H. Richard Lamb et al. eds., 1992).

12. *See* Lewis A. Opler, *The Use of Drugs and Other Somatic Treatments, in* THE COLUMBIA UNIVERSITY COLLEGE OF PHYSICIANS AND SURGEONS COMPLETE HOME GUIDE TO MENTAL HEALTH 63, 65 (Frederic I. Kass et al. eds., 1992).

13. *See* Michael Sheehy & Francine Cournos, *What Is Mental Illness?, in* THE CO-LUMBIA UNIVERSITY COLLEGE OF PHYSICIANS AND SURGEONS COMPLETE HOME GUIDE TO MENTAL HEALTH, *supra* note 12, at 3-4.

14. *See* Jonathan M. Silver & Stuart Yudofsky, *Violence and Aggression, in* THE COLUMBIA UNIVERSITY COLLEGE OF PHYSICIANS AND SURGEONS COMPLETE HOME GUIDE TO MENTAL HEALTH, *supra* note 12, at 385-86.

15. *See* CHARLES A. SALTER & JEFFREY L. SALTER, ON THE FRONTLINES: COPING WITH THE LIBRARY'S PROBLEM PATRONS 111 (1988).

16. *Id.* at 112-15.

17. Bruce A. Shuman, *Down and Out in the Reading Room: The Homeless in the Public Library, in* PATRON BEHAVIOR IN LIBRARIES: A HANDBOOK OF POSITIVE AP-PROACHES TO NEGATIVE SITUATIONS, *supra* note 9, at 3, 9.

18. *Id.*

19. *Id.*

20. MARK R. WILLIS, DEALING WITH DIFFICULT PEOPLE IN THE LIBRARY 24 (1999).

21. *Id.* at 25.

22. *See* ANNE M. TURNER, IT COMES WITH THE TERRITORY: HANDLING PROBLEM SIT-UATIONS IN LIBRARIES 42-43 (1993).

23. *See* James H. Clark, *Making Our Buildings Safer: Security Management and Equipment Issues*, 11 LIBR. ADMIN. & MGMT. 157, 158-59 (1997).

24. *See* Thomas W. Shaughnessy, *Security: Past, Present, and Future, in* SECURI-TY FOR LIBRARIES: PEOPLE, BUILDINGS, COLLECTIONS 1, 23 (Marvine Brand ed., 1984).

25. *See* Keller, *supra* note 4, at 165.

26. Salter & Salter, *supra* note 9, at 42-43.

27. *See* Bruce A. Shuman, *Designing Personal Safety into Library Buildings*, AM. LIBR., Aug. 1996, at 37, 38; ALAN JAY LINCOLN, CRIME IN THE LIBRARY: A STUDY OF PATTERNS, IMPACT, AND SECURITY 138-141 (1984).

28. *See* Keller, *supra* note 4, at 164-65.

29. *See* Clark, *supra* note 23, at 160.

30. *See* Randall L. Atlas, *Designing Crime-Free Environments: Making Our Buildings Safer*, 11 LIBR. ADMIN. & MGMT. 88, 90-91 (1997).

31. *See* Robert L. Willits, *When Violence Threatens the Workplace*, 11 LIBR. ADMIN. & MGMT. 166, 168 (1997).

32. *See* Salter & Salter, *supra* note 9, at 37.

33. *See* Linda A. Morrissett, *Developing and Implementing a Patron Behavior Policy, in* PATRON BEHAVIOR IN LIBRARIES: A HANDBOOK OF POSITIVE APPROACHES TO NEGATIVE SITUATIONS, *supra* note 9, at 135, 136-37.

34. *See* Salter & Salter, *supra* note 9, at 29; Willis, *supra* note 20, at 119. For more information on policies concerning food and drink in the library, see the article in this volume by Jessie Cranford, *"Library Police": Drafting and Implementing Enforce-able Library Rules*.

35. *See* SECURITY AND CRIME PREVENTION IN LIBRARIES (Michael Chaney & Alan F. MacDougal eds., 1992); *see also* Linda A. Morrissett, *supra* note 33, at 137; John Newman & Chris Wolf, *The Security Audit*, COLO. LIBR., Spring 1997, at 19.

36. *See* Rianna Schroeder, *Library Rules, Policies, and Library Security*, NEB. LIBR. ASS'N Q., Spring 1999, at 16, 17-18.

37. *See* TURNER, supra note 22, at 113. This book includes sample procedures and policies.

38. *See* Salter & Salter, *supra* note 9, at 30. "The point is to prohibit specific types of behavior, not types of people. Policies should address patrons' behavior rather than their status. Libraries should not restrict or bar individuals solely because they look like 'bums' or 'weirdos'." *Id.*

39. Kreimer v. Bureau of Police for the Town of Morriston, 958 F.2d 1242 (3d Cir. 1992).

40. Brinkmeier v. City of Freeport, No. 93 C 20039, 1993 U.S. Dist. LEXIS 9255 (N.D. Ill. July 2, 1993); *see also* Lieber v. Village of Spring Valley, 40 F. Supp. 2d 525 (S.D.N.Y. 1999); New York v. Kern & Miller, 289 N.Y.S.2d 71 (Nassau County Ct. 1968); Vrndavan v. Malcolm, No. 64839, 1994 Ohio App. LEXIS 1103 (March 17, 1994).

41. *See* Katherine Malmquist, *Legal Issues Regarding Library Patrons, in* PATRON BEHAVIOR IN LIBRARIES: A HANDBOOK OF POSITIVE APPROACHES TO NEGATIVE SITUATIONS, *supra* note 9, at 95, 95-99; *see also* Stuart Comstock-Gay, *Disruptive Behavior: Protecting People, Protecting Rights*, Wilson LIBR. BULL., Feb. 1995, at 33; Richard Danner, *From the Editor: Public Access to the Law*, 79 L. LIBR. J. 163 (1987); Barbara J. Snow, *When Goals Collide: Planning and Implementing a Restricted Access Policy at the University of Michigan Law Library*, 84 L. LIBR. J. 387 (1992); *ACRL Guidelines for the Preparation of Policies on Library Access: A Draft*, 53 COLLEGE & RES. LIBR. NEWS 709 (1992).

42. Thomas M. Steele, *Managing Legal Liability*, 11 LIBR. ADMIN. & MGMT. 94, 97 (1997).

43. *Id.* at 94-98.

44. *See* Barbara Bintliff & Al Coco, *Legal Aspects of Library Security, in* SECURITY FOR LIBRARIES: PEOPLE, BUILDINGS, COLLECTIONS, *supra* note 24, at 83, 106; *see also* PHILIP D. DICKINSON, WORKPLACE VIOLENCE AND EMPLOYER LIABILITY (1997); BERNARD D. REAMS, JR. & ERWIN C. SURRENCY, INSURING THE LAW LIBRARY: FIRE AND DISASTER RISK MANAGEMENT (1982); RENEE RUBIN, AVOIDING LIABILITY RISK: AN ATTORNEY'S ADVICE TO LIBRARY TRUSTEES AND OTHERS (1995); Carol B. Allred, *Negligence Law for Libraries*, 77 L. LIBR. J. 195 (1985); Silva E. Barsumyan, *Premises Liability*, NEW JERSEY LIBR., Spring 1988, at 9; Carol Kristl, *Rape of Teenager Raises Security Issues*, AM. LIBR., Sept. 1996, at 15; Joseph J. Mika & Bruce A. Shuman, *Legal Issues Affecting Libraries and Librarians: Employment Laws, Liability & Insurance, Contracts, and Problem Patrons*, AM. LIBR., Jan. 1988, at 26; Thomas Steele, *Law of Premises Liability as Applied to North Carolina Libraries*, N.C. LIBR., Spring 1991, at 9; Jonathan S. Tryon, *Premises Liability for Librarians*, 10(2) LIBR. & ARCHIVAL SECURITY 3 (1990).

45. Colleen McLaughlin, *Salt Lake City: A Model*, LIBR. J., Aug. 1994, at 37.

46. *Id.*

47. *See* Kitty Smith, Serving the Difficult Customer, A How-To-Do-It Manual for Library Staff 139 (1994).

48. *E.g.*, After repeated difficulties with a problem patron, the University of Nebraska Law College conducted in-service staff training with University of Nebraska Police Director Ken Cauble, and University Employee Assistance Program Director Nancy F. Myers.

49. *See* Salter & Salter, *supra* note 9, at 20.

50. *See* Smith, *supra* note 47, at 145. "Among the most useful [items] for planning interpersonal skills training in a library context are Barbara Conroy, *Library Staff Development and Continuing Education: Principles and Practices* (Littleton, CO: Libraries Unlimited, 1978); Sheila Dainow and Caroline Bailey, *Developing Skills with People: Training for Person to Person Client Contact* (Chichester: John Wiley and Sons, Ltd., 1988); *Guidelines for Quality in Continuing Education for Information, Library and Media Personnel* (Chicago: ALA/Continuing Education Subcommittee of the Standing Committee on Library Education, January 12, 1988); Charles A. Salter and Jeffrey L. Salter, *On the Frontlines: Coping with the Library's Problem Patrons* (Englewood, CO: Libraries Unlimited, 1988); and *Staff Development: A Practical Guide* 2nd ed., Ed. Anne G. Lipow and Deborah A. Carver (Chicago: ALA, 1992)." *Id.*

51. *See* Smith, *supra* note 47, at 14.

52. *See* Nathan M. Smith, *Active Listening: Alleviating Patron Problems through Communication*, *in* Patron Behavior in Libraries: A Handbook of Positive Approaches to Negative Situations, *supra* note 9, at 127.

53. *See* Smith, *supra* note 47, at 6, 15, 29, 30, 39; Tom R. Arterburn, *Librarians: Caretakers or Crimefighters?*, Am. Libr., Aug. 1996, at 32, 33; Rhea Joyce Rubin, *Anger in the Library: Defusing Angry Patrons at the Reference Desk (and Elsewhere)*, 31 Reference Libr. 39, 39-47 (1990); Willis, *supra* note 20, at 31-39.

54. *See* Rubin, *supra* note 53, at 40. *See also* Smith, *supra* note 47, at 48-50.

55. *See* Smith, *supra* note 47, at 33, 51, 57, 60-61, 67.

56. *See* Silver & Yudofsky, *supra* note 14, at 391-92.

57. *Id.* at 392.

58. *Id.*

59. *See* Salter & Salter, *supra* note 9, at 41; Morrissett, *supra* note 33, at 143; *see also* Salter & Salter, *supra* note 50, at 155-60 (containing examples of various levels of documentation).

60. <http://www.law.utoledo.edu/lavalleylibrary/darndt/endnotes.html>.

61. Additional Sources of Information (in reverse chronological order):

Monographs

Christine A. Adamec, How to Live with a Mentally Ill Person: A Handbook of Day-to-Day Strategies (1996).

Office for Intellectual Freedom, American Library Ass'n, Intellectual Freedom Manual (5th ed. 1996).

Michael P. Nichols, The Lost Art of Listening (1995).

Academic Libraries in Urban and Metropolitan Areas: A Management Handbook (Gerard McCabe ed., 1991).

ANN CATHERINE PAIETTA, ACCESS SERVICES: A HANDBOOK (1991).

OFFICE OF MANAGEMENT SERVICES, ASSOCIATION OF RESEARCH LIBRARIES, BUILDING SECURITY AND PERSONAL SAFETY (SPEC Kit no. 150) (1989).

BRUCE A. SHUMAN, RIVER BEND REVISITED: THE PROBLEM PATRON IN THE LIBRARY (1984).

Journal Articles

Lyn Hopper & Ruth E. O'Donnell, *50 Simple Things You Can Do to Improve Your Library's Security–Ok, It's Really 51*, 110 UNABASHED LIBR. 22 (1999).

Bruce A. Shuman & Stephen L. Hupp, *Library Security and Safety Handbook*, LIBR. J., Sept. 15, 1999, at 118 (book review).

Bruce A. Canal, *Libraries Attract More Than Readers: Investing in Library Safety*, 17(1) IND. LIBR. 15 (1998).

Michael Lorenzen, *Security Issues in the Public Libraries of Three Midwestern States*, 37 PUB. LIBR. 134 (1998).

Steven P. Fisher & Thomas K. Fry, *Security and Emergency Preparedness in a University Library: Planning Works*, COLO. LIBR., Spring 1997, at 9.

Cameron Johnson, *(In)security Is Our Business: Sentinels of the Stacks We Have Known*, ALKI, Mar. 1997, at 26.

David Luurtsema, *Dealing with Book Loss in an Academic Library*, 14(1) LIBR. & ARCHIVAL SECURITY 21 (1997).

Glenda Ann Thornton, *Guarding Against Chaos: Establishing and Maintaining Library Security*, COLO. LIBR., Spring 1997, at 27.

Glenda Ann Thornton, *Security in Libraries: A Concern for Everyone*, COLO. LIBR., Spring 1997, at 5.

U.S. Dep't of Labor, *Violence on the Job–Guidelines*, 102 UNABASHED LIBR. 24 (1997).

Arthur James Anderson, *Showdown*, LIBR. J., Mar. 1, 1996, at 59. (Library security following a mugging; with discussion.)

Carol D. Billings, *Rights and Obligations of a Librarian*, LLA BULL., Winter 1996, at 128.

Steve E. Ezennia et al., *Antisocial Acts in Libraries: The Nnamdi Azikiwe University Library's Experience*, 13(2) LIBR. & ARCHIVAL SECURITY 19 (1996).

David H. Johansson, *Library Materials Theft, Mutilation, and Preventive Security Measures*, 15(4) PUB. LIBR. Q. (1996).

Leonard Kniffel, *Facing Up to an Insecure Reality*, AM. LIBR., Aug. 1996, at 27.

Erma D. Ulmer, *Electronic Security Systems in Arkansas Academic Libraries*, ARK. LIBR., June 1996, at 3.

Thomas B. Witt, *The Use of Electronic Book Theft Detection Systems in Libraries*, 6(4) J. INTERLIBRARY LOAN, DOCUMENT DELIVERY & INFO. SUPPLY 45 (1996).

Patricia J. Davis, *Libraries in Crisis: Safety and Security in Today's Library; Or, I've Seen Fire and I've Seen Rain*, 71 TEXAS LIBR. J. 90 (1995).

Susan Kamm, *A Rose Is Not Necessarily a Rose: Issues in Public Library Security*, 13(1) LIBR. & ARCHIVAL SECURITY (1995). (Inglewood Public Library, California.)

Metta Nicewarner & Shelley Heaton, *Providing Security in an Urban Academic*

Library, 13(1) LIBR. & ARCHIVAL SECURITY 9 (1995). (University of Nevada-Las Vegas)

Robert J. Belvin, *Crime and Security in New Jersey Public Libraries*, 27 N.J. LIBR., Fall 1994, at 11. (Survey on crimes and security guards.)

Jane Lopes Crocker et al., *"Security" in the Smaller Academic Library*, 27 N.J. LIBR., Fall 1994, at 6.

Bruce E. Ford et al., *Security at the Newark Public Library*, N.J. LIBR., Fall 1994, at 17.

Barry V. Lipinski, *A Practical Approach to Library Security*, N.J. LIBR., Fall 1994, at 19. (Based on experience at two Rutgers libraries.)

Sheryl Owens, *Proactive Problem Patron Preparedness*, 12(2) LIBR. & ARCHIVAL SECURITY 11 (1994).

Terrance G. Shults, *Library Security: A Selected Bibliography*, 27 N.J. LIBR., Fall 1994, at 20.

Lillian Gerhardt, *Safe at Work?: Library Security Strategies for Staff Protection*, SCH. LIBR. J., Feb. 1993, at 4.

Guidelines for the Development of Policies Regarding Patron Behavior and Library Usage, LIBR. J., Mar. 1, 1992, at 51.

Nina Lyon & Warren Graham, *Library Security: One Solution*, N.C. LIBR., Spring 1991, at 21.

Nathan M. Smith & Irene Adams, *Using Active Listening to Deal with Patron Problems*, 30 PUB. LIBR. 236 (1991).

Elena Cevallos & Charles Kratz, *Training for Public Services*, 12(2) J. LIBR. ADMIN. 27 (1990).

Robert Chadbourne, *The Problem Patron: How Much Problem, How Much Patron?*, WILSON LIBR. BULL., June 1990, at 59.

Will Manley, *Facing the Public*, WILSON LIBR. BULL., Feb. 1990, at 61.

Bruce A. Shuman, *Problem Patrons in Libraries–A Review Article*, 9(2) LIBR. & ARCHIVAL SECURITY 3 (1989).

Herbert S. White, *Send These, the Homeless, Tempest-Tost to Me*, LIBR. J., Feb. 15, 1989, at 146.

Robert H. Abrams & Donald J. Dunn, *The Law Library's Institutional Response to the Pro Se Patron: A Post-Faretta Review*, 1 W. NEW ENG. L. REV. 47 (1978).

All in a Day's Work:
What's a Reference Librarian to Do?

Sandra B. Placzek

Sandra B. Placzek is Head of Public Services and Assistant Professor of Law Library at the Marvin and Virginia Schmid Law Library, University of Nebraska College of Law, Lincoln, NE 68583 (E-mail: splaczek2@unl.edu).

[Haworth co-indexing entry note]: "All in a Day's Work: What's a Reference Librarian to Do?" Placzek, Sandra B. Co-published simultaneously in *Legal Reference Services Quarterly* (The Haworth Information Press, an imprint of The Haworth Press, Inc.) Vol. 19, No. 1/2, 2001, pp. 41-56; and: *Emerging Solutions in Reference Services: Implications for Libraries in the New Millennium* (ed: John D. Edwards) The Haworth Information Press, an imprint of The Haworth Press, Inc., 2001, pp. 41-56. Single or multiple copies of this article are available for a fee from The Haworth Document Delivery Service [1-800-342-9678, 9:00 a.m. - 5:00 p.m. (EST). E-mail address: getinfo@haworthpressinc.com].

SUMMARY. Although reference librarians today have much in common with yesterday's counterparts, their days are much more hectic. Technological advances, changes in law and society, demands from a diverse group of library users, and an increased workload make time and stress management important issues to explore. This article examines reference librarianship in the academic environment, discusses how reference librarianship has changed, and offers suggestions on coping with the stresses those changes have caused. *[Article copies available for a fee from The Haworth Document Delivery Service: 1-800-342-9678. E-mail address: <getinfo@haworthpressinc. com> Website: <http://www.HaworthPress.com> © 2001 by The Haworth Press, Inc. All rights reserved.]*

I. INTRODUCTION

Librarianship as a profession is in the midst of an evolution that impacts the work of reference librarians on a daily basis. Today's answers to the questions of *who* wants the information; *what* information do they want; *where* is the information; *why* is the information needed and *how* is the information found and communicated are vastly different than in the past. Reference librarians today also face two additional challenges: user expectations of instant information and the level of informational and technological sophistication those users bring to the reference desk. When countless other demands on a reference librarian's time are added to traditional duties, a picture emerges of a reference librarian's "day" that today varies tremendously from yesterday's counterpart.

II. TRADITIONAL DUTIES

In the past, legal reference was primarily a paper-based information profession. Questions were posed and answers provided through the reference librarian's knowledge of library resources. In addition to the physical materials located in the library, those resources might include: telephone calls to appropriate individuals, agencies, and organizations; an understanding of what services and information each publisher provided; and a determination of when information would be in print.

Speed was an understood concept: as soon as possible. That usually meant as fast as the information was printed and could be personally retrieved, received in the mail, or acquired through other means of transmittal. Speed of transmission was not defined by fax or high-speed Internet connections. Reference librarians not only oversaw and responded to reference inquiries, they also created bibliographies, kept abreast of current events (through newspapers, advance sheets, legislative services, participation in tours and seminars, etc.), maintained vertical files, instructed on the use of library resources, and prepared legislative histories.[1]

Today's reference librarians still have many things in common with reference librarians of yesterday. Although some of the resources are different, the duties have increased, and the speed of information retrieval has accelerated, one constant remains true: there is never enough time to accomplish everything that needs to be done. "The commodity which most of us never seem to have in sufficiency is time."[2]

III. TODAY'S RESPONSIBILITIES

What has changed? Reference librarians still perform all the duties noted above. How and why is a reference librarian's "day" today any different than a "day" in the past? The changes impacting reference librarians today can be summed up by exploring four categories: changes in the law, changes in society, changes in technology, and changes in the publishing environment.

A. Changes in the Law

Law and the legal profession experienced tremendous growth in the last half of the twentieth century[3] that may continue in the twenty-first century as Americans become an increasingly litigious society.[4] Not only are the number of lawyers and cases commenced on the rise, but both "the Law" and the legal profession are undergoing a transformation. Areas of practice are expanding and new areas, such as cyberlaw, are developing. Increased specialization is the norm, with more and more lawyers focusing their practice in one particular area.[5] This expansion of legal topics and specialization by practitioners directly impacts reference librarians.

To effectively aid library users who are learning about those new areas or who specialize in a particular area, reference librarians need a basic understanding of the changing character of the law. New materials need to be investigated and quantified–is this something the library has and will it be helpful? What area of the law is this new emerging topic most like and are there any resources already in the library to help or will it be necessary to purchase new materials? At the most basic level, reference librarians need to be conversant in these areas to even conduct a reference interview.

B. Changes in Society

Society in general is much more sophisticated today, and as a result law library users are much more savvy. The expansive growth in communication and information transmission, often referred to as "information overload," is one of the causes for that sophistication. Society is bombarded with "the Law" in television, movies and bestsellers. Newspapers, news shows, and documentaries detail the intricacies of high-profile cases, as evidenced by media exposure during the O.J. Simpson trial. Reference librarians face library users who are much more familiar with legal matters because of that exposure as well as being more demanding and specific in their reference needs.

C. Changes in Technology

Perhaps the biggest change impacting reference work today is technology. Colleagues communicate through personal e-mail; discussion lists offer a forum for posting and responding to questions;[6] e-mail reference services provide distance reference;[7] Westlaw and LEXIS permit access to materials not available in the library; and the Internet has become a treasure trove of both free and fee based legal information.[8] CD-ROMs, DVDs, and copy machines also are examples of technological advances, as are fax machines, cell phones, pagers, and voice mail.

Although these technological advances provide reference librarians with a number of very current information retrieval avenues, they also place more demands on a profession that lacked adequate time to accomplish everything as far back as 1953.[9] Reference librarians must learn and become comfortable in the use of each new technology introduced into the legal reference world and be able to use those resources efficiently and effectively. The learning curve expectation is high, with reference librarians providing instruction in the use of many resources in both class sessions and on an individual basis, often not long after their introduction.

D. Changes in the Publishing Environment

Because the impact on the services reference librarians provide is less obvious, many librarians may not realize how the shifts in the publishing environment affect their work. In 1977, there were at least twenty-three independent legal publishers. Today there are primarily three large companies: Thomson Corporation, Reed-Elsevier, and Wolters Kluwer.[10] Why is this important and how does the decrease in legal publishers affect reference services? Reference librarians rely on both the quality of the information found in print resources and the time when those print resources will be available. Rising print costs, cessation of publication of particular resources, confusing invoices, and decreased quality of customer service directly impact the work reference librarians do.

If the information printed in a resource is incorrect and the customer service department has no experience with the resource or lacks a sufficient understanding of the librarian's question, finding the correct information for a library user may be an impossible task. To address these and other vendor related issues, the American Association of Law Libraries (AALL) formed the Committee on Relations with Information Vendors (CRIV). Volunteers from the AALL membership serve on this committee and work to "facilitate communication between AALL and information vendors, foster a cooperative working relationship between librarians and publishers, monitor complaints and provide suggestions to vendors, and keep AALL members informed of developments in legal publishing."[11] CRIV newsletters are published three times a year in issues of the *AALL Spectrum* and online.[12]

IV. USER EXPECTATIONS

A. Faculty

In an academic environment, faculty expectations vary.[13] While some faculty members are comfortable conducting their own research and exploring library resources, other faculty members require more assistance from the reference librarians. Faculty may call upon librarians to perform online searches, conduct classes or workshops on the use of electronic resources, assist with audio/visual needs, provide legal research instruction, locate resources or information, or provide one-on-one instruction with particular resources.

Although most faculty members give adequate preparation time to reference librarians, others may expect any of the services above with little or no advance warning. As a result, reference librarians may often find themselves juggling other duties while trying to prepare a class or find materials at a moment's notice. In addition, reference librarians may be the first contact for faculty members concerning why the library lacks particular resources necessary for their research, putting the reference librarian in the position of explaining tight budgets and lack of resources.

B. Staff

Library and law school staffs also have expectations even if they may be less easily identifiable. Contributing to law school newsletters, tracking down invoices, troubleshooting computers, and explaining updating instructions are a few areas where staff members expect assistance from reference librarians. Particularly in the area of updating, reference librarians are often consulted when questions arise concerning pocket parts, loose-leaf filing, and the removal of legislative service pamphlets because they are primary users of the materials. Reference librarians not only understand how the materials are organized and updated, but also the topics covered within the resource.

C. Students

If staff expectations are often less easily identifiable, student expectations are the easiest to ascertain. In some respects, students expect the reference librarian to have the answer to everything or to obtain it for them. They rely on reference librarians to provide instruction in the use of library materials, both in the classroom and individually, and to find even the most obscure materials. Additionally, as a friendly face in a confusing environment, a reference librarian can become a sounding board–an ear students can bend if they become bogged down in their legal studies or life in general while in law school. "Being a reference librarian is sort of like being a bartender without the sticky beer mess and the drunks."[14]

D. Pro se/General Public

In some respects the expectations of pro se users and the general public are similar to those of law students: someone to give an immediate answer. This category of library users usually comes to the reference desk with the expectation of having the librarian provide a formbook or an answer to a very specific legal question. One of the challenges reference librarians face with this group of users is explaining what services a reference librarian can provide and having the library user leave the reference desk understanding that the librarian can help them find the answer, but cannot give them the answer in many circumstances. "In our Reference Department, we–like most law librarians–steer clear of interpreting or explaining the law to public patrons. Instead we help them use the library and other resources."[15]

Another challenge librarians face in meeting the expectations of this group of users is the reference interview. Pro se patrons and the general public usually have a difficult time articulating their questions–either they provide too much information or not enough. This can be frustrating for the user because the question is obvious to them, and frustrating for reference librarians because they cannot elicit the information they need to help the user answer the question. Because of the limitation of resources, a lack of understanding of what a reference librarian can do, uncertainty in what they need, and difficulty in understanding legal materials, this group of users is often frustrated and leaves the library with unfulfilled expectations.

E. Attorneys/Legal Community

The expectations of attorneys are perhaps the most difficult to define. Because many members of the legal community were once law students, their expectations are often influenced by that experience. One expectation is that the library will have all the resources they need, everything from an expensive, multi-volume practitioner's treatise to briefs from a different state's courts. Many individuals new to the profession assume that privileges denied to them as students will now be permitted. They may expect to check out items that do not circulate, and they can be difficult when their requests are denied by the reference librarian.

One of the most difficult challenges reference librarians face with this group is communication. Attorneys and members of the legal community sometimes assume that reference librarians can answer difficult questions with only a few pieces of the puzzle. Their reticence in communicating leads to frustrated expectations. Disappointments arise when the answer they receive from the librarian is not what they want. When further questioning by the reference librarian reveals more information, however, the reference librarian often can then find what the attorney needs.

F. Director/Administrator

An entirely separate aspect of a reference librarian's day involves other duties and responsibilities assigned by the law library director/ administrator that are independent of reference. These duties may include participation on university or professional committees, work on the library's web page, serving as public safety contact for the library, or editing the law library newsletter. Many reference librarians in an academic environment are in tenure track positions where they must meet tenure requirements such as publishing, working in local and national professional organizations, participating in continuing legal education (CLE) programs, and serving the university community through committee work.

V. CASE STUDY-REFERENCE LIBRARIAN DUTIES

Why are there never enough hours in a day? What does a reference librarian do that makes time and the lack thereof such a precious commodity? The previous sections outlining library users and their expectations give an inkling of some of the challenges faced by reference librarians on a daily basis. At the Schmid Law Library at the University of Nebraska College of Law, three librarians share the title and job description of Reference Librarian. While all three spend hours working at the reference desk, attending a weekly librarians' meeting, teaching legal research in the fall, coordinating Westlaw and LEXIS training in the spring, and providing informational brown bag seminars, each has responsibilities and duties not detailed in the job description.

One librarian focuses on electronic services, and is responsible for e-mail maintenance, creating discussion lists for classes each semester, serving as Westlaw and LEXIS contact, and maintaining the law college's career services web site. Another of the three librarians is the audio/visual (AV) librarian, coordinating AV requests from both the faculty and the law school community. This librarian also serves on the university staff development committee, working with librarians from the four other libraries in the university system to promote staff development through workshops and programs. She created and maintains a Technology Index and web page, and works with the technical services department to index and organize unpublished opinions of the state court of appeals.

The third reference librarian assisted in the creation of the law college/law library web site and now maintains it. She serves on the ERPG (Electronic Resources Program Group) committee with members of the other libraries on campus, collects and formats the library's contributions to the law school's bi-weekly newsletter, and works with the law library director in presenting an Internet segment in many state CLEs. Because the positions are tenure track, each librarian is also encouraged to publish and work on projects to include in their tenure review files.

While the duties listed above are typical, reference librarians in other institutions may perform different duties and have other responsibilities. In 1997 Frank G. Houdek compiled a series of essays for the Law Library Journal entitled "A Day in the Law Library Life."[16] A review of those "days" shows that reference librarians also attend a variety of meetings, provide training on the use of library resources, trouble-shoot computers, load software, respond to e-mail reference inquiries, provide last minute instruction, create and publish newsletters, review admissions files, and provide a sympathetic ear to law students.[17]

While reference duties and responsibilities vary from institution to institution, one point is obvious from the comparison of the duties of the three librarians at the Schmid Law Library and a review of the articles in the day-in-the-life series: the duties of a Reference Librarian are time consuming and include some tasks that may be difficult to define.

VI. HOW TO GET IT ALL DONE

So how do reference librarians do it all and maintain their sanity? It is often a challenge, moving from one crisis to another while simultaneously putting out any fires that may ignite along the way AND addressing reference queries. Are there any solutions to what often seems a chaotic mess? Perhaps nothing will alleviate the fast pace aspect of the job, but there are ways to help reduce the inherent pressure.

A. Time Management and Organization

1. Controlling Time

One way to create a better balance and accomplish more is through time management and organization. Time management can be as simple as creating a prioritized list of goals for the day or as complicated (initially) as taking a critical look at the way the job is approached, evaluating where time is wasted, and making a conscious effort to change and break bad work habits.

Books by J. Wesley Cochran and Alec Mackenzie can help a librarian understand time management techniques.[18] While a thorough explanation of their methodologies is beyond the scope of this article, some of techniques they suggest can be implemented. Individuals interested in exploring time management techniques in more detail and incorporating the suggestions into their daily routine should consult the Cochran and Mackenzie books.[19]

On a very basic level, time management is about controlling time instead of being controlled by time. One way to begin to take control of time is to set goals for the day by writing them down with as much specificity as possible, while being realistic about what can be accomplished. Priorities should be assigned to the tasks to ensure that the most important things are completed first. Each task is checked off when complete, and the list is reviewed at the end of the day. One of the important points that Cochran makes in his book is that librarians often focus on what they have not accomplished instead of what they have completed.[20] Librarians should be sure to recognize and feel a sense of satisfaction for finished tasks and not dwell on unfinished ones; this will be a subconscious reminder to continue to make a daily list as well as a way to alleviate unwanted stress.

Librarians may want to explore the possibility of emulating other faculty members by posting office hours. This idea can be discussed with an immediate supervisor or the law library director to determine if it would be feasible. Set office hours, in addition to the time spent working at the reference desk, provide a reference librarian with a specific block of time to work on other duties–uninterrupted. Once the hours are determined they should be prominently displayed on the office door or window if possible. A notice about office hours can be added to phone mail/voice mail messages so callers know that their messages may not receive an immediate response. Although a reference librarian's job is by its nature public service oriented, there are times when it is necessary to work on tasks uninterrupted. Setting office hours encourages interruptions at known, specific times and permits the accomplishment of other tasks with little or no interruption. Having other reference librarians available to provide reference services during that time should make office hours an achievable goal for the entire reference staff.

One of the challenges faced by reference librarians, particularly those who also may work with acquisitions, is the arrival of unscheduled visitors.[21] The problem with unscheduled visitors is not only that time is spent conversing with the visitor, but time is spent shifting gears to return to the task that was interrupted. How can a reference librarian deal with unscheduled visitors? Often it is impossible to avoid these interruptions, but some suggestions for cutting down on them include: closing the door; anticipating and scheduling appointments; having an open door policy during certain times and making those times known, much like the office hours concept.

2. Organizing the Workplace

In addition to the suggestions above, other ways to become more organized and manage time better focus less on the individual and more on the environment. One method is to organize or create a reference log or record. An updated version of the reference record suggested by Margaret E. Hall can be used;[22] many reference librarians already use a similar reference log or record today. For those that do not have such a system, a file on the server can be created that can be accessed from the reference desk so that entries for difficult, interesting or time-consuming reference questions can be made. As much detailed information as possible should be included to assist the next reference librarian asked the question. If no server is available the file can be placed on the hard drive of the reference computer or on a disk kept at the reference desk. A paper reference log also is an alternative. This technique can help manage time better by alleviating the need to "recreate the wheel" by researching a question that may have already been answered by a colleague.

Obvious resources should not be overlooked. One group of resources in today's electronic world is traditional paper reference materials. A librarian should know what reference resources are available and frequently used in the library, and have them within easy access of the reference desk. Learning the state, local, and specialty resources and reviewing them periodically to avoid outdated material can make answering many questions easier.[23] The online catalog can be explored for new or particularly interesting materials, and the library's call number system can be reviewed for easier access to the collection. Taking a little time every day to explore the library and the collection can increase one's depth of knowledge as well as provide a therapeutic break from normal tasks.

Communication with other reference librarians inside the library and out can be a key in creating essential networks. Reference stories should be shared and colleagues' publications read. Subscribing to Law-lib and other law library/reference related discussion groups can help a librarian stay current while the listserv archives serve as a reference resource.[24] Making and maintaining contacts in both local and national organizations provides resources that are of incalculable value if they are ever needed.

B. Stress Management

1. Identifying Stress Factors

Stress often plays a major role in a reference librarian's day. Because stressful situations are not often easily resolved, they can consume more time than a reference librarian can afford. This, in turn, can create more stress on the personal level and lead to focus problems and even burnout.[25]

One of the ways to help alleviate stress is to become more organized and aware of wasted time. Once ways to become more organized and avoid wasting time are identified, they can be implemented into a daily routine and help reduce the stress that comes from an out-of-control feeling or the inability to complete tasks. One of the benefits of the time management techniques mentioned above is the reduction in stress. "Rather than allowing ourselves to be placed in positions of constant stress and then teaching ourselves coping techniques, we focus instead on managing our time more effectively. This way we prevent most of the stress that time shortages inflict on us. So time management is stress management of the highest order."[26]

In addition to implementing time management techniques, stress can be relieved in other ways as well. Reference librarians should not be afraid to say, "I don't know." One of the traps reference librarians fall into is assuming they know or should know the answer to any question posed, or if not, at least where to find the answer. One way to ease the stress brought on by not being able to readily find an answer or identify a resource that would help answer the question is to say "I don't know," and then work with the library user to find the answer.[27]

One of the most stressful situations for a reference librarian is dealing with difficult library users.[28] When facing a difficult library user it may be appropriate to ask for help or indicate that an immediate answer cannot be given. A basic communication problem could result in both the reference librarian and the user becoming increasingly frustrated and short tempered. To prevent these situations, a buddy system with the other reference librarians should be established so that a backup is on hand to step in. This will remove both the reference librarian and the library user from a stressful situation.

2. Reducing Stress

Two key techniques can help relieve the stress inherent in any workday. First, time should be set aside for non-library activities. A daily exercise routine is one way many librarians maintain a sense of balance and reduce stress. Some follow a structured daily exercise class regime, while others take walks over lunch and return with a new perspective on work. Another activity is taking classes, perhaps during lunch or at some other time during the day, which may broaden a librarian's horizon and provide a creative, stress-relieving outlet. Many universities provide tuition reimbursement, which encourages employees to take classes. Socializing through occasional lunch dates with friends or the celebration of staff birthdays and accomplishments is another way to provide a break in the normal job routine.

Some libraries have a "grub day" on a Friday every third month or so as a time to catch up on the little routine tasks that accumulate. Staff come in jeans or casual clothing and use the day to clean desks, attack piles on the desk that have been growing, reorganize files, or just attend to little things that have been tabled for lack of time.

Librarians also should explore outside interests, such as starting a book club with colleagues; finding something that fascinates them and beginning a collection;[29] attending on-campus events, speeches or presentations; or becoming involved in community activities or organizations. The goal is to avoid having work become so all consuming that other interests fall to the wayside.

Second, maintaining both a sense of humor and perspective is essential to alleviating stress. It is easy to become overwhelmed by the demands and deadlines that come with being a reference librarian; keeping work in perspective and being able to laugh about frustrations or problems will help ease that pressure. In discussing her mentor Jane Stewart, Barbara C. Holt illustrated the importance of laughter in relieving stress, "Lighten up. You'll last longer. At least once a week, something occurred that made us laugh so hard that we cried. These weren't necessarily big things or even things that were all that funny. But Jane's humorous approach to the frustrations and miscommunications that regularly occur in any setting helped us through many a stressful time."[30]

VII. CONCLUSION

Although the basic principles and duties of reference librarianship have remained constant, technological changes and changes in both the legal profession and society have placed increasing demands on reference librarians. Avoiding or reducing stress and working to manage time better are two ways to better address those demands. Adopting some of the suggestions in the time management section–perhaps trying a prioritized daily to-do list or critically looking at what eats up time during the day–are ways to begin exploring the time and stress crunches many librarians face. Reference librarians need to be aware of ways to more effectively use time; avoid stress through time management, humor or other methods; and take advantage of activities that can provide professional and personal satisfaction.

NOTES

1. For historical perspectives on legal reference, see Margaret E. Hall, *Reference Work in a Law Library*, 31 L. LIBR. J. 238 (1938); Matthew A. McKavitt, *The Layman and the Law Library*, 33 L. LIBR. J. 324 (1940).

2. *Reference Work in Law Libraries–A Panel Discussion*, 46 L. LIBR. J. 448, 451 (1953) (statement by A. Elizabeth Holt regarding law library services to the community).

3. ABA statistics report 135 law schools in the 1963-64 academic year awarded 9,638 J.D. or LL.B. degrees and 10,788 individuals were admitted to the Bar. During the 1999-2000 academic year, 182 law schools awarded 39,071 J.D. or LL.B. degrees; bar admission statistics for the academic year 1998-99 show 55,481 individuals were admitted. American Bar Ass'n, *Legal Education and Bar Admission Statistics, 1963-1999* (visited June 12, 2000) <http://www.abanet.org/legaled/statistics/le_bastats.html>.

4. On the federal trial court level, 168,800 civil cases commenced in 1980; that figure rose to 265,200 in 1997. Criminal cases commenced for the same period rose from 28,000 in 1980 to 48,700 in 1997. U.S. CENSUS BUREAU, U.S. DEP'T OF COMMERCE, STATISTICAL ABSTRACT OF THE UNITED STATES, table 372 (119th ed. 1999) <http://www.census.gov/statab/www>.

5. For an interesting discussion on this phenomena in the Chicago area, see John P. Heinz et al., *The Changing Character of Lawyers' Work: Chicago in 1975 and 1995*, 32 L. & SOC'Y REV. 751 (1998).

6. *See, e.g.*, LAW-LIB@ucdavis.edu; TEKNOIDS@listserv.law.cornell.edu. For a listing of law library related discussion lists, see Lyonette Louis-Jacques, *Lists for Law Librarians* (last modified Feb. 26, 2000) <http://www.lib.uchicago.edu/~llou/lawlists/lawlibs.txt>. For a listing of law related discussion lists, see Lyonette Louis-Jacques, *Law Lists* (last modified Feb. 1, 1999) <http://www.lib.uchicago.edu/~llou/lawlists/lawlists.2-99.html>.

7. *See* Washington State Courts, *State Law Library, Need Help Finding Information?* (visited June 3, 2000) <http://www.courts.wa.gov/lawlib/needhelp.htm>. For additional information on e-mail reference services, see the article in this volume by Beth Smith, *Enhancing Reference Services Through Technology*.

8. For examples of materials that discuss using the Internet for legal research or illustrate the information available for legal researchers on the Internet, see generally T.R. HALVORSON, LAW OF THE SUPER SEARCHERS: THE ONLINE SECRETS OF TOP LEGAL RESEARCHERS (2000). For additional information, see *The Super Searchers Web Page* (visited June 5, 2000) <http://www.infotoday.com/supersearchers>. Other examples include: ERIK J. HEELS & RICHARD P. KLAU, LAW LAW LAW ON THE INTERNET: THE BEST LEGAL WEB SITES AND MORE (1998) and JERRY LAWSON, THE COMPLETE INTERNET HANDBOOK FOR LAWYERS (1999).

9. *See Reference Work in Law Libraries–A Panel Discussion, supra* note 2.

10. Kendall F. Svengalis & Frank G. Houdek, *Member's Briefing: The New Age of Legal Publishing*, AALL SPECTRUM, July 1999, at 19, 22.

11. *Dealing With the New World of Legal Publishing: How AALL Can Help*, AALL SPECTRUM, July 1999, at 20.

12. *See id.* at 21. For an example of the newsletter, see THE CRIV SHEET: THE NEWSLETTER OF THE COMMITTEE ON RELATIONS WITH INFORMATION VENDORS, May 2000, *in* AALL SPECTRUM, May 2000. For more information regarding CRIV, see AALLNET, *CRIVPage* (last modified May 26, 2000) <http://www.aallnet.org/committee/criv/>.

13. For an overview of some of the issues law librarians face in providing faculty services, *see* Robert S. Payne, *Answering Faculty Research Requests*, AALL SPECTRUM, April 2000, at 10-11.

14. Jean McKnight, *My Day at Work (and You're Welcome to It!)*, 89 L. LIBR. J. 192, 194 (1997). Part of the *A Day in the Law Library Life* series compiled by Frank G. Houdek.

15. Mary Whisner, *Practicing Reference . . . Golf Buddy Reference Questions*, 91 L. LIBR. J. 413, 413 (1999).

16. Frank G. Houdek, *A Day in My Law Library Life, Circa 1997*, 89 L. LIBR. J. 157 (1997).

17. *See id.*

18. J. WESLEY COCHRAN, TIME MANAGEMENT HANDBOOK FOR LIBRARIANS (1991); ALEC MACKENZIE, THE TIME TRAP (3d ed. 1997).

19. *See* COCHRAN, *supra* note 18; MACKENZIE, *supra* note 18.

20. COCHRAN, *supra* note 18, at 18.

21. *See* MACKENZIE, *supra* note 18, at 103-13.

22. Hall, *supra* note 1, at 239.

23. *See* Robert C. Berring, *How to Be a Great Reference Librarian*, 4 LEGAL REFERENCE SERVICES Q. 17 (1984) (discussing resource awareness).

24. Law-lib is hosted by the University of California-Davis at law-lib@ucdavis. edu with archives at UC Davis Law Library, *Archive of the Law-Lib Electronic Discussion List* (last modified June 2000) <http://lawlibrary.ucdavis.edu/LAWLIB/lawlib. html/>.

25. For a discussion on law librarians and burnout, see Veneese C. Nelson, *Burnout: A Reality for Law Librarians?*, 79 L. LIBR. J. 267 (1987).

26. MACKENZIE, *supra* note 18, at 15-16.

27. For an excellent discussion of saying "I don't know," see Mary Whisner, *Celebrating the Virtues of Saying "I Don't Know,"* 91 L. LIBR. J. 861 (1999).

28. For more information on this topic, see the article in this volume by Donald Arndt, Jr., *Problem Patrons and Library Security.*

29. To see what other law librarians collect, see Frank G. Houdek, *What Law Librarians Collect*, 91 L. LIBR. J. 577 (1999).

30. Barbara C. Holt, *All I Really Need to Know I Learned from My Mentor*, 91 L. LIBR. J. 218, 219-20 (1999). Part of the *"Meet My Mentor": A Collection of Personal Reminiscences* series compiled by Frank G. Houdek.

Creating and Using Web Resources
to Train Attorneys:
An Experience with the State Bar

W. David Gay
Jim Jackson

W. David Gay is Head of Public Service (E-mail: wdgay@comp.uark.edu), and Jim Jackson is Reference Librarian (E-mail: jrjack@comp.uark.edu) both at the University of Arkansas Law Library, Fayetteville, AR 72701-1201.

[Haworth co-indexing entry note]: "Creating and Using Web Resources to Train Attorneys: An Experience with the State Bar." Gay, W. David, and Jim Jackson. Co-published simultaneously in *Legal Reference Services Quarterly* (The Haworth Information Press, an imprint of The Haworth Press, Inc.) Vol. 19, No. 1/2, 2001, pp. 57-73; and: *Emerging Solutions in Reference Services: Implications for Libraries in the New Millennium* (ed: John D. Edwards) The Haworth Information Press, an imprint of The Haworth Press, Inc., 2001, pp. 57-73. Single or multiple copies of this article are available for a fee from The Haworth Document Delivery Service [1-800-342-9678, 9:00 a.m. - 5:00 p.m. (EST). E-mail address: getinfo@haworthpressinc.com].

57

SUMMARY. The experience of producing a web-based CLE program is shared by two academic law librarians who teamed with a practicing attorney to deliver the training. The focus is on teaching lawyers to effectively find and use materials on the Internet using a hands-on web-based CLE. The insights gained from taking web-based legal instruction "on the road" are explored along with the challenges presented by well-intentioned administrators and those wishing to profit from CLEs who may thwart good planning and organization. Dependable technical support and control of the process and environment are not only desirable but necessary. Selected web site URLs used in training are included and future directions for this type of training are examined. *[Article copies available for a fee from The Haworth Document Delivery Service: 1-800-342-9678. E-mail address: <getinfo@haworthpressinc.com> Website: <http://www.HaworthPress.com> © 2001 by The Haworth Press, Inc. All rights reserved.]*

I. INTRODUCTION

Lawyers' interest in the World Wide Web is creating a need and an opportunity for training in how to effectively find and use materials on the Internet. Librarians in law schools, law firms, bar associations, and other organizations can help meet the demand for these services by providing specialized sessions for members of the bar. For some libraries this presents the possibility of partnering with another group, such as a local or state bar association, to offer continuing legal education (CLE) programs. The results of the cooperative efforts can provide benefits and offer challenges to both organizations.

The Young Law Library at the University of Arkansas School of Law designed a CLE program to train lawyers in web resources. The subjects for the program were "Legal and Related Sites on the Web" and "Some Considerations Re Law and Law Practice on the Internet." A web site was designed and posted[1] which contained discussion about and links to sites covered in the CLE, which will be referred to as the CLE site in this article. Some of the CLE presentations were done in partnership with the Arkansas Bar Association.

Development of the program began in 1998 though the efforts of two academic law librarians, David Gay and Jim Jackson, and Mac Norton, a practicing attorney and adjunct professor of law.[2] Programs were conducted in computer labs in three locations between September 1998 and June 1999. The lawyers taking the courses followed the presentations in two ways. They worked at individual personal computers by viewing links from the CLE site as those links were discussed and demonstrated by the presenters. At the same time, the lawyers also viewed a large screen on which those sites were shown from a video data projector. If the lawyers became temporarily lost, presenters reviewed the path of links on the large screen which allowed the lawyers to duplicate that path on their personal computers and become current.

The purpose of this article is to convey what was learned from the three CLE presentations, which may help readers carry out similar programs. Almost all of this discussion also applies to law firm librarians presenting similar materials in their firms.

II. PLANNING THE PROGRAM

The increasing use of the World Wide Web by attorneys and the proliferation of legal sites presents an opportunity to help lawyers learn about web resources. Although one-on-one instructional sessions can help, they are inefficient in light of the rapid rise in web use and the improved teaching approach available through CLE courses. Most state CLE requirements supply a captive audience of lawyers who prefer useful information that can be practically applied. The advantage of a CLE course is that training can be provided in a group setting by covering basic web sites and answering questions. If that training is done from a web site such as the CLE site described in this article,[3] there is an opportunity for reinforcement and the economy of group training.

There is a distinction between planning which sites to include in a CLE course, and planning which links to include in a CLE site to teach that course. All of the sites visited in a presentation also will be among the many more that make up the CLE site. However, because of time constraints, not all of the CLE sites can be covered in a presentation. Therefore, for program purposes, the presenters must select sites that can be covered in the time allowed for the program and which are important to the trainees.

Most law librarians have a list of web sites they consider essential and some they consider more or less important. Personal preference plays a role in whether a given site is used instead of another, particularly when the two duplicate information. Other choices about sites arise from which state jurisdiction is being considered, and in a law firm, from the firm's use of internal sites or an intranet. Readers who would like to review a list of web sites can consult sources such as Diana Botluck's *The Legal List*[4] or the sites listed on the Super Searchers web site.[5] The presenters found that the following sites were the most helpful.

A. Legal Web Site Selections

1. Federal Statutory and Legislative Material
Government Printing Office   http://www.access.gpo.gov/su_docs
Thomas   http://thomas.loc.gov/

2. Federal Case Law
Federal Court Locator   http://vls.law.vill.edu/Locator/
                                   Fedcourt.html

3. Federal Agency and Administrative Information
Federal Web Locator   http://www.infoctr.edu/fwl/
Federal Agency Index   http://www.washlaw.edu/doclaw/
                                   executive5m.htm

For statutory and legislative material the Government Printing Office site should be included.[6] Another site that contains statutory and legislative information is the Library of Congress site known as Thomas after Thomas Jefferson.[7] The Federal Court Locator maintained by the Villanova School of Law contains information and links to federal case law and courts.[8] Two sites that contain federal agency and administrative law information are The Federal Web Locator,[9] maintained by the Center for Information Law and Policy, and The Federal Agency Index[10] maintained by the Washburn School of Law.

4. State Law Sites
Findlaw State Resources   http://www.findlaw.com/11stategov/
                                   index.html
State Law, State Government   http://www.washlaw.edu/uslaw/
                                   statelaw.htm
Administrative Codes/Registers   http://www.nass.org/acr/index.
                                   htm
Kansas Supreme Court   http://www.kscourts.org/kscases

State law web resources can be placed into two categories for purposes of CLE presentations. First are sites that offer links to all of the different states. These include the Findlaw State Resources site,[11] the State Law, State Government and Legislative Information site[12] from Washburn, and the Administrative Codes and Registers site[13] maintained by the National Association of Secretaries of State. Links from these eventually lead to information for individual states.

Second, direct links to the particular state jurisdiction covered by the CLE course should be provided. Lawyers should know about the Findlaw and Washburn sites and know they can follow links to get to a particular state site, and a demonstration of that can be included in the presentation. However, there is not enough time during a presentation for prolonged navigation. If, for example, the CLE course is for Kansas lawyers, a direct link should be provided to Kansas case law[14] and to each particular site covered in the presentation.

B. Program Web Site Considerations

The CLE site[15] contains links to all the web sites included in the presentations and to additional sites which cannot be covered because of time constraints. It is also a tool for repetition and reinforcement. Simply knowing the URL,[16] the student can return to revisit familiar sites and look at new material. Because the material is posted on the web, students are offered a hands-on learning experience. There is no substitute for this arrangement if the objective is to create a quality product that will provide the greatest benefit to the learner. Because students can return to the site at any time, librarians can stay in contact with members of the bar, which has public relations benefits for the library and law school. In a law firm library, it can provide a way for lawyers to maintain closer contact with librarians than they otherwise might.

If a firm librarian is already training on LEXIS, Westlaw, or Loislaw, adding sessions on web legal resources offers another avenue to needed materials. Although there may be duplication from the web and an online vendor, the web at times offers more current material. If a firm pays an online vendor on a per-search or time-of-use basis, locating the same material for free on the web may save money.[17]

C. Development Details and Logistics

1. *Personnel.* When a librarian does CLE training, several people must be included in the planning process. At a law school, staff mem-

bers connected with CLE must be involved. If the training is through the auspices of the state bar association, the association's CLE director must be contacted. Depending on where the training site is located, those whose jobs are relevant to using that site must be included. Every person who is going to conduct the training must participate. Involving technical support personnel is essential because of the potential problems that come in using computers and lab facilities. In a law firm, if there are staff who have analogous positions other than the librarian, they must be involved.

2. *Facilities.* When a remote facility is used, a site visit well in advance of the training should be made to insure that everything is ready or will be ready. If an advance visit is not possible, there is a good chance something will go wrong, and there are any number of somethings that can go wrong, not the least of which is a network problem at a remote facility. Although assurances may be given by the lab operator at that facility, a trip to the location will allow the presenters to see what their trainees will see during the presentation, the computers that will be used and how well they work or do not work, the size and layout of the room, the actual number of places available for attendees, as well as any number of other things that only a trip to the facility can reveal. The preview trip should be done at least a week in advance so there is enough time to make adjustments if problems are found. However, regardless of how ready the facility may seem a week before the presentation, it should be checked again a day or two before the presentation.

3. *Coordination.* The best personnel arrangement may be to team librarians with a practitioner. In this case the attorney was a well-respected practitioner[18] who also serves as an adjunct professor specializing in Internet law. If the three are compatible and can work well together, a balanced perspective from both an academic and a practitioner perspective can provide legitimacy for those members of the bar who may be skeptical of academic types. Also, this format allows all to participate in a course which can be planned and conducted for three hours of CLE credit without being overly burdensome on any one presenter. This structure provides flexibility and balance, and it allows the presenters to divide responsibilities and to individually contribute when appropriate.

4. *Equipment.* A video data projector allows the students to follow along with the presenter. One presenter can operate the projector while

another stands next to the screen, points, and talks. A third presenter can circulate through the room offering assistance to the students who are watching the video data projector's screen and working from the CLE web site. It is best if each lawyer sits at a computer and follows the course of the program to get the full effect. If there are not enough individual computers, as long as there is adequate space, two lawyers can share a workstation. If more people register for the program than there are computers, they can share. On the other hand, if that would result in crowding, the number of registrants should be limited.

5. *Marketing*. Besides using a web site similar to the CLE site and hands-on instruction, other factors can make the course attractive. If the CLE course can be scheduled with other CLE programs, or if there are sporting or other special events scheduled, attendance might increase. Another attraction may be a kindred subject that can be combined with teaching web legal resources as part of the same CLE program. For example, if a law school offers a course on Law and the Internet, that program could be divided into segments with web resources as one part conducted by the librarians, and the other segment taught by the Law and the Internet presenter. The course would be worth more CLE hours and, therefore, more attractive to the bar.

D. Non-Legal Web Sites

Besides legal information, lawyers need information related to law, such as health and business. At some point they may need information on travel, weather, ways to find people, or news and local information, all of which reflect the non-legal but very practical side of law practice. The table of contents from the CLE site[19] includes links to agriculture, business, health and medicine, and other sites. The sites included at the CLE site and discussed here were selected by the presenters as being most helpful for their programs but not necessarily as the most important.

1. *General News*
   The New York Times   http://www.nytimes.com
   The Washington Post   http://www.washingtonpost.com

2. *Statistical Information*
   FedStats   http://www.fedstats.gov

3. *Miscellaneous Sites*

Weather	http://cnn.com/WEATHER/cities.sc.html
Expert Witness Information	http://www.nocall.org/experts.htm
U.S. Census Bureau	http://www.census.gov/econ/www/
American Bar Association	http://www.abanet.org/lawlink/home.html
Yahoo People Search	http://people.yahoo.com/
Mapquest	http://www.mapquest.com/
My Virtual Reference Desk	http://www.refdesk.com/

For general news sources, *The New York Times*[20] and the *Washington Post*[21] are essential. If a gateway to local media sources[22] exists for the geographical area in which the CLE is being conducted, it should be included too. One or more of the statistical sites shown on the CLE site[23] under part 4[24] should be included, as well as search engines and perhaps meta search engines listed under part 5.[25] The more important miscellaneous sites from part 6[26] include a weather site, an expert witness site, the U.S. Census Bureau, the American Bar Association, Yahoo People Search, Mapquest, and My Virtual Reference Desk.[27]

Agricultural law was selected because the National Center for Agricultural Law Research and Information is located at the law school and because Sally Kelley[28] maintains the Center's homepage,[29] which is an excellent gateway to legal information on the web. Any speciality from the librarian's law school or firm should receive similar treatment. Academic, as well as government or public libraries, have staff with subject expertise and should not be overlooked in suggesting materials on special subjects for the trainees.

4. *Business Sites*

CEOExpress	http://www.ceoexpress.com/
Hoover's Online	http://www.hoovers.com/
Edgar	http://www.sec.gov/edgarhp.htm
Wall Street Journal	http://interactive.wsj.com/home.html

Lawyers also need business information. The business reference librarian[30] at the University of Arkansas' Mullins Library was consulted because of her subject expertise and her suggestions were followed in choosing business web sites linked to the CLE site.[31] When relying on the expertise of others, permission should be obtained to use the material and the assistance acknowledged.

Important business sites include CEOExpress,[32] a gateway to a variety of business and related information; Hoover's Online;[33] Edgar,[34] which is a publication of the Securities and Exchange Commission; and the Wall Street Journal Interactive Edition.[35] Although the latter is a subscription site, it and other subscription sites were included in the business information section because they contain helpful information and some lawyers may choose to use them. Other essential sites are those specific to the jurisdiction for which the presentation is aimed, such as state-wide business publications.

5. *Health and Medicine*

Medlars/Medline	http://www.nlm.nih.gov/databases/freemedl.html
Health Law Research Gateway	http://lawlib.slu.edu/HealthCenter/Research/RESEARCH_INDEX.HTM

Health and Medicine includes at least two essential sites: the Medlars/Medline database[36] which is maintained by the National Library of Medicine, and the Health Law Research Gateway[37] maintained by the St. Louis University Center for Health Law Studies.

E. Special Subject Sites

International and Foreign Law	http://www.lib.uchicago.edu/e/law/home.html
U.S. Patent and Trademark Office	http://www.uspto.gov

International and foreign law was accorded subject treatment with inclusion of one of the most comprehensive sites, the D'Angelo Law Library at the University of Chicago.[38] The last special subject category included was intellectual property with the prime resource being the U.S. Department of Commerce Patent and Trademark Office.[39]

Arrangements were made with three fee-based legal web resources for complimentary access to their products for purposes of the CLE:

Loislaw,[40] Quick Law America,[41] and VersusLaw.[42] These resources were not promoted and no time was given to them in the presentation, but their URLs were provided so the lawyers could investigate them on their own if they so chose.

F. Internet Law

The other major division of the CLE was entitled, "Some Considerations Re Law and Law Practice on the Internet"[43] and it was addressed solely by its author, Mac Norton.[44] The session covered practice issues such as accuracy and timeliness of web information, attorney-client e-mail, confidentiality, ethics, attorney-client privilege, encryption, attorney web pages and advertising, e-mail solicitation, electronic filing and service, and others.[45]

Early in the CLE planning process the presenters had decided to make the course as practical as possible, bearing in mind the preference of lawyers for CLE courses that are informative and can be directly applied to their work. The practice-oriented nature of this section met those needs. In general, for the entire CLE course the presenters chose to include web sites they personally used doing legal and related research, web sites and subjects they had previously covered with law students, questions practicing lawyers asked, and information which in the judgment of the presenters lawyers need to know.

G. Target Audience

Besides trying to limit the presentation to practical matters, the presenters had to decide at which level the course would be taught. As a group, older lawyers who had been in practice for a while often had less knowledge about the web and computers than more recent law school graduates. As a result, the longer-in-practice group could benefit from a more basic course emphasizing the mechanics of using computers and the web than the course that was actually taught. Consideration was given to offering such a rudimentary course but the decision was made to present an intermediate course, although the presenters knew they would be limiting their audience. As a practical matter, both levels of courses could not be provided simultaneously or sequentially on the same program. The course could not be all things to all people.

III. PRESENTATION AND SITE COMPARISONS

The three presentations conducted at different locations revealed certain practical considerations that librarians should be aware of and observe in their own situations if similar programs are undertaken. First, because of the need for computers and computer lab requirements for the programs, each location must have dependable technical support. The presenters should have first-hand working experience with the technical support personnel and support personnel should have previously provided computer lab support for groups or CLE programs. Support personnel should be paid and located nearby for easy communication. The site should be close enough for preliminary visits by the presenters.

Second, the facility must be able to comfortably accommodate the number of trainees that register for the course, including enough space, adequate temperature control, and other amenities at the site. If there is not enough space for the number of registrants, no attempt should be made to somehow adapt to the overage: the sponsors must either schedule additional training times, but not on the same day, or turn some away.

A. First Site–Local

The first presentation was conducted at a nearby site with excellent technical support and proven ability to set up a computer lab for a group. A contract was made for their services. It was easy to communicate with them, to have several preliminary visits, and to establish a clear understanding of the requirements for the program. The site regularly conducts continuing education programs and its managers knew what was necessary for a successful program. This was the most successful of the three programs.

The only significant negative was the high demand for the program beyond what the facility could accommodate. Because of the large number of registrants, the presenters agreed with the CLE sponsor the week before the program to conduct a second three-hour session after a break. Although it worked, it did not work well because even with three presenters working in tandem, the course was too long to repeat in the same day. The quality level of the first session could not be maintained as the day wore on.

B. Second Site–Community College

The second presentation was conducted further away at a community college's computer lab. Because the presenters were satisfied with the format from the first presentation and because student evaluations also reflected that satisfaction, the same format was followed. The overall average rating for the first program was 4.55 out of 5.00. The average for oral presentation and course material for the second program was 4.32 out of 5. Typical of the comments received were: "These guys did a good job. Knew their subject . . . " "Probably the most important training in legal and law-related and law-necessary research since Legal Bibliography. . . . "

The second program did not work as well as the first. Because of a greater geographical distance, although a preliminary site visit was made, the distance prohibited easy communication and sufficient site visits to insure adequate preliminary arrangements. The site was provided at no cost by well-intentioned college administrators, but good intentions are no substitute for proficient computer support, and one usually gets what one pays for. Lab air conditioning did not function, which required the introduction of fans making it difficult for the trainees to hear.

There were problems with lab software, and at one point the network went down, although the presenters were able to continue with a segment of the program that did not require the live CLE site. Too many trainees were admitted to the lab and it was overcrowded. CLE sponsors generally want to maximize the financial return from programs, so the incentive for them is to pack in as many as possible, which is not necessarily unreasonable except for a program such as this where the computer lab's environment is of critical importance.

C. Third Site–Remote

The same format was followed but the location of the third presentation was farthest away and it was the least successful. The major problem was that the lab did not work because the network connection was never established. The CLE sponsor contracted for the lab and network connection. Because of the geographical distance, the presenters could not visit, arrange for, or oversee the necessary preliminaries. Planners should understand that the less they control in the computer lab's set up and organization, the less reliable their tools will be.

Well after the program was scheduled to begin, a substitute modem connection was arranged so that one computer could access the CLE site, which could then be projected onto a screen for the trainees to see. The presenters conducted the program as best they could without the trainees being able to track the presentation on their own computers. The essential hands-on experience was missed. The URL of the CLE site was repeatedly emphasized to the trainees with the suggestion that once they later reached that site on a working web browser, they would be able to visit the sites in the presentation. In addition, a handout listing the various web sites was distributed to the trainees.

The lesson from the third presentation and to a lesser extent from the second is not to depend on someone with whom there is no work history and whose quality is unknown. Although the problems were beyond the presenters' ability to influence and "not our fault," and although that explanation was given and accepted by the trainees who nevertheless gained some benefit from the program, those trainees cannot help but at some level associate the presenters with the problems.

The presenters can spell out their expectations to the CLE sponsor before the program's registration materials are mailed or posted. If the sponsors are unwilling or unable to comply with the requirements set out by the presenters, the responsibility lies with the sponsors should they go forward with the program anyway.

IV. FUTURE CONSIDERATIONS

Web-based legal information is readily available, and not just from the major legal database vendors. Providing training for web-based legal information to the bar and bench, in addition to technologically savvy law students, is a major responsibility. Individuals and institutions who risk taking the lead in new training venues, including the Internet, have the most at stake in how this educational process develops. From the presenters' experience, instruction is best accomplished hands-on, using a live web page which is maintained for later use.

One important question to address in planning is which aspects the presenter can and cannot control. The presenter can manage the content and therefore the accuracy of the information. The location of resources and the file server which stores the information can be controlled. The organizational and the presentation skills of the presenters are a given.

Some aspects are more difficult to control. Flexibility is an essential skill in dealing with the unexpected. The facility location for the program in general and specifically the lab setting may be outside the presenters' jurisdiction. Even if one has an unlimited budget and computer labs with the necessary space, hardware and technical support may not be easily available. And even when a lab has been scheduled for a presentation, one cannot know for sure it will be available when needed. Computer hardware and software upgrades often are scheduled during down times when outsiders, such as presenters, are more likely to have access to the lab. And because of those upgrades, the network may be less stable. What is not within the presenters' control makes using a lab problematic and must be part of the planning equation.

What is the alternative to the live, web-based, hands-on approach to training which is not always easy away from a home institution? Distance education is the hot topic in higher education today, including legal education, and offers an alternative approach to the scenarios described above. Both student and teacher are in front of cameras or monitors, whether attached to individual workstations or arranged for a group. Distance education solves the problems of traveling to remote sites, relying on unfamiliar technology in new locations, and contending with the unknown of "technical support," an oxymoron at times, as well as with a host of other ills. But it also severely limits the amount of one-on-one contact and individual problem solving which is crucial to teaching in any setting. Arturo L. Torres and W. Clinton Sterling offer a great road map for those unfamiliar with the distance education literature in the legal environment.[46]

There are other problems with distance education and other alternative means of electronic CLE delivery, such as whether CLE certification will be permitted by accrediting groups. This issue has been raised and state bar associations and other CLE providers are addressing alternative methods of delivery. States are accepting the delivery of CLE in many forms. CLE Online.com in Texas provides a good summary of states approving online programs.[47]

Another question concerns how to deliver the traditionally required paper handouts for a CLE in a distance education setting. Because the material can be included on the web, CLE attendees can print any handout material. How is CLE attendance verified from a remote site? Encryption developments are making electronic signatures verifiable which makes remote certification workable for those accrediting bodies skeptical of actual attendance in a non-traditional setting. Moreover, in the legislative arena, the Electronic Signatures in Global and National Commerce Act (E-SIGN) should pave the way for jurisdictional standardization in the usage of electronic signatures.[48] The Corporation for Research and Educational Networking (CREN)[49] is an example of a group of educational institutions currently providing electronic verifications through a "certificate authority service."

V. CONCLUSION

In order to have a successful remote web-based CLE program, a hands-on learning experience for trainees is essential. There is no substitute for this arrangement if the objective is to create a quality program that will provide the greatest benefit to the participants. Thorough planning with everyone involved including preliminary site visits prior to the program is necessary. In this undertaking control by the presenters cannot be overemphasized. Planners should understand that the less they control in the computer lab's setup and organization, the less reliable the lab will be. Good environmental controls and adequate space in the teaching environment are a must. Reliable, dependable technical support is not just desirable but necessary.

Good intentions are no substitute for proficient computer support; hiring qualified technical support may be less costly in the long run than using site-provided staff, especially if site personnel are not familiar with the demands of the program. Construction and maintenance, including updating the web site for the CLE, provide benefits for attendees and a teaching tool for subsequent instruction to other audiences. The problems of taking web-based legal instruction "on the road" away from the home environment where the trainer is in control can be solved. Securing acceptance of distance education alternatives by bar associations and remote certification by the legal community are challenges that provide librarians with opportunities to showcase their expertise. Librarians can become leaders in providing web-based legal training.

NOTES

1. David Gay et al., *Legal and Related Sites on the Internet* (last modified Oct. 11, 1999) <http://law.uark.edu/new/cle.html>.

2. M.N. "Mac" Norton is a member of the Wright, Lindsey and Jennings Law Firm, Little Rock, Arkansas.

3. Gay, *supra* note 1.

4. DIANA BOTLUCK, THE LEGAL LIST: RESEARCH ON THE INTERNET (1997). *See also* Mark Voorhees & Wayne Lovett, *Surf's Up: Guide to the Best Web Sites for Lawyers*, NAT'L L.J., Apr. 3, 2000, at B12.

5. Information Today, Inc., *The Super Searchers Web Page* (visited Apr. 21, 2000) <http://www.infotoday.com/supersearchers/>. The URLs listed in the site also are found in T.R. HALVORSON, LAW OF THE SUPER SEARCHERS: THE ONLINE SECRETS OF TOP LEGAL RESEARCHERS (2000).

6. Superintendent of Documents, U.S. Government Printing Office, *GPO Access* (visited Apr. 17, 2000) <http://www.access.gpo.gov/su_docs>.

7. Library of Congress, *Thomas: Legislative Information on the Internet* (visited Apr. 17, 2000) <http://thomas.loc.gov>.

8. Villanova Internet Legal Research Compass, *Villanova Federal Court Locator* (visited Apr. 17, 2000) <http://vls.law.vill.edu/Locator/Fedcourt.html>.

9. Center for Info. Law & Policy, *Federal Web Locator* (visited Apr. 17, 2000) <http://www.infoctr.edu/fwl/>.

10. Paul A. Arrigo, *Federal Agency Index* (visited Apr. 17, 2000) <http://www.washlaw.edu/doclaw/executive5m.htm>.

11. Findlaw, *Findlaw State Resources* (visited Apr. 17, 2000) <http://www.findlaw.com/11stategov/index.html>.

12. Joe Hewitt, *State Law, State Government and Legislative Information* (visited Apr. 17, 2000) <http://www.washlaw.edu/uslaw/statelaw.htm>.

13. National Ass'n of Secretaries of State, *Administrative Codes and Registers* (visited Apr. 17, 2000) <http://www.nass.org/acr/index.htm>.

14. Martin Wisneski & Pam Tull, *Kansas Supreme Court/Kansas Court of Appeals Opinions* (visited Apr. 17, 2000) <http://www.kscourts.org/kscases>.

15. Gay, *supra* note 1.

16. *Id.*

17. BOTLUCK, *supra* note 4.

18. *See supra* note 2.

19. *See supra* note 2.

20. The New York Times Co., *The New York Times on the Web* (visited Apr. 15, 2000) <http://www.nytimes.com>.

21. The Washington Post Co., *Washingtonpost.com* (visited Apr. 15, 2000) <http://www.washingtonpost.com>.

22. Network of Ark., *My Hometown* (visited Apr. 15, 2000) <http://www.state.ar.us/ina/myhometown.html>.

23. Gay, *supra* note 1.

24. *Id.*

25. *Id.*

26. *Id.*

27. *Id.*

28. Research Associate Professor, University of Arkansas School of Law.

29. Sally Kelley, *National Center for Agricultural Law Research and Information* (visited Apr. 15, 2000) <http://law.uark.edu/arklaw/aglaw/>.

30. Donna Daniels, Associate Librarian, University of Arkansas Libraries.

31. Gay, *supra* note 1.

32. The CEO Express Co., *CEOExpress* (visited Apr. 15, 2000) <http://www.ceoexpress.com/>.

33. Hoovers, Inc., *Hoovers Online* (visited Apr. 15, 2000) <http://www.hoovers.com/>.

34. U.S. Sec. & Exch. Comm'n, *EDGAR Database of Corporate Information* (visited Apr. 15, 2000) <http://www.sec.gov/edgarhp.htm>.

35. Dow Jones & Co., *wsj.com: The Wall Street Journal* (visited Apr. 15, 2000) <http://interactive.wsj.com/home.html>.

36. U.S. Nat'l Library of Med., *United States National Library of Medicine* (visited Apr. 16, 2000) <http://www.nlm.nih.gov/databases/freemedl.html>.

37. St. Louis Univ. Ctr. for Health Law Studies, *Health Law Research Gateway* (visited Apr. 16, 2000) <http://lawlib.slu.edu/HealthCenter/Research/RESEARCH_INDEX.HTM>.

38. University of Chicago Library, *D'Angelo Law Library* (visited Apr. 16, 2000) <http://www.lib.uchicago.edu/e/law/home.html>.

39. U.S. Patent & Trademark Office, *United States Patent and Trademark Office* (visited Apr. 16, 2000) <http://www.uspto.gov/>.

40. Law Office Info. Sys., Inc., *LOIS.com* (visited Apr. 16, 2000) <http://www.loislaw.com/>.

41. Quick Law Am., Inc., *Quick Law America* (visited Apr. 16, 2000) <http://www.currentlegal.com/>.

42. Versus Law, Inc., *VersusLaw* (visited Apr. 16, 2000) <http://www.versuslaw.com/>.

43. Gay, *supra* note 1.

44. *See supra* note 2.

45. Gay, *supra* note 1.

46. Arturo L. Torres & W. Clinton Sterling, *Will Law Schools Go the Distance?: An Annotated Bibliography on Distance Education in Law*, 91 L. LIBR. J. 655 (1999).

47. Educational Online Network, Inc., *CLE Online.com* (visited Apr. 28, 2000) <http://www.cleonline.com/clecred.html>. David Kroll, Program Director for Professional Development at the Texas State Bar and Chair of the Technology Committee for the Association of Continuing Legal Education (ACLEA)2, was especially helpful in providing this information.

48. Electronic Signatures in Global and National Commerce Act, Pub. L. No. 106-229, 114 Stat. 464 (2000) (to be codified in 15 U.S.C. § 7001).

49. Corporation for Res. & Educ. Networking, *CREN* (visited Apr. 16, 2000) <http://www.cren.net/>.

Taking Time for Legal Research Instruction at the Reference Desk

Paul A. Arrigo

Paul A. Arrigo is Government Documents, Reference Coordinator and NT Administrator at Washburn University School of Law Library, 1700 College Avenue, Topeka, KS 66621 (E-mail: zzarri@washburn.edu).

[Haworth co-indexing entry note]: "Taking Time for Legal Research Instruction at the Reference Desk." Arrigo, Paul A. Co-published simultaneously in *Legal Reference Services Quarterly* (The Haworth Information Press, an imprint of The Haworth Press, Inc.) Vol. 19, No. 1/2, 2001, pp. 75-98; and: *Emerging Solutions in Reference Services: Implications for Libraries in the New Millennium* (ed: John D. Edwards) The Haworth Information Press, an imprint of The Haworth Press, Inc., 2001, pp. 75-98. Single or multiple copies of this article are available for a fee from The Haworth Document Delivery Service [1-800-342-9678, 9:00 a.m. - 5:00 p.m. (EST). E-mail address: getinfo@haworthpressinc.com].

SUMMARY. Different types of legal research techniques can be used at the reference desk with the goal of assisting the patron in learning research skills while helping alleviate reference desk congestion. Guidelines are provided to help the librarian decide which type of instruction to use at the reference desk based on time available and staffing constraints in the library. Also considered are the information gathering needs of the primary clientele of the library. *[Article copies available for a fee from The Haworth Document Delivery Service: 1-800-342-9678. E-mail address: <getinfo@haworthpressinc.com> Website: <http://www.HaworthPress. com> © 2001 by The Haworth Press, Inc. All rights reserved.]*

I. INTRODUCTION

When a patron arrives at the library and asks a question, is the answer delivered on a silver platter? Does the patron leave with great awe at the magical information gathering skills of the reference librarian, or does the patron leave with some ability to perform future research with little assistance from the librarian? Is the role of the reference librarian that of teacher or magician? It all depends on what is expected by the patrons and librarians as well as any staffing or physical constraints in the reference department in question. Ideally, all librarians should strive to teach patrons to better help themselves, if only to relieve the librarian from the burden of being the primary source of information.

Librarians can teach legal research at the reference desk in several ways ranging from one-on-one instruction to teaching an entire legal research course. Harvey Sager notes that bibliographic instruction includes: giving library tours; delivering classroom lectures, presentations or demonstrations on information gathering skills and resources; developing and teaching credit and non-credit library courses; co-teaching or providing course integrated library instruction; developing print, media, and multimedia library instruction materials; and even creating and implementing library signage systems.[1] More examples could be included depending on the creativity of the librarian. Sager further defines bibliographic instruction as, "In the broadest sense, bibliographic instruction, or library user education, might include any and all educational activities planned, designed and employed to enhance the independent information gathering and synthesizing of information seekers."[2]

This article points out the different types of legal instruction that can be performed at the reference desk with the goal of enabling the patron to learn to use research tools. It also takes into consideration the information gathering needs of patrons as well as their willingness to be instructed at the reference desk.

II. THE REFERENCE INTERVIEW

Before choosing a legal research method to assist a patron, it is critical to know the patron's informational needs and level of interest in receiving legal research instruction. One of the best ways to gain this information is through the reference interview. The reference interview is an art that includes some of the following components: eye contact, gestures, posture, facial expressions/tone of voice, remembering, avoiding premature diagnosis, reflecting feelings verbally, restating or paraphrasing contents, using encouragers, giving opinions/suggestions, asking open questions, and closing the conversation.[3]

From the reference interview the librarian must discover exactly what the patron needs to answer his or her question. The librarian must be aware of non-verbal as well as verbal communication with the patron. The teaching reference interview goes a step further than the regular reference interview by determining how much help the librarian should give the patron and how much research the patron should or can conduct. The best way the librarian can determine a patron's informational needs and receptiveness to legal research instruction is to focus on those needs and verbal and non-verbal clues.

A. Recognizing Patron Attributes

Knowing the patron's classification (faculty/staff member, law student, attorney, public patron, etc.) and the information gathering tendencies for that type of patron are important when conducting a reference interview. General information about a patron group can help identify past research tendencies and may indicate whether this patron would be more or less receptive to instruction than another type of patron.

Patron profiles are described below along with sample reference interviews for each type of patron. The librarian in each situation uses the profile to determine how best to provide instruction on a particular research tool.

1. Law Students

Most students could use some instruction when it comes to legal research, especially in the first year. A delicate balance exists, however, because the librarian must enable law students to do their own research, since they will need to have those skills when they begin clerking and practicing law. The librarian must train them and then let them do the research on their own. The reference interview can provide a good opportunity for the librarian to teach the law student. Most students are interested in learning how to research, but sometimes only to obtain the direct answers to their problem. More motivated students, however, will want to learn everything they can when conducting legal research. A typical exchange might include the following dialogue.

> *Law Student:* I need to know the blood alcohol level for DUI conviction in all fifty states.
> *Law Librarian:* All fifty states?
> *Law Student:* Yes, all fifty states!
> *Law Librarian:* What type of project are you working on?
> *Law Student:* I am doing this for the attorney I am clerking for.
> *Law Librarian:* Why don't you try searching the *Subject Compilations of State Laws* by Nyberg[4] to access that information or perhaps search a web site maintained by organizations directly impacted by drunk drivers?[5]
> *Law Student:* Thanks!
> *Law Librarian:* Do the attorneys at your firm ask these multi-state legislative questions often?
> *Law Student:* Well, I have been there two months and this is the third question like that.
> *Law Librarian:* In the future, no matter what the subject is, just remember to check the *Subject Compilations of State Laws* and look for related organizations on the Internet.

The librarian then helps the student conduct the search and shows how to use the Nyberg book to access data in the future.

Analysis: Although the librarian knew the patron was a law student and could have stopped after mentioning the resources, taking the additional step of asking how the information would be used enabled the librarian to determine that the student would benefit from instruction. The student had the time to learn what the librarian wanted to teach. The librarian recognized that it would be worthwhile to teach the student how to find the information upon discovering that the student conducts this type of search often.

2. Law Firm Partners

Most law firm partners are very busy handling client matters. They do not have the time to learn legal research techniques at the reference desk, as illustrated below.

Partner: Leslie, I need to know how much the Xerox Corporation is worth? I will need their annual report and 10k report. Please e-mail it to me within the next two hours so I can prepare for a deposition tomorrow!
Librarian: O.K. Pat I will get right to it.

Analysis: The partner made this an easy interview. The librarian did not need to ask anything or even show an interest in teaching how to do the research as was evident in the urgency of the request. The partner did fit the librarian's profile for the type of patron who does not have time to do the research or learn to do it. In the law firm setting the librarian knows the priority is to find the information; teaching can come later.

3. Public Patrons

The public patron usually needs the most instruction and handholding, but many libraries may not want reference librarians spending a great deal of time with public patrons. Sometimes public patrons are so new to an area of law that they need to sit down with a legal treatise or a legal self-help book. These types of books will give the patron some understanding of the legal terminology to help explain their needs to the librarian as noted in the following example.

Joe Public: My son recently got a divorce and my wife and I would like to know what our visitation rights are as grandparents. We want to still see our grandchild but our son's wife refuses to let us see her. What can we do?

Librarian: In what state did your son get the divorce?

Joe Public: Minnesota.

Librarian: How much time do you have? This could take awhile.

Joe Public: We're retired so we have as much time as you would like to give us.

Librarian: Well let's start by. . . .

Analysis: This time the librarian was direct in asking how much time they had to address this question. The patron responded by saying they had all the time in the world. This may be more than what the librarian bargained for, but the librarian did create an opportunity to show the couple how to conduct their research on this area of law. Due to their lack of knowledge of the legal process the librarian could direct them to the self-help materials dealing with grandparent rights to get them started.[6] Once they had read more on the issue they could come back for more information.

This librarian also knew that they were public patrons and would require quite a bit of instruction. By directing them to self-help materials and asking them to come back after reading them she enabled them to learn more about the legal process and subject area of the law so they could decide if they needed more help.

B. Determining the Receptiveness to Instruction: Strategies for Recognizing Verbal and Non-Verbal Clues

Classification of the patron helps the librarian recognize past research tendencies but does not help the librarian identify the patron's most immediate needs or motivations. If librarians are inflexible in their preconceived ideas of the needs for a particular type of patron, they may miss an opportunity to teach a patron or even worse, teach an uninterested patron. Observing the verbal and non-verbal clues sent by the patron is critical if librarians are to determine the patron's receptivity to instruction on that day. What a reference librarian did right and wrong is illustrated in the following reference interview with a faculty member.

Most law school faculty members are independent and unique.

They may be very good at legal research themselves and are experienced in using the tools. Some may need more assistance in using newer electronic resources. They usually prefer one-on-one to group instruction. Their time schedule may not be as pressed as a law firm partner, so they may have time for instruction if they are interested.

> *Faculty:* Kyle, I need to get the Supreme Court case on abortion that came down today. I need it as soon as possible so I can share it with my class this afternoon. I'll be leaving for a meeting in a few minutes.
>
> *Librarian:* Sure, let me show you how to find this information in the future. You know that the Supreme Court decisions have been on the Internet for the last five years. It is so amazing how technology has really allowed us to get access to the latest information. The best places to go for the latest Supreme Court decisions are the Cornell site[7] or the official court site.[7] Decisions appear there before they are posted on LEXIS or Westlaw. If Thomas Jefferson were alive today, he would be shocked to see how fast this information is delivered.
>
> *Faculty:* Thanks, I have to go.

Analysis: The librarian in this example, knowing that faculty members are receptive to learning, just continued to talk even though the faculty member was in a hurry. Needless to say the faculty member lost interest and probably became annoyed because he did not have time for a lengthy explanation. The librarian should have recognized that the faculty member was pressed for time.

III. DETERMINING THE LEVEL AND TYPE OF INSTRUCTION NEEDED

Once the librarian determines the patron's receptiveness to instruction based on the patron's classification and verbal and non-verbal clues, the next step is to determine what type of instruction is needed. This can be determined by identifying the informational needs of the patron. "The information need has a great deal to do with determining if there is a justification for teaching how to use a particular tool, or set of tools, or leaving the patron to do most of the searching alone."[9]

A. Basic Statistical Information and Fact Finding

Factual information is retrieved from various sources that are too numerous for most patrons to learn. Often the information required will only be requested once by the patron and never needed again. Guiding the patron to the needed information is probably a more productive route than attempting instruction for a tool that the patron may not need again.

B. Topical Subject Searches

A subject search will require more instruction than a fact-finding search. Based on the subject knowledge of the patron, the librarian may want to begin by directing the patron to a legal encyclopedia such as *American Jurisprudence Second* or help locate law journal articles that deal with the subject area. Patrons need to be taught how to search these sets as well as how to find the cases cited by these secondary sources. If patrons are unsure of which subject area to search, referring them to legal treatises or West Group's Nutshell series might be a good place to start.[10]

C. Primary Law Search Updating

Patrons searching for laws should be told that updating must be done to make sure each law is still valid. This necessitates instructing the client on how to update primary materials. For example, a patron might come into the library with a citation for Executive Order 11197 written by President Lyndon B. Johnson in 1965 concerning the establishment of the President's Council on Equal Opportunity. If the librarian located the executive order and let the patron leave with only that information, the librarian may have failed to fully address the patron's needs. The librarian should point out that executive orders can be amended or superceded and therefore should be updated.

In this case the patron can be guided to one of several sources to update the executive order. The fastest approach may be to search the Internet site for the National Archives and Records Administration (NARA) for *Executive Orders-Disposition Tables-Administration of Lyndon B. Johnson (1963-1969)*[11] which indicates the order was revoked. The table in the *Codification of Presidential Proclamations and Executive Orders* provides that same information as does the *Code of Federal Regulations: Title 3-The President, 1964-65 Cumulation.* A similar process using pocket parts, supplements, citators, or electronic sources must be utilized for updating other types of primary materials, including state and federal cases, regulations and state laws.

A good series that provides helpful hints on teaching legal research at the reference desk and often covers updating the law is the "Teachable moments" column in *Perspectives: Teaching Legal Research and Writing.*[12]

D. Electronic Resources

Electronic research has revolutionized the way the law is researched, but many patrons do not know how to effectively perform electronic searches. Some patrons, particularly older ones, might be unaccustomed to using a computer and may require some additional assistance. Others know how to search the computer but need more training to obtain better results. The computer has reemphasized the importance of providing legal research instruction at the reference desk, especially since some publications can be found only in electronic format, as explained in part VI of this article.

E. Sample Reference Interviews

Several teaching interviews are given below followed by an analysis of whether the librarian responded correctly to the type of information required by the patron.

1. One-Time Need

Faculty: I need to find out the total number of black women entrepreneurs in the United States and their average salary level.
Librarian: Do you only want the latest information? How far back should I go with this information?
Faculty: I would like to have data from the last ten years.
Librarian: I will get on that right away.

Analysis: Here the librarian made the right decision not to provide any type of legal instruction since the information requested was not likely to be needed again by the faculty member. The librarian would check census data and look at the *Glass Ceiling Commission Reports* to see if there have been any updates.[13]

2. Basic Instruction

Public Patron: I am evaluating a person who has applied to live in one of my rental homes. Where can I find information on his credit history? *Law Librarian:* Well, we do have Internet access to the local county district court docket, which will allow you to see any actions that have been taken on this individual. Would you like to use this resource?
Public Patron: You bet, but I am not too handy with computers. Could you get me started?
Law Librarian: Sure, first I need to log into the computer with the library user ID and password. Here is the district court docket homepage. All you need to do is to type in the plaintiff's first and last names and the computer search engine will pull up any cases concerning your prospective renter. If you don't get any results, be sure to type his last name and first initial. He might have used a different version of his first name for the case.

Analysis: Although this person had limited computer skills, little instruction was needed. The Internet site for the docket information was very user friendly. All that was needed was to type in the person's first and last name. The librarian just highlighted the limitations of the search engine and then let the patron search it.

3. Directional Responses

Law Student: I need to find 24 C.F.R. § 27.100 and make a copy for my law firm.
Librarian: O.K., it is in the documents area of the library. You can find it at the back wall. Good luck and have a nice day!

Analysis: The librarian should have wished the patron much luck, for when he returns to his law firm since he will likely need it. What did the librarian do wrong? The librarian did not notify the patron that the regulation needed to be updated by checking the latest *List of CFR Sections Affected* (LSA) covering title 24. The student then needed to check the Cumulative List of Parts Affected in the last issue of each month's Federal Register since the last LSA was printed and in the most recent Federal Register. This updating also could be done by going to the U.S. Government Printing Office site, *GPO Access*,[14] which provides the most current status of any regulations. At the law firm the clerk may be admonished for his lack of research skills and the librarian may be criticized for not telling the patron that regulations need to be updated.

Once the librarian has conducted the reference interview, identified the patron's classification, recognized the patron's receptivity for instruction, and ascertained the patron's informational needs, the research instruction technique must be selected that would best apply in the situation. In order to do that the librarian must know the strengths and weaknesses of the various legal reference instruction techniques. The section below will point out some of the most often used techniques and identify what informational needs they address. For a more extensive collection of legal research techniques the reader can consult the work by Gary L. Hill, *Survey on Legal Research Instruction*.[15]

IV. TECHNIQUES AND TOOLS
FOR REFERENCE DESK INSTRUCTION

A. The Library Providing Basic Services

A library with limited resources provides basic services by striving to teach as many as efficiently and expediently as possible so as to not to overburden the reference desk or the patron. The techniques below may or may not require much preparation beyond the time at the reference desk and are probably used most by the small, one-person library. A library without a large staff and considerable resources but with high reference demands may have difficulty in providing extensive legal research instruction at the reference desk. Listed below are some of the options available.

1. Training Provided by Vendors

When the librarian is overwhelmed with other administrative tasks, representatives of the online vendors such as LEXIS and Westlaw can be utilized to train students, law clerks, interns and new attorneys in those services. Vendor representatives are knowledgeable about system features and are experienced trainers. This technique is not performed at the reference desk but can help alleviate some reference questions and better equip the library's primary patrons to conduct their research.

2. One-on-One Instruction

Through the use of the teaching interview the librarian can provide one-on-one instruction in how to use a resource such as the Index to Legal Periodicals CD-ROM so patrons will be able to do research for themselves in the future. Elaine and Edward J. Jennerich describe the one-on-one interview in six steps:

> (1) Find out what the user wants, (2) Answer the question and only the question, (3) If the answer is too brief for the user to continue, the librarian should explain more to the user than was asked, (4) Be patient but brief with the user, (5) Indicate your willingness to assist users once they have tried things out on their own for a while, and (6) If the user is still frustrated, make an appointment with the user.[16]

Ann Fox has said that it is "best to err on the side of giving too little information than too much."[17] One-on-one sessions also can be scheduled away from the reference desk to allow the librarian to be more relaxed, which in turn will relax the patron (especially faculty members and attorneys).

Teachable moments are those times when the reference librarian can show a patron how to research and use a particular tool. One example of that is to show a student or a member of the public how to update a United States Treaty using *Treaties in Force* to see if there were any amendments since the original treaty was signed.[18] Teachable moments may be the ideal way to teach patrons legal research at the reference desk.[19] They could be considered a component of the one-on-one instruction technique.

3. The Intranet

Law firm librarians often use the law firm's intranet for legal research instruction. The librarian can send e-mail messages to attorneys notifying them of new searching techniques. The intranet allows attorneys to access more electronic information from their desktops than from the library. A front-end system could be used to help attorneys identify which electronic resource would contain the most appropriate content for the topic they are researching. Although the initial development of the intranet, as well as its maintenance, can be quite time consuming, one study suggests that the overall time savings can equate to twelve minutes per day per employee.[20]

If law clerks or student interns need training, the firm may ask a local law school to help train them to more efficiently search LEXIS, Westlaw, and the frequently used print materials. A clerking seminar or brown bag session might be a good vehicle for research instruction.

4. Online Tutorials

The librarian from a small firm also could use the online and CD-ROM tutorials that come with search software. For example, LOIS-LAW has a good search tutorial and help screens on its Internet site.[21] Because most people do not have the time or the patience to complete the tutorial, this method is underutilized. If the librarian is swamped with reference questions, however, a tutorial can be helpful as an interim aid until the librarian can provide assistance.

5. Handouts

Handouts can succinctly answer the most frequently asked questions, often on a single sheet of paper. Maps of the library, copier policies, and online catalog instructions are examples of the types of information that can be covered in handouts which can be provided in hard copy or on a web page.

B. The Larger Library's Expanded Opportunities

1. Teaching Legal Research in Upper Division Courses

Larger libraries often have staffing levels that make it possible to provide more legal research instruction than smaller law libraries. One technique is to develop a bibliographic instruction course with a faculty member, especially in an upper division course. Professor Lee Vaughn at the University of Washington developed a research component in several of her upper division classes. She said the only way law students are able to grow and develop the necessary legal research skills is by using legal research instruction techniques in all courses, including upper divisional specialty courses.[22] Mary Whisner, Professor Vaughn's librarian cohort, discovered the importance of having the law professor present while the librarian instructs the class to give the research component more credibility.[23]

2. Library Signage and Maps

Providing good signage throughout the library is another subtle form of instruction by helping answer frequent directional questions. Developing a map of the library for patrons as a separate handout or part of a bookmark, pamphlet or brochure also is helpful. A map or diagram of the library could be posted on the library's home page for those who might want to review the library's layout before coming to the library.

3. Research Guides and Handouts

Research guides and one-page handouts should be brief with as much white space as possible. Guides can be loaded on the Internet so that users can learn how to do legal research by reading an explanation of a web resource and then directly linking to that resource. These guides are very helpful for a patron to peruse while waiting for the reference librarian.

C. The Research Library with Extensive Resources

1. In-House Expert Systems

For larger libraries which have sufficient staffing, in-house creation of computer-assisted legal research (CALR) tools may be a possibility. For example, Professor I.T. Hardy created Lexpert, an "expert system for giving advice about legislative history research."[24] He noted that others could adapt his design for other types of CALR programs:

> [U]seful expert systems can be created for law library research that do not depend on highly complex software to deliver the system to

its end users. Most conventional expert systems rely on software to draw conclusions each time an end user asks a question. The fact that the system must draw conclusions each time makes such expert systems flexible and powerful, but also means that they are computing intensive and, hence, require more powerful computer hardware than most hypertext systems require. The software complexity in Lexpert's hypertext approach shows up only in the development cycle and even this consists in the integration of a large number of individual tools, each of which is fairly simple and understandable in its own. The particular distribution software for Lexpert is a straightforward and reliable hypertext reader program that requires minimal computing hardware.[25]

Expert systems like these could be used at reference by having patrons sit down and work through the program while the librarian is helping other individuals. The patron always can ask for assistance. This type of tool may be best used in conjunction with a research and writing course, similar to computer-assisted legal instruction (CALI) exercises.[26]

Washburn University School of Law Library developed a computer-assisted expert system on how to search for patents. Washburn is a satellite library to the Kansas State Patent Depository Library at Wichita State University. Washburn has an agreement with the Kansas Technology Enterprise Corporation to conduct patent searches for the citizens of Northeast Kansas.[27] Since these patrons are members of the public and not the library's primary clientele, an expert system was developed in which the patrons access the electronic CD-ROM collection with as little assistance from the librarians as possible. That system explains the patent searching process and then connects patrons to the CD-ROMs they need to conduct the search. The public benefited from the tool, which only took a month to create, and librarians were free to handle other matters.

2. Front-End Systems

Development of a front-end system can help various clients in a large library, especially one that has a large number of electronic resources. With a large selection of databases available, it may be difficult for users to identify which resources would best answer their specific needs. Washburn University School of Law Library, for example, has over 50 different electronic resources available by clicking a series of hierarchical folders from faculty desktop computers. So many resources are provided that professors had difficulty knowing which tool would best answer their questions.

A front-end system was created in which a descriptive abstract was written about each research tool with a direct link to that tool.[28] Subject descriptors were added to the abstract so the professors could search by subject. The abstracts were then indexed using the Internet indexing tool IsysWeb.[29] Professors can enter the subject of interest to find the electronic resources that could best answer their questions. They can read the abstract and decide which tool is best for them and then access that resource directly. This type of system acts as a mini-reference librarian for professors and users who are not physically in the library and have no direct access to the librarian's assistance. Law students seeking assistance at the reference desk also find this tool helpful.

3. Internet Research and Writing Web Courses and Resources

Internet course development is another tool in teaching legal research. Law professors are beginning to create online legal research pages. For example, Cornell University's Legal Information Institute at http://www.law.cornell.edu gives an overview of several legal topics and then provides links to Internet legal resources beginning with primary materials and providing links to other organizations dealing with the same topic.

A course page on Legal Literature and Librarianship by Professor Ted Tjaden of the University of Toronto can be a helpful resource. This site covers statutes and regulations, case law, secondary legal resources, and legal materials for Canada, Britain and the United States at http://www.fis.utoronto.ca/courses/LIS/2133/techqn.htm. The E.B. Williams Law Library at Georgetown University has a legal research and writing site at http://www.ll.georgetown.edu/lr/rs/leglwrite.html.[30] Several legal research and writing course pages are posted on the Jurist site at http://jurist.law.pitt.edu/cour_pgs.htm. Additional sites are provided in the appendix.

V. EFFECTIVE INSTRUCTION TECHNIQUES FOR SPECIFIC REQUESTS

Once a librarian knows the possible instruction techniques, the next step is to determine when to use them. During the reference interview the librarian should be able to determine which method will address the patron's specific information needs. The samples below will help explain how the librarian can adapt the instruction techniques to meet the patron's needs.

A. Fact Finding

One-on-one instruction is an option when the patron requires specific factual information. Librarians may invite the interested patron to watch how they access the information, such as by showing the patron how to use Internet search engines when looking for facts. The librarian also could educate the patron on the limitations of information found on the Internet, including concerns of authenticity and accuracy. The following dialogue illustrates one approach.

Law Student: I need some statistical information concerning the number of people living below the poverty level in Kansas.
Librarian: What do you need to do with this information?
Law Student: I am trying to do some research on the Social Security Act and how much it truly helps people in Kansas and I think knowing the number people below the poverty level over the last 15 years would be very helpful.
Librarian: That sounds like a very interesting question. Lets start by . . . . [Ring] Oh, excuse me I have a phone call. While I am gone you can take a look at this handout on Statistical Resources on the Internet and try searching for poverty level information from one of those sites. I will be back to help you a bit later.

Analysis: If the reference librarian is too busy to provide immediate service, the patron can be given a handout of the top statistical Internet sites. This list would include clearinghouses of federal and state statistical resources on the Internet.[31] The patron could then access these sites while waiting for the reference librarian. If a handout is not available, the patron could be directed to the FedStats home page at http://www.fedstats.gov/.

B. Subject Searching

Faculty: Dana, I am searching for some information on biomedical ethics. Do you know where I can find such information? How do I

go about even locating such information? Bioethics is not a subject
I am familiar with.
Librarian: Why don't you try this in-house index of our Internet
subscriptions. Just type in the subject of bioethics and see which
resource would best answer your question. If you have any trouble
searching the site once you are there, please let me know and I will
help you.
Faculty: O.K. I'll do it. Thanks!

Analysis: In this example the librarian obviously works in a library
with a large staff and extensive electronic resources. Dana can point
the patron to the in-house front-end system. Not every librarian has
access to such sophisticated information tools so providing the faculty
member with one-on-one instruction on searching the library catalog
for treatises on bioethics is another useful technique. Dana could have
located a law professor's bioethics course Internet home page and
from there the faculty member could access various bioethics web
sites.

C. Primary Legal Resource Updating

Public Patron: I need a copy of the Supreme Court case of *Kansas
v. Hendricks*. It concerns the Kansas Sexual Predator Act.
Librarian: O.K. Let's look at the Supreme Court Digest. The case
can be found in 521 U.S. 346. But you may wish to see if there is
any negative history on this case.
Public Patron: What do you mean by negative history?
Librarian: Negative history is any subsequent case law that has
either amended or overruled the case you are interested in. This will
determine if the case is still good law or not.
Public Patron: How do I find out if there has been any negative
history on this case?
Librarian: You can access *Shepard's United States Citations:
United States Reports*. Let me show you how this works.

Analysis: In this example the librarian just performed one-on-one
instruction. If the library has extensive electronic resources, the patron
could have been directed to a computer-assisted legal instruction program on searching Shepard's Citators. A Shepard's online tutorial on
conducting the search also could be accessed from Shepard's home
page.[32]

D. Electronic Searching

Law Student: I need to find out how many states have legislation that requires gun owners to have a safety lock on all handguns. I searched the all-states legislative database in Westlaw but could not find any reference to those laws. What am I doing wrong?

Librarian: Tell me what search strategy you used and we can see what might have gone wrong.

Law Student: I searched for "gun owner!" and "safety lock" in the all-states legislative database.

Librarian: You may want to use other synonyms for gun, such as weapon, handgun, pistol, etc. and trigger lock as well as safety lock. For example, you might try: gun or weapon or handgun or pistol or revolver or firearm /5 safety or trigger /5 lock. You also might look at some of the Internet sites that have compilations of gun control laws.[33]

Analysis: In this example the librarian worked with the patron to refine the search strategy by suggesting just a few changes in query formulation. The librarian's response of one-on-one electronic training was effective.

VI. IMPACT OF TECHNOLOGY ON TEACHING RESEARCH AT THE REFERENCE DESK

As technology becomes more of a factor in legal research, the reference librarian must be able to recognize not only when to use electronic resources but also how to use them more effectively. The librarian must not become so immersed in the technology as to miss out on identifying which format is best for the situation at hand. An acknowledged weakness of CALR system design is that relevant documents may be missed.[34] Thus, CALR must be used as part of an integrated research strategy which incorporates the use of several research tools.[35] Certain types of CALR searches are more effective than others; they are best for retrieving specific words, products, or entities (highly relevant results) and less effective when searching for abstract concepts.

The effectiveness of computer retrieval systems is judged by comparing recall versus precision.[36] When conducting a narrow search, the computer will retrieve some highly relevant results, yet many other relevant cases in the database are not retrieved. In contrast, when performing a broader search to produce higher recall, the user is left with many false hits.[37] CALR can be used to gather those highly relevant cases (precision). Shepardizing the case (forward chaining) and accessing those cases cited by the relevant case (backward chaining) address recall.[38]

Law library patrons are becoming even more sophisticated in accessing electronic information. Reference librarians must continue to steer patrons in the right direction and give them the road map to find the information they need.

VII. GUIDELINES FOR REFERENCE DESK INSTRUCTION

Elaine and Edward Jennerich suggest the following procedures to make a teaching interview flow more smoothly.[39]

1. Simplify. As the intermediary between the complex organization of the library and the patron, the librarian must simplify services, tools and technology as much as possible. Do not burden the patron with detailed explanations of how a particular reference tool works, for example, unless a lengthy explanation is absolutely needed. Also, never ask the patron to learn more sources than are necessary to answer the specific question at hand. In other words, a teaching interview is not intended to be all-inclusive library instruction, but instruction for the purpose of helping a patron meet specific information needs.
2. If you tell patrons that you (or some other librarian) will get back to them, be sure to do so. It is easy to get sidetracked in assisting other patrons, but politeness and the success of the interview demand that you follow up with the first clients.
3. Work alongside patrons for a while to make sure they understand what they have been told and how to use the resources (whether online or in other formats).
4. Do not try to teach a patron who refuses to be taught. Just because a school librarian, for example, believes that students should be taught how to use the library does not mean that every student feels the same way.[40]

Several additional factors need to be weighed before providing legal research instruction at the reference desk. Most of these factors deal with the patron's specific needs and apparent receptiveness to instruction.

1. *How much time does the patron have?* A patron in a hurry is not going to be receptive to any type of instruction during the reference interaction. The librarian can usually tell if the patron is in a hurry by listening carefully and observing body language.
2. *How often does the patron use the library collection?* If the patron is a regular user, providing legal instruction may be worthwhile. If the patron is a one-time visitor, then giving legal instruction may not be necessary.
3. *How much instruction should the librarian provide?* Deciding what instruction would most benefit the patron requires that the librarian listen carefully to the needs of the patron. The librarian should not douse the patron with a fire hose if all that is needed is a sip of water. Giving too much information can confuse the patron. The appropriate level can be discovered through the reference interview.
4. *Would the patron be open to legal research instruction at a later time?* If the patron does not have the time now, making an appointment for more detailed instruction later may be a possibility.
5. *Is the patron uncomfortable learning new research skills at such a public place as the reference desk?* Some individuals are more comfortable learning in a more private setting. If faculty members or law firm partners do not want to appear unknowledgeable to their colleagues and subordinates, the librarian should be perceptive of that concern and consider working with them in their offices.
6. *What legal research techniques has the patron preferred in the past?* If the librarian knows that a patron prefers to read one-page handouts rather than be instructed one-on-one, then the librarian should provide him with the appropriate handout. A handout can be especially helpful for busy faculty members or associates.

VIII. CONCLUSION

Legal researchers normally consult a reference librarian to find the information they need. A reference librarian, like the wise guru, will not give the patron the answers, but will ask them the right questions enabling them to discover the truth for themselves. The reference librarian's job is to enable patrons to find information for themselves and equip them to focus on the types of resources they need. If the librarian does not have time in the reference desk setting to provide that assistance, it is essential to develop tools that will teach the patrons in settings outside the reference desk, including when the patron seeks assistance electronically.

Librarians must determine what type of legal research methods will best meet their patrons' needs. Librarians can decide the best way to provide legal research instruction at the reference desk once they discover the patron's informational needs and receptivity to instruction though careful listening and recognition of non-verbal clues.

NOTES

1. Harvey Sager, *Implications for Bibliographic Instruction, in* IMPACT OF EMERGING TECHNOLOGIES ON REFERENCE SERVICE AND BIBLIOGRAPHIC INSTRUCTION 51 (1995).

2. *Id.* at 50.

3. ELAINE ZAREMBA JENNERICH & EDWARD J. JENNERICH, THE REFERENCE INTERVIEW AS A CREATIVE ART 11 (2d ed. 1997).

4. SUBJECT COMPILATIONS OF STATE LAWS 1998-99: AN ANNOTATED BIBLIOGRAPHY (Cheryl Rae Nyberg ed., 2000). The volumes in this set, which currently is published annually, provide coverage back to 1960. For more information on the series, see Boast/Nyberg, *State Legal Information Center* (visited June 23, 2000) <http://www.state-laws.com>.

5. James B. Reed et al., National Conference of State Legislatures, *State Legislative Progress in Improving Traffic Safety,* 1997 (visited June 8, 2000) <http://www.ncsl.org/programs/esnr/transer8.htm#alcohol>. *Drunk Driving Defense.com* <http://www.drunkdrivingdefense.com/frames/linksframe.htm> provides access to many of the pro- and anti-drunk driving special interest groups. The Georgia Insurance Information Service has a news release in 1997 entitled *State-by-State Blood Alcohol Content Levels: Existing Blood Alcohol Content Levels for Drunken Driving in the 50 States and the District of Columbia,* <http://www.giis.org/bac-us.htm>. Finally, the National Conference of State Legislatures has some additional information on its web site entitled *News Release: State Drunk Driving Laws: The .08 Debate* <http://www.ncsl.org/programs/press/pr980330.htm>.

6. *See* TRACI TRULY, GRANDPARENTS' RIGHTS (2d ed. 1999). This work is from Sphinx Publishing. Libraries serving public patrons often collect a number of titles from Nolo Press, one of the largest publishers of legal self-help books. Nolo.com, *Law for All* (visited June 23, 2000) <http://www.nolopress.com>. The Nolo.com Self-Help Law Centers include an article by Liza Weiman Hanks, *Grandparent Visitation Rights* (visited June 23, 2000) <http://www.nolo.com/encyclopedia/articles/div/grandparents.html>.

7. *Legal Information Institute's Supreme Court Collection* (visited June 8, 2000) <http://supct.law.cornell.edu/supct/>.

8. *See* <http://www.supremecourtus.gov/>.

9. JENNERICH & JENNERICH, *supra* note 3, at 50.

10. The West Nutshell series provides a brief overview of a particular area of law with topical coverage ranging from Accounting to Workers' Compensation. A listing of the more than 100 titles in the Nutshell series is available from <http://lawschool. westgroup.com/products/leg/nutshell.htm>.

11. NARA, *Executive Orders–Disposition Tables–Administration of Lyndon B. Johnson (1963-1969)* (last modified May 1, 2000) <http://www.nara.gov/fedreg/eo_lbj. html>.

12. *See, e.g.,* Lydia Potthoff, *Teachable Moments . . . How Do You Update the Code of Federal Regulations?*, 5 PERSP.: TEACHING LEGAL RES. & WRITING 28-29 (1996). *Perspectives* is provided to librarians at no charge by West Group. For the past few issues and subscription information, see West Group, *Perspectives: Teaching Legal Research and Writing newsletter* (visited June 23, 2000) <http://www. westgroup.com/librarians/perspec/perspec.htm>. The fall 1999 issue includes a cumulative index for the first seven volumes.

13. Catherwood Library, *E-Archive: Glass Ceiling Commission* (visited June 8, 2000) <http://www.ilr.cornell.edu/library/e_archive/gov_reports/glassceiling/default.html? page=home>. The Glass Ceiling Commission was created in 1991 as a part of the Civil Rights Act of 1991 as a 21-member body appointed by the President to investigate barriers and promote employment opportunities and advancement for women and minorities. Another site called *Glassceiling.org* at <http://www.glassceiling.org/ ns.html> promises to provide 19 years of data (1980-1998) from an average of 217 Fortune 500 corporations each year. The release of data is scheduled for 2001.

14. GPO Access provides the updated LSA at <http://www.access.gpo.gov/nara/ lsa/aboutlsa.html>.

15. GARY L. HILL, SURVEY ON LEGAL RESEARCH INSTRUCTION (1998).

16. JENNERICH & JENNERICH, *supra* note 3, at 58.

17. Ann Fox, *Reference IS BI*, OLA Q., Fall 1998, at 6.

18. U.S. DEP'T OF STATE, TREATIES IN FORCE (1999).

19. More examples of teachable moments can be found in the regular series by that same name in *Perspectives: Teaching Legal Research and Writing. See supra* note 12; *see also* Edward Grosek, *Teachable Moments . . . How Can I Find a United States Treaty?*, 7 PERSP.: TEACHING LEGAL RES. & WRITING. 29-30 (1998).

20. Nancy M. Nelson, *Shifting Currents from the World Wide Web to Your Own Intranet*, PLL PERSP., Summer 1998, at 8 (summarizing the July 1997 AALL Program).

21. *Loislaw.com* (visited June 8, 2000) <http://www.loislaw.com/>.

22. Mary Whisner & Lea Vaughn, *Teaching Legal Research in Upper Division Courses: A Retrospective from Two Perspectives*, 4 PERSP.: TEACHING LEGAL RES. & WRITING 72 (1996).

23. *Id.* at 76.

24. I.T. Hardy, *Creating an Expert System for Legislative History Research: Project CLEAR'S "Lexpert,"* 85 L. LIBR. J. 239 (1993).

25. *Id.* at 272.

26. *See* The Center for Computer-Assisted Legal Instruction, *CALI* (visited June 23, 2000) <http://www.cali.org/>.

27. Kansas Technology Enterprise Corporation is a quasi-state agency created from lottery money for economic development in Kansas.

28. Washburn Univ. School of Law, *Legal Reference Indexes* (visited June 8, 2000) <http://198.252.9.108:8081/indexesa-f.html>.

29. For more information on IsysWeb, see < http://www.isysdev.com>.

30. Michael G. Walsh, *Legal Research and Writing Resources on the Internet*, 44 Prac. Law. 9 (1998). For additional online resources useful to writers, such as *Roget's Thesaurus* and *William Strunk's The Elements of Style*, see Bartleby.com, *Great Books Online* (visited June 23, 2000) <http://www.bartleby.com/index.html>.

31. For statistical information, see Federal Interagency Council on Statistical Policy, *FedStats* (visited June 23, 2000) <http://www.fedstats.gov/>; U.S. Dep't of Commerce, *Census Bureau* (visited June 23, 2000) <http://www.census.gov/>; U.S. Dep't of Commerce, *Stat-USA/Internet* (visited June 23, 2000) <http://www.stat-usa.gov/>; University of Michigan Documents Center, *Statistical Resources on the Web* (visited June 23, 2000) <http://www.lib.umich.edu/libhome/Documents.center/stats.html>.

32. *See How to Shepardize: An Interactive Tutorial* (visited June 8, 2000) <http://helpcite.shepards.com/howtoshep/howto1.htm>. Westlaw's KeyCite is another citator option if the library provides that service to the public.

33. For listings of Child Access Prevention (CAP) laws, see National Conference of State Legislatures, *Child Access Prevention Laws* (visited June 23, 2000) <http://www.ncsl.org/programs/press/schoolviolence/cap.htm> or the Center to Prevent Handgun Violence, *State Summaries* (visited June 23, 2000) <http://www.handguncontrol.org/laws/cap.asp>.

34. June Stewart, *CALR's Role in the Legal Research Process*, 15 Legal Reference Services Q. 109 (1996).

35. *Id.* at 121.

36. Daniel P. Dabney, *The Curse of Thamus: An Analysis of Full-Text Legal Document Retrieval*, 78 L. Libr. J. 5, 15 (1986).

37. *Id.* at 16.

38. Stewart, *supra* note 34, at 122.

39. Jennerich & Jennerich, *supra* note 3, at 50.

40. *Id.*

APPENDIX
Selected Legal Research and Writing Sites

Site Name	URL
Internet Lawyer: Legal Resources on the Net	http://www.internetlawyer.com/til/research/start.htm
Law News Network	http://www.law.com
Legal Research and Writing (Florida State)	http://www.law.fsu.edu/library/courseconnections/index.html
Legal Research Web Lecture Index (LEXIS)	http://lawschool.lexis.com/weblec/lrw/top.htm
Nettech, Inc. Excellent Legal Resources	http://www.nettechinc.com/lawlinks.htm

Law Library Tours in an Information Age:
Format, Effectiveness and Function

Deborah M. Keene
Holliday Gordon

Deborah M. Keene is Associate Dean for Library and Technology at George Mason University School of Law, Arlington, VA 22201 (E-mail: dkeene@gmu.edu). Holliday Gordon is Information Services Librarian for Morris, Manning & Martin, 1600 Atlanta Financial Center, 3343 Peachtree Road, N.E., Atlanta, GA 30329 (E-mail: hgordon@mmmlaw.com).

[Haworth co-indexing entry note]: "Law Library Tours in an Information Age: Format, Effectiveness and Function." Keene, Deborah M., and Holliday Gordon. Co-published simultaneously in *Legal Reference Services Quarterly* (The Haworth Information Press, an imprint of The Haworth Press, Inc.) Vol. 19, No. 1/2, 2001, pp. 99-114; and: *Emerging Solutions in Reference Services: Implications for Libraries in the New Millennium* (ed: John D. Edwards) The Haworth Information Press, an imprint of The Haworth Press, Inc., 2001, pp. 99-114. Single or multiple copies of this article are available for a fee from The Haworth Document Delivery Service [1-800-342-9678, 9:00 a.m. - 5:00 p.m. (EST). E-mail address: getinfo@haworthpressinc.com].

SUMMARY. The virtual library poses challenges for law librarians in developing effective library orientation programs. Survey results from law librarians in academia and in law firms reveal how basic library orientation is conducted in light of the proliferation of electronic resources. The types of additional instruction being required, such as training in computer-assisted legal research and web searching, are examined along with the perceived effectiveness of the initial library tours. *[Article copies available for a fee from The Haworth Document Delivery Service: 1-800-342-9678. E-mail address: <getinfo@haworthpressinc.com> Website: <http://www.HaworthPress.com> © 2001 by The Haworth Press, Inc. All rights reserved.]*

I see our role as being sort of like a guide. We recommend and provide information on local and exotic travel along with prices for various packages. We make recommendations and we prepare people for travel to their destinations. If they decide not to personally take the trip we can "travel" for them but the results may not be as good in most cases as firsthand experience.[1]

I. INTRODUCTION

Today in most academic and firm law libraries, one of the key responsibilities of the library staff is to provide library orientation to new students and associates. This orientation usually takes the form of a physical tour of the library and may include other types of instruction. Over the years, librarians have experimented with a variety of formats for the orientation tour ranging from audiotape to videotape and physical tours to virtual tours. This article examines how librarians conduct basic orientation tours and offers some observations on the continuing effectiveness of these tours, given the proliferation of electronic resources and the changing role of reference librarians in the information age.

In order to gather data for this article, a short survey was e-mailed to selected librarians from 50 law schools and 50 large law firms. In addition, the same survey was e-mailed to law-lib, the largest law library listserv.[2] Sixty librarians returned the survey, and the responses were equally divided between academic and firm libraries.

II. ACADEMIC LAW LIBRARIES

A. Provision of Orientation Tours to New Students

The results of the survey of academic librarians indicate that the overwhelming majority of academic law libraries provides basic orientation tours to their new law students. This orientation tour typically introduces the students to the library's physical arrangement and includes information on library policies, services, and the collection. Students are often given a library guide, maps, and other handouts at the beginning of the tour.

Some libraries provide more in-depth instruction during the initial orientation by teaching students to use online resources such as the Web, the online catalog, or LegalTrac, as well as key print resources such as digests, statutes, Shepard's citations and ALRs. Other libraries integrate the tour into the legal research program and instead of doing one big tour of the library, they provide a series of short instructional tours on the different areas of the collection.

According to the survey, few libraries do not provide tours or some type of introductory library instruction. However, in these few instances, the tours were conducted by other groups such as students from the Student Bar Association or instructors in the legal research and writing program. In some schools, students are given several library tours during their first year. The library staff may conduct the initial tour but the legal research and writing instructor might give a more in-depth tour or series of tours later in the semester.

B. Orientation Tours as a Requirement

Over two-thirds of the academic libraries surveyed require that new first-year students participate in the initial orientation tours. This mandatory requirement may change from year to year in some libraries as they experiment with different ways of inducing students to attend the tour. In many libraries the tour is a mandatory part of the legal research and writing program, but this requirement may not be enforced equally by all legal writing instructors. The tour is more likely to be required if the library staff is also responsible for teaching legal research.

Most libraries perform the tours at the beginning of the school year.

However, some libraries give the tours later in the semester in short segments as students are introduced to various legal materials through the legal research program. Many libraries also provide orientation tours to visiting, transfer, and advanced degree students, or to special groups such as new law journal staffs or faculty research assistants. However, these tours tend to be optional. Some libraries also offer tours in conjunction with regular law school classes or seminars in specialized areas such as taxation, labor law, or international law.

C. Format of the Orientation Tours

1. Walk-Around: Group or Individual

Almost all of the academic law libraries that responded to the survey conduct group tours. A few libraries require that students take individual self-guided tours. Libraries try to keep group sizes down to a manageable level, but the size often depends upon the format and the amount of time allotted. Many libraries provide one-on-one tours to students upon request. The survey responses indicate that all of the libraries that provide orientation to their new students use the traditional walk-around tour.

Almost all of the tours are led by one library staff member who walks a group of students through the library. In some cases, the tour guide escorts the group around to different key areas where another staff member gives a short lecture on the services or features of that area. In other instances, the students gather for a preliminary lecture before they are guided through the library. The length of these tours varies but tends to be no longer than one hour.

Two libraries that responded to the survey use self-guided walk-around tours. One of these libraries makes the self-guided tour a mandatory part of the legal research course and requires the student to answer questions about the location of services and collections that they encounter during their tour. The other library offers a voluntary self-guided tour that provides students with more in-depth instruction than the group walk-around.

2. Audio and Video

According to the survey results, there is currently very little use of audio-visual formats for orientation tours. Only one of the libraries that responded to the survey uses a multimedia format for its tours. The University of Michigan uses self-guided audiotapes for new first-year students; this is a required part of the legal research and writing course. A new audiotape is created each year by the staff, and the tour takes 90 minutes to complete. Each student receives a written guide as well. A couple of other libraries tried using audiotapes but stopped due to problems with keeping the tapes up-to-date and because of a dislike of the format by students.

In 1987, the Emory Law Library produced a seven-minute musical video tour[3] that was used for several years until the library's new building project began construction. The video was done in "rap" style and was popular with students at the time it was produced. However, the library decided not to try to bring the video up-to-date, as the video was a "one-of-a-kind" that could not easily or inexpensively be redone.

3. Web- or Computer-Based

A quick look at the web sites of the members of the Association of American Law Schools reveals that most academic law libraries are using the World Wide Web as a means of distributing information about their libraries. Almost all libraries have their library guides on the web and many also post maps and location guides to their collections.[4] Many libraries have extensive collections of their research guides or pathfinders posted on their sites.[5] Some libraries also post their newsletters or new acquisitions lists.[6] A number of library web sites have suggestion boxes or allow their own law students to send questions to the reference desk. One library posts a "Research Tip of the Week,"[7] and another library provides their users with the ability to customize an electronic research page.[8]

Only a handful of libraries have put up "virtual" library tours on their web sites. These virtual tours generally consist of photographs of the library with descriptive text.[9] Many more law schools' sites provide virtual tours of their buildings, which often include a few pictures of the library.[10] Law schools with new buildings are most likely to include these virtual tours, and several buildings under construction use webcams to provide live video feed of their construction sites. A few law schools use RealVideo[®] or QuickTime[™] to provide a tour of their building or to post a promotional video.[11] These videos may include brief footage of the library.

The library survey revealed only one instance of a non-web based computer program for library tours. One university law library uses Microsoft PowerPoint in lieu of a physical walk-around to provide a tour to their students.[12] This presentation consists of photographs with important information about the library. The students may also participate in an optional physical walk-around.

D. Perceived Effectiveness of Tours

All of the librarians who responded to the survey indicated that their tours are either "effective" or "somewhat effective" in providing orientation to the library. None of the respondents judged their tours to be either "very effective" on "ineffective." The degree of effectiveness does not seem to be influenced by whether or not the tour is mandatory or by the format or the tour. Neither does the judgment of effectiveness hinge on whether or not the librarians teach in the legal research program. Having a reasonable expectation for the tour does have some influence over the perceived value of the tour. One of the librarians who stated that their tours were "effective" indicated that their "goal is just general orientation, nothing more." Another librarian wrote that their tours have become more effective since the students were required to turn in a written set of answers to questions about the tour.

Many libraries focus on just the "essentials" and keep detail about research tools to a minimum. Other libraries emphasize only the research tools that students will have immediate use for in connection with their classes. Of the librarians who responded that the tours were only "somewhat effective," one indicated that "students cannot cope with this much new information," and another stated that "they [students] only listen some of the time, not knowing how much it will help them." One librarian summarizes the goal of their tours as "we don't expect students to remember all of the details but just to get a better 'feel' for the place and to feel more comfortable asking questions."

E. Responsibility for Other Types of Instruction

Aside from the traditional introductory library tour and orientation to print materials, survey results reveal that academic libraries also are providing a number of other types of library instruction in the use of online and computer resources. Two-thirds of the libraries teach students to use the on-line catalog. One-half of the libraries provide training in e-mail and web and Internet research. About a quarter of the libraries provide instruction in the use of CD-ROMs.

Training in these online resources is often part of the initial orientation tour or may be incorporated into the legal research program. In some libraries, training in e-mail and the web is done on a one-to-one basis at the request of the student. One library offers lunchtime workshops on the Internet. In another case, the main campus does the e-mail training, but the library provides a number of handouts on how to use the system. About half of the libraries surveyed teach LEXIS and Westlaw to new students. In some cases where the library does not provide the initial training, they may do one-on-one training when asked or provide advanced or specialized classes.

III. LAW FIRM LIBRARIES

A. Provision of Orientation Tours to New Associates

All but one of the law firms represented in the survey conduct library tours to new associates. At the firm not providing tours, the librarian explained that while a tour of the library facilities is not given, the librarian is responsible for giving a fifteen-minute presentation about library services and facilities during the new associates' orientation to the firm. The librarian's rationale for not giving library tours is that, in her opinion, actual use is the best way for a new associate to learn his or her way around the library. She observed that after the first few research projects, associates become very comfortable using the library.

B. Orientation Tours as a Requirement

Tours are required as a part of the firm's orientation of new associates in the majority of law firm libraries surveyed. Invariably, the tours are conducted during the first few days after associates begin work at the firms. In some instances, requiring associates to attend tours is apparently more a matter of form than substance. One librarian noted that at her firm, even though new associates are required to take tours

of the library, many fail to participate. The appearance of new associates for the "required" tours, according to the librarian, depends largely on the influence of the hiring committee, the firm's support of the library, and the individual associate's research habits.

Two of the firms surveyed require new associates to take tours while not making tours a requirement for attorneys hired laterally from other law firms. In this instance, the perceived value of the library tour seems to rest more on introducing new attorneys to law firm libraries in general rather than familiarizing them with the specific library and its collection, services, and librarian.

One survey response indicates that lack of familiarity with a law firm library's services and facilities may very well breed contempt, particularly in the case of lateral hires. The librarian observed that lateral hires at her firm do not take part in tours, often failing even to pick up library maps. These laterals are most likely to be critical of the library, comparing its collection and its services to those of their former firms' libraries in a negative manner.

C. Format of the Orientation Tours

1. Walk-Around: Group or Individual

More than a third of the law firm libraries surveyed offer physical tours of their facilities on both group and individual bases. The remaining libraries are evenly split between offering only group tours or only individual tours.

A number of firm libraries responding to the survey noted that the decision on whether to conduct an individual or group tour depends on the circumstances of the hiring of the new associate. Since the majority of these firm libraries conduct tours as a part of law firm orientation, the librarians by necessity must give tours on an as-needed basis. In cases where several attorneys are hired at the same time, the tours are conducted in groups. Single-attorney hires inevitably lead to individual tours.

2. Self-Guided, Audio, and Video

Law firm librarians participating in the survey eschew the use of tours that do not require personal contact with the new attorneys. None of the survey participants uses self-guided, audio, or video tours as a means of introducing new attorneys to their libraries. Several librarians, however, emphasize the use of memoranda outlining library policies and procedures, handouts created specifically for firm practice areas, and other forms of orientation packets as crucial parts of their tours.

One firm librarian commented that the real value of giving tours lies in the opportunity to establish a rapport with the new associates and to encourage them to consult the librarian when they have research questions. A personal tour is obviously a better vehicle for establishing this rapport than a self-guided, video, or audio tour.

3. Web or Computer-Based

Three survey participants indicated that they conduct web tours. However, in the comments attached to their answers, they seemed to equate the idea of a web tour with a tour of the legal research resources present on their intranets and on the World Wide Web. Web-based tours of the physical facilities of law firm libraries are not mentioned in any of the responses to the survey nor are they evident from searches conducted on the web.

D. Perceived Effectiveness of Tours

The majority of law firm librarians participating in the survey consider their library tours to be either effective or very effective. Approximately twenty percent of the survey respondents rate their tours as very effective. More than half of the librarians judge that they had been effective in their provision of tours. The remaining quarter of the survey responses indicate that the librarians feel that their tours had only been somewhat effective.

In some of the surveys, dissatisfaction with the effectiveness of the tours seems to be linked with the reticence of attorneys to participate in the tours or to attend subsequent training sessions on legal resource materials. The attorneys simply do not want to spend time on library tours or instruction.

Indeed, lack of time is an ever-present reality of attorneys' lives. In order to support the firm and to establish themselves in the firm's hierarchy, lawyers must maintain high billable hours.[13] Non-billable time is invariably spent networking and working on firm committees. On the whole, attorneys are not encouraged to spend time on functions that cannot be billed to a client. Training sessions are not billed and therefore are perceived as an ineffective use of the attorneys' time.[14]

E. Responsibility for Other Types of Instruction

From the survey results it is very clear that law firm librarians' instructional efforts extend far beyond physical tours of their libraries. Of the twenty-seven libraries responding to the survey, only one restricted its additional instruction to training on LEXIS and Westlaw. The majority of survey respondents either teach or supervise the teaching of both LEXIS and Westlaw to new attorneys. More than half of the survey participants conduct instruction on intranet, web-based, and CD-ROM resources at their firms, as well as provide training on their online catalogs. Involvement in e-mail training is negligible, typically being left to firms' management information systems (MIS) departments.

Other types of instruction offered by the surveyed law firm libraries include sessions on traditional legal resources such as encyclopedias and digests; classes geared toward specific practice groups within their firms; and instruction in the use of specialized databases like LiveEdgar.[15] Two librarians surveyed emphasized instruction on billing practices and effective legal research as an integral part of their jobs.

Training on firm intranets constitutes another type of instruction provided by firm librarians. In one firm responding to the survey, the librarian conducts training on the firm's online catalog, state legal resources, and basic Internet searching via intranet modules.

The efforts of law firm librarians to provide additional instruction seem to be part and parcel of an attitude that while the library tours are at the very least somewhat effective in educating the attorneys about using the libraries, they simply are not enough. One survey respondent explained the dilemma in the following way:

> [H]ow do you convince folks of the need to spend more than a half-hour on orientation or research training? It's like pulling teeth to get them to come to training sessions once they have been given work assignments. Even the promise of food won't bring them in like it used to.

Several of the survey participants have responded to this dilemma by offering instruction on electronic resources other than Westlaw and LEXIS upon request and tailoring each session to meet the individual attorney's needs. One librarian observed that attorneys seem to learn better in their own environment, so she offers training on a one-on-one basis in attorneys' offices.

IV. GUIDELINES FOR LIBRARY TOURS

In order to determine what makes a library tour successful, one must first determine what constitutes a library in the information age and what goals should be set in providing library tours in the new millennium. The proliferation of electronic legal resources and the reduction in the physical space of law libraries have transformed the concept of what constitutes a library. As Carolyn Ahearn, a Washington, D.C., law firm librarian related during an American Association of Law Libraries Roundtable in 1996:

> My day-to-day work and the reality of shrinking physical space for my library has propelled me out of thinking of the library as a place and into focusing on the library as the services we offer, be it books, online/Internet access or assistance, or providing directions to Capitol Hill.[16]

Libraries are no longer merely the physical space they inhabit. They comprise innumerable resources in a wide variety of formats, and the goals of library tours, by necessity, should reflect this change. Imparting details regarding the holdings, both hardcopy and electronic, during orientation tours is clearly impossible and ultimately undesirable.

The principal goal of law library tours, in both an academic and a law firm setting, is to encourage the use of the library and the librarian in legal research. Tours of the physical space of the law library should be geared toward making new patrons comfortable in the facility and aware of how the expertise of the librarian can help them in their research. Details about the collection and the use of computer-assisted legal research tools should be the subject of handouts and subsequent tours and instruction.

With this goal in mind, the following guidelines will greatly enhance the effectiveness of library tours.

1. *Marketing.* All librarians should conduct orientation tours not only for the education of their patrons but also to market their libraries and establish themselves as sources of information. In giving the tours, librarians should establish their authority and professionalism, holding themselves out as the best resource a student or new associate could have in researching the law. By establishing a rapport with incoming students and attorneys, librarians enhance the value of not only their libraries but also the law schools or firms in which they work.

2. *Necessity.* Library tours should be a required part of the new law student or associate's orientation. The librarian should convince the administration of the necessity and value of library tours as a means to enhance the new associates' and law students' effectiveness in legal research.

3. *Flexibility.* In providing library tours, flexibility is the key. Providing informative access to the library should not be limited to orientation. Librarians should be willing to conduct tours of the collection on an as-needed basis, providing group tours, individual tours, or subject-oriented tours upon request. Librarians should use self-guided tours to supplement, not replace, personal tours. The availability of personal tours enhances the library's value to the law school or law firm while providing students and attorneys access to one of the most valuable assets of any library, its librarians.

4. *Creativity.* A physical walk-around of the facility is highly recommended in order to increase the comfort level of new students and associates. Librarians should feel free to be creative and use audio-, video-, and web-based tours but should realize that additional expenditures of time and money will be needed to keep those tours up-to-date. It is very important to fit the format of the tour to the particular audience. If physical tours cannot be required, tours should be offered in as many media formats as possible.

5. *Reinforcement.* Librarians should set realistic expectations of what their tours can accomplish. Time constraints often reduce the effectiveness of tours, but use of "reinforcements" such as handouts, guides, and the library's web site (or intranet) offer the patrons concrete, on-the-spot guidance after the tours. Using "reinforcements" goes a long way in establishing the librarian as a knowledge expert and in encouraging students and attorneys to seek out the librarian when they need help.

6. *Training*. Librarians should offer training in legal resources in all formats available, hard-copy and electronic. Teaching students and attorneys in the use of legal resources or even e-mail demonstrates the expertise of the librarian and emphasizes the librarian's availability as a source of information and instruction. This ultimately enhances the legal research capabilities of the student or attorney.

V. CONCLUSION

Library tours should encourage new patrons to use the library and take advantage of the services library personnel can provide. As users become more familiar with the physical facility and the expertise available from the staff, they should make more effective use of those resources. Some of the key considerations in providing tours include the need to market library services, provide essential information to new patrons, adapt to the special information requirements of users, tailor the type of tour to the expected audience, reinforce the tour with handouts and other follow-up materials and information, and offer training in the various formats in which legal resources are provided.

VI. SURVEY RESULTS

A. Academic Law Libraries

1. Does your library provide orientation tours to new students?
   Yes–90% (27)   No–10% (3)
2. Are new students required to participate in the tours?
   Yes–78% (21)   No–22% (6)
3. How are most tours conducted?
   Group–26; Individual–6; Self-guided–3; Other–1
4. What format(s) do you use for your tours?
   Physical walk-around–27; Videotape–0; Audiotape–1;
   Computer-based–2; Web-based–2
5. How effective do you think your library tours are in providing orientation to the library?
   Very Effective–0; Effective–48% (13);
   Somewhat Effective–52% (14); Ineffective–0

6. What other types of instruction do you provide to your new students?
   Online Catalog–19; LEXIS–15; Westlaw–16; E-Mail–15;
   Web/Internet Research–15; CD-ROM–7; Other–1

B. Law Firm Libraries

1. Does your library provide orientation tours to new associates/clerks?
   Yes–96% (26)   No–4% (1)
2. Are new associates/clerks required to participate in the tours?
   Yes–85% (23)   No–15% (4)
3. How are most tours conducted?
   Group–17; Individual–16; Self-guided–0; Other–3
4. What format(s) do you use for your tours?
   Physical walk-around–26; Videotape–0; Audiotape–0;
   Computer-based–0; Web-based–2; Not Applicable–1
5. How effective do you think your library tours are in providing orientation to the library?
   Very Effective–19% (5); Effective–54% (14);
   Somewhat Effective–27% (7); Ineffective–0
6. What other types of instruction do you provide to your new associates?
   Online Catalog–15; LEXIS–21; Westlaw–21; E-Mail–8;
   Web/Internet Research–14; CD-ROM–15; Other–9

NOTES

1. *The Future of the Law Firm Library: The AALL Electronic Roundtable*, 89 L. LIBR. J. 99, 128 (1997).

2. Deborah Keene, *Survey on Library Tours* (last modified Jan. 17, 2000) <http://lawlibrary.ucdavis.edu/LAWLIB/Jan00/0303.html>.

3. Law Library, Emory Univ., *Just Ask* (visited May 26, 2000) <http://www.law.emory.edu/LAW/justask/justask.html> (containing a viewable example on the web in RealVideo®). *Just Ask* received the 1989 AALL Publications Award, Non-Print.

4. *See, e.g.*, Law Library, University of Ariz., *Law Library Map* (visited May 26, 2000) <http://www.law.arizona.edu/library/librarymap.html>; Pappas Law Library, Boston Univ., *Collections, Maps & Guides* (visited May 26, 2000) <http://www.bu.edu/lawlibrary/info>; Beeson Law Library, Samford Univ., *Maps of Library* (visited May 26, 2000) <http://lawlib.samford.edu/maps.shtml>.

5. *See, e.g.*, D'Angelo Law Library, University of Chicago, Research Guides (visited May 26, 2000) <http://www.lib.uchicago.edu/e/law/resguide.html>; Law Library, Duke Univ., Research Guides (visited May 26, 2000) <http://www.law.duke.edu/lib/libser/publicat/researchGuides>; Law Library, University of Minn., Research Guides and Pathfinders (visited May 26, 2000) <http://www.law.umn.edu/library/tools/pathfinders/pathfinders.html>.

6. *See, e.g*, Taggart Law Library, Ohio N. Univ., *Acquisitions Lists* (visited May 26, 2000) <http://www.law.onu.edu/library/acquisitions/index.htm>; Law Library, Suffolk Univ., *Publications* (visited May 26, 2000) <http://www.law.suffolk.edu/library/pubs/index.html>; Law Library, Univ. of S. Cal., *Law Library Newsletter* (visited May 26, 2000) <http://hal-law.usc.edu/newsletters/library>.

7. Law Library, Rutgers Univ., Camden, *Quick Guides to Research Questions* (visited May 26, 2000) <http://lawlibrary.rutgers.edu>.

8. Marshall-Wythe Law Library, College of William & Mary, *My Law Library* (visited May 26, 2000) <http://www.wm.edu/law/law_library>.

9. *See, e.g*, Law Library, University of Akron, *Law Library Picture Tour* (visited May 26, 2000) <http://www.uakron.edu/law/picturetour/pictour.html>; Edward Bennett Williams Law Library, Georgetown Univ., *Virtual Tour* (visited May 26, 2000) <http://www.ll.georgetown.edu/lib/ebwtour.html>; Law Library, Southwestern Univ. Sch. of Law, *Pictorial Tour* (visited May 26, 2000) <http://www.swlaw.edu/d/05.shtml>; Warren E. Burger Library, William Mitchell College of Law, *Tour* (visited May 26, 2000) <http://www.wmitchell.edu/library/tour/welcome.html>.

10. *See, e.g*, Brooklyn Law Sch., *Virtual Tour* (visited May 26, 2000) <http://www.brooklaw.edu/tour/>; Dickinson Sch. of Law, *Virtual Tour* (visited May 26, 2000) <http://www.dsl.edu/vtour/vtour.html>; Florida State Univ. College of Law, *Virtual Tour* (visited May 26, 2000) <http://www.law.fsu.edu/vtour>; University of Wis. Law Sch., *Law School On-Line Tour* (visited May 26, 2000) <http://www.law.wisc.edu/tour>.

11. *See* New York Univ. Sch. of Law, *Virtual Tour Intro Movie* (visited May 26, 2000) <http://www.law.nyu.edu/virtualtour/>; Ohio State Univ. College of Law, *Video Tour* (visited May 26, 2000) <http://www.acs.ohio-state.edu/units/law>; Washington Univ. Sch. of Law, *A 'Day in the Life' at Washington University School of Law* (visited May 26, 2000) <http://ls.wustl.edu/qtlifewuls>; College of William & Mary Sch. of Law, *Admissions Video: The Right Choice* (visited May 26, 2000) <http://www.wm.edu/law/admissions/video>.

12. E-mail from Gregory Ivy, Associate Director, Southern Methodist University Law Library (Jan. 18, 2000) (responding to the library tours survey and giving a brief summary of use of PowerPoint-based presentation at Southern Methodist University Law Library) (on file with author).

13. *See* Sheila M. Nielsen, *Teaching Old Dogs New Tricks in the Information Age*, *in* MANAGING THE LAW LIBRARY 1999: FORGING EFFECTIVE RELATIONSHIPS IN TODAY'S

LAW OFFICE 94-95 (1999); *see also A Firm-by-Firm Sampling of Billing Rates Nationwide*, NAT'L L.J., Dec. 27, 1999, at B12.

14. Nielsen, *supra* note 13, at 94-95.

15. *LiveEdgar* is a web-based database developed by Global Securities Information, Inc. *See* Global Sec. Info., Inc., *LiveEdgar* (visited May 26, 2000) <http://www.gsionline.com/news.html>.

16. *See supra* note 1, at 112.

Making Electronic Resources
Available to Patrons

Robert M. Linz

Robert M. Linz is Information Technology Coordinator at Ave Maria School of Law, 3475 Plymouth Road, Ann Arbor, MI 48105-2550 (E-mail: rmlinz@avemarialaw.edu).

The author wishes to thank Suzanne L. Cassidy, Acting Director at Mercer University Law Library, for her assistance in writing this article.

[Haworth co-indexing entry note]: "Making Electronic Resources Available to Patrons." Linz, Robert M. Co-published simultaneously in *Legal Reference Services Quarterly* (The Haworth Information Press, an imprint of The Haworth Press, Inc.) Vol. 19, No. 1/2, 2001, pp. 115-132; and: *Emerging Solutions in Reference Services: Implications for Libraries in the New Millennium* (ed: John D. Edwards) The Haworth Information Press, an imprint of The Haworth Press, Inc., 2001, pp. 115-132. Single or multiple copies of this article are available for a fee from The Haworth Document Delivery Service [1-800-342-9678, 9:00 a.m. - 5:00 p.m. (EST). E-mail address: getinfo@haworthpressinc.com].

SUMMARY. As law schools build interactive web sites for teaching and administrative functions, law libraries must continue to develop useful and resource-rich web sites of electronic materials for their patrons. This article examines issues and practical considerations for implementing Internet and CD-ROM resources in a library and provides a basic review of the media available. Suggestions for building an Internet or Intranet site are included as is an explanation of how to use database-driven tools to create an integrated environment. *[Article copies available for a fee from The Haworth Document Delivery Service: 1-800-342-9678. E-mail address: <getinfo@haworthpressinc. com> Website: <http://www.HaworthPress.com> © 2001 by The Haworth Press, Inc. All rights reserved.]*

I. INTRODUCTION

Law schools are engaged in a technology revolution. Law faculty have seized upon Internet technology to create virtual learning environments.[1] These Internet environments are populated with discussion groups, chat rooms, listservs, PowerPoint presentations, computer-assisted learning exercises, and a host of web-based transformations including class assignment boards, course pages, reading lists, and exams.[2] In addition to appealing to a generation of computer-assisted learners, law schools also are responding to the reality that tomorrow's attorneys need to be technologically savvy in their law practices.[3]

As students view their law school's web site as their gateway to classroom and administrative materials, they expect to access all forms of legal research tools, not just Westlaw and LEXIS, through the law library's web site and computer workstations. The library literature includes many articles on the forthcoming virtual library[4] which review the virtual library's theory, technology,[5] limitations,[6] and impact upon the role of librarians.[7] This article examines issues and practical considerations for a library to provide Internet and CD-ROM resources to its patrons.

II. INTERNET RESOURCE CONSIDERATIONS

A. Introduction

Information service vendors have all staked their claim on Internet turf. The chief development officer for LOIS[8] reported that 80% of

LOIS subscriptions in 1998 were on the Internet while the remaining 20% were on CD-ROM.[9] Thompson Corporation anticipated that its Internet revenues would double in 1999.[10] The Computer Industry Almanac projects there will be more than 133 million Internet users in the United States and more than 318 million users world-wide by the end of the year 2000.[11] One survey reported that online retailers expected a 300% growth in revenue for 1999.[12] It is little wonder that electronic resources on the web hold such an appeal to libraries and patrons alike. Patrons are lured by the idea of limitless information resources continuously available through their computers. Libraries gain access to a vast array of information sources using relatively simple and inexpensive technology.

B. Basics

The key Internet technology for the user is the web browser. Invented in 1990, the browser enables web users to read documents formatted in hypertext markup language (HTML), the language of the web.[13] Today, the two primary web browsers are Microsoft's Internet Explorer and Netscape's Navigator, which is a subsidiary of America Online.[14] Both browsers are very similar in form and function and provide comparable viewing experiences. However, the two browsers do interpret certain elements of web pages differently. The library web site developer who wishes to extend the library's services to the broadest range of users must make an effort to ensure that the web site is properly viewable in both browsers.

Obtaining and installing a browser is easy since both can be freely downloaded from the web.[15] If an Internet connection is too slow for efficient downloading, Netscape can be purchased on CD-ROM from Netscape's web site. Internet Explorer comes bundled with various applications and operating system CD-ROMs and can also be purchased on CD-ROM from Microsoft's web site.[16] Once obtained, the software can be loaded onto the library's server for further distribution. Technology personnel can run the software's installation program to provide easy access from individual computers.

To finish setting up a web-based resource for patrons, the library needs to provide two additional items. The first is a link to the resource's web site, which will be discussed in detail below. The second is to obtain from the vendor the means by which patrons can access the service. The service can either be restricted to the library's users through the library's IP address range[17] or through a password or both. If the vendor can restrict access using IP addresses, the library need only provide the vendor with its IP address range. This range can be obtained from the library's technical support staff or Internet Service Provider (ISP). If library patrons need a password to access the resource, a procedure to provide that password will be needed. For example, the password could be kept at the Reference or Circulation Desk or e-mailed to a list of patrons.

One trend in Internet technology is to provide web content to wireless devices. These devices include cell phones and hand-held computers like the Palm VII.[18] Companies are busily creating new web sites to facilitate the exchange of information with these devices.[19]

III. CD-ROM RESOURCE CONSIDERATIONS

A. Introduction

In 1998 over 10,000 commercial titles were available on CD-ROM.[20] As the Internet proves to be a superior means of database access, the need for libraries to add CD-ROM servers should decline.[21] Many libraries, however, still possess large collections of CD-ROMs and wish to provide its patrons with access to these materials.[22] Several options are available to make these resources available.

B. Basics

The library first needs to install the CD-ROM software and data onto a publicly available workstation that need not be connected to the network. While this solution offers advantages of security and license compliance, it restricts the use of the CD-ROM software title to one specific location in the library. This option may be acceptable if the staff wants the CD-ROM near the reference librarian or other similar materials. However, it may not be flexible enough for in-house patrons, such as faculty and students. Assuming the library owns sufficient licenses, one solution is to install the software onto multiple workstations by copying the data onto the workstation's hard drive. A more sensible solution would be to network the title and place the various workstations on the network. This permits multiple, simultaneous access but requires a CD-ROM server.[23]

Networking CD-ROMs is a difficult and time-consuming task. The data is distributed to client workstations by connecting through the library's network to a CD-ROM server. The CD-ROM title can either be placed in a CD-ROM drive on the server, tower, or jukebox or copied to the server hard drive. If a tower or jukebox is used, theses devices are connected physically to a server which runs special software that identifies the titles in the CD-ROM drives and makes those titles available to workstations on the network. Copying, or caching as it also is called, the titles on the server's hard drive produces the same result but provides faster access to the data at a lower cost[24] than other media but requires adequate space on the drive.

CD-ROM towers save hard drive space but are more expensive. Towers can be linked together to form even larger capacity CD-ROM solutions up to the system limit. Another option is a jukebox, which can be used to network from 100 to 600 CD-ROMs. A jukebox is connected to the server just as a tower would be but can only provide access to a few CD-ROMs at a time as disks are swapped to and from the drives as needed.[25]

Although the jukebox data is accessible to the server, software is needed on the server to provide the client workstations access to the data itself. Creating a networked CD-ROM server solution can be a daunting task. A turnkey CD-ROM server solution can be purchased if adequate funds are available. These turnkey products house the titles and server software and plug into the library's network for immediate use. In light of costs and complexity of this option, loading CD-ROMs on a server's hard drive may be a more attractive solution.

C. CD-ROM Client Considerations

Once the CD-ROM server set-up is complete, individual titles will need to be installed on the workstations. The library will need to consult the vendor's CD-ROM installation instructions to learn how that particular title should be installed. Some titles, such as LOIS, only require that the workstation contain a link or shortcut to the title's program file. This shortcut can be placed as an icon on the client's desktop. By double-clicking on the icon, the user launches the program. Other titles require that a small piece of the installation actually occur on the client workstation itself. In these situations some program files are installed to the client and a link is created to the title program and data on the CD-ROM server.

In order to use networked CD-ROMs the user must be able to log on to the network and access the software and data on the server. The network administrator must provide the user with sufficient permissions to use the title while at the same time preventing a malicious user from accessing other resources. Assigning appropriate rights to user accounts authorized to access the resources can provide this level of permissions. Members of the general public, however, usually will not have accounts on the library's network and libraries may not want to issue public patrons a temporary account. One solution is to create a public account so that one workstation is continuously logged in to the network using that account. The workstation can be configured to automatically log in using that account or a library staff member can log the workstation onto the network each day.

As the need for larger capacity disks increases, a clear trend is developing to replace CD-ROMs with DVDs. DVD stands for digital versatile disc or digital videodisc. DVDs have a storage capacity that ranges from 4.7 gigabytes to 17 gigabytes compared to 650 megabytes for CD-ROMs.[26] DVD drives also read CD-ROM disks and are becoming increasingly common in new computers. As DVDs replace CD-ROMs in the next few years, CD-ROMs may become as common as 5 1/4 inch floppies.[27]

IV. CONSIDERATIONS OF INTERNET VS. CD-ROM

A few short years ago libraries might have provided almost all of their electronic resources via CD-ROM or with dial-up access in the case of databases such as Westlaw or LEXIS. Today, access to these resources is increasingly provided through the Internet. In determining whether a library should purchase resources via the web or CD-ROM the library must weigh the ease of access to the title against maintenance considerations. Web-based resources provide simple set-up and configurations. As noted above, library patrons need only a computer with a web browser and Internet connection. Once in place, almost all of the updating is done by the vendor at its web site.

Relying only on the web has two drawbacks. The first is that the resource is not available if the library loses its connection to the vendor's web server if the library's Internet connection fails. A library may lose its Internet connection for a number of reasons, many of which are not controlled by the library or even its Internet service provider. Slow access speed is a related problem as the increased congestion of users and web sites, particularly companies leveraging the Internet for commercial use, makes the Internet painfully slow at times. Users facing delays may abandon a non-responsive resource and assume it is not working.

A library also may lose access to the resource if the vendor's web server is down or if the vendor has lost its connection to the Internet. A well-prepared vendor can alleviate some of this risk by using redundant servers and connections to the Internet. For example, OCLC utilizes both redundant server architecture[28] as well as multiple connections to the Internet[29] to maintain system availability.

A second drawback to vendor-provided web-based resources is that the library loses control over the resource itself. The vendor may change the resource's information content, user interface or technology. As with all new product releases, librarians need to be aware of new coverage and learn the new product interface. However, the vendor's new release may take advantage of new web-based technology that requires newer web browsers or computers with increased hardware resources. The new version of Westlaw.com, for example, requires a computer with at least 64 MB RAM and updated browsers.[30]

As Westlaw has done, a vendor who chooses to upgrade its online product in this way should either continue to provide access to the older, less technology-intensive web site or provide ample warning so that the library can upgrade its hardware should it decide to continue to provide access to the product. Librarians should keep abreast of these product developments through newsletters, publications, listservs, conferences, product literature, and vendor contact.[31]

CD-ROM server solutions have many drawbacks as noted previously. First, they are difficult and time-consuming to set up. The library staff may not have the expertise to complete the task. Second, they require a great deal of maintenance. As new CD-ROM titles are released, these titles need to be installed on the CD-ROM workstation or server. Certain titles may require the client software to be updated by the library's technical support staff. A large CD-ROM server installation can take hours of maintenance each week and requires the full attention of an employee.

Even with these considerations a library may decide that the title is too important to be without access even for a short period of time. In that case the library may decide to tolerate the maintenance issues of

CD-ROM resources and provide the resource in both Internet and CD-ROM format.

V. DELIVERING INFORMATION SERVICES TO CLIENTS

A. Introduction

Once web or CD-ROM resources are selected and installed, they must be made available to the library's patrons. The role of the reference librarian is to provide access to and instruction in various information resources. Those duties may include selecting sources, producing written guides and other instruction materials, and teaching patrons how to use the resources.[32] While these roles will continue to be important in the delivery of electronic resources, librarians' duties may expand to include being a database developer, copyright and license coordinator,[33] as well as interface designer.[34] In this last role, librarians can use their knowledge of electronic resources and their experience in assisting patrons in performing searches to improve information delivery. The primary delivery systems now in use are the desktop computer and the Internet or Intranet web site.

B. Workstation Desktop

The Microsoft Windows 95/98/NT desktop offers a platform through which electronic resources can be organized, explained, and launched. First, the desktop itself or the start menu can be used to organize program icons on the patron workstation. The icons should be logically grouped before being placed on the desktop or start menu. Folders can be created and descriptively named to house groupings of icons, such as "Legal Research Databases." Second, detailed explanations can be created of the resources. As with the program icons, these descriptions can be placed in the desktop or start menu folder. Finally, the active desktop feature of Windows 95/98 can be used to create a page describing the resources of each icon. The page is created as an HTML document, saved to the computer's hard drive, and is made a part of the desktop background. The page is always visible.

C. Web Sites

Although configuring the workstation desktop is helpful for accessing resources such as CD-ROM research applications, creating a library web site may be the most common means to deliver electronic resources. With a little HTML programming,[35] librarians can develop informative and attractive web pages for electronic resources. These web pages can either be part of the library's public Internet page or customized and expanded for use on the parent organization's Intranet page.

The first step is to determine the site's content. Then, a flexible structure must be developed to accommodate that content and other information that may be added in the future. Finally, the site should take advantage of the experience of reference librarians to build an environment of links and helpful guides.[36] These web pages should contain descriptions of the resources as well as links to the resources. Librarians can develop new research guides or convert existing ones to HTML so patrons can access them at the click of a mouse.

1. Design Tips

By reviewing a number of web sites a developer should have a good idea of which features to emulate and which to avoid. One site that helps by displaying examples of poor web site design is WebPages-ThatSuck.com. Articles and books on web site design can be informative as well.[37]

Links. In creating a site the developer should ensure that each page has a consistent look and feel. This consistency can be achieved through colors, repetitive images, and navigation links. Navigation links and menus should always be in the same place. Navigation links that enable the patron to move between the major sections of the web site should use the same location and wording on every page of the site. Although content links that help a user navigate and locate information in a particular section of the site can certainly change from section to section, they should remain constant for all of the pages within that section. Finally, each page should contain the library's name and address.

Frames. Because much of the page remains constant throughout the site, some developers like to place the navigation links in one or more frames. Frames permit multiple pages to be viewed at the same time in separate windows or frames. The content of some frames can remain constant while the content in other frames changes. With that in mind, a developer may place a site's navigation links in a frame at the top or side of the page. Every page then would have the same links and the page could be completed with minimal effort. This approach is particularly attractive when a navigation link needs to be updated since only one link would have be to changed instead of having to change the link on each page of the site.

HTML Tables. Despite these apparent advantages, frames have drawbacks. Frames are often awkward to implement because the designer has no control over the viewer's screen size. The user of a small screen may have to scroll within the frame to view the entire page in that frame. Web pages can be coded so they can be displayed within a frame but that makes it more difficult for users to view the contents of the site. More importantly, HTML tables can provide the same design advantages as frames. Many sophisticated sites that appear to use frames may be using tables.

One apparent disadvantage of a table is that it is not as easy to update changed navigation links, although the designer has two options. One is to use a sophisticated HTML editor to search the entire site for specific link strings and replace them. Though this approach has some risks, its careful application can result in updated links in a matter of minutes. The second option is to create page templates that contain the navigation links for the site or a section of the site. Each page, therefore, will not only contain the main text presented on that page but also contain the navigation template pages.

HTML tables provide incredible flexibility and control. Although a table can be designed to occupy a certain percentage of the user's screen, a better solution is to set the width of the table to a width of no greater than 600 pixels. This width will display a table on a VGA monitor without requiring the user to scroll horizontally to view the contents of the table. SVGA and higher resolution monitors also will have no problem displaying the table. The other advantage of using tables is the precise control provided over the width of the columns within the table. HTML tables are flexible enough that rows or columns can be joined to properly format data or a new table can be created within an existing table's data cell. If the web designer eliminates the table border by setting the border's width attribute to zero, the table structure will be completely transparent to the end user.

Colors. Use of color in a web site design should be consistent. First, colors provide visual clues about the structural design of the web site. For example, the highest-level pages may contain a background that is completely white. The next lower level of pages may change that color to yellow. While the user is navigating more deeply into the site, an observant user will be aided as to their location within the site. Second, colors can also be used to denote navigation bars from headings and the textual content of the page. When these clues are consistently used throughout the site, the user's information-seeking experience will be aided by the logic of the site. Third, standard or nearly identical colors should be used to denote active and visited links that contrast with the normal page color.

Text. Judicious use of text on the web site can be very helpful. Patrons use library pages to locate information, not to be dazzled with graphics. A web designer certainly should use graphics that enhance the site's usefulness but these should be used consistently throughout the site and be a small file size so downloading is easy and quick. White space and horizontal lines also can enhance site navigation. Another advantage of pages containing mostly text is that visually impaired individuals can read it more easily using assistive technology.[38]

Menus. Appropriate use of drop-down and slide-out menus can greatly aid the web user. These menus provide the user with a great many choices while using very little screen real estate, as when the user must choose menu fields such as state of residence or age group. However, some users believe that drop-down menus prevent them from finding information. Users who quickly scan a page looking for information may not bother to drop the menu and view its choices. Designers may want to restrict their use of such menus to logically-related lists of items or clearly indicate what types of items are to be found in the list without requiring the user to display the list.

Visually Impaired Users. As noted before, visually impaired users may view the site with the aid of assistive technology, which reads the text of a page. If images contain alternative text and links that are descriptive,[39] these users will be able to make more effective use of web materials.

2. Database-Driven Web Sites

Database-driven pages should be used wherever possible. In a database-driven web site, the web pages or portions of them are generated by merging the content in a database with code on the web page in two steps. First, data needing to be accessed through the web site must be added to one or more tables in a database. Any open database connectivity (ODBC) database such as Microsoft Access should work. Second, the database needs to be accessible to the library's web server. Web pages should be written using a code that can access the data in the database as the user requests it with the web page acting as a template. The creation process is greatly aided using web site development packages such as Allaire's Cold Fusion.[40] This program provides both the database application server that resides on the web server and an optional HTML editor with the Cold Fusion code that calls the data from the database. Another option is Microsoft's Active Server Pages.[41]

Advantages. Although the creation of a database-driven web site is a little more labor-intensive initially, it saves work in the long run as information can be more easily reused and managed. First, information from the database can be used to generate a number of different pages without having to code the data in each of those pages. For example, a library may create a database of legal information sites. Using the data in the table, a page can be produced that lists the sites by practice area while another page sorts the sites by jurisdiction. Second, the web site's content can be more easily managed. Web-based forms can be created so that librarians and others can modify the content in the tables. Since the web site developer creates the pages dynamically, librarians do not need to know HTML code nor have a program to create web pages in order to modify page contents. Entire web sites can be developed using tools such as Cold Fusion.

Topical Resources. A library can take advantage of a database-driven web site in making various electronic resources available to patrons. For example, a library could create a database of research materials. One table could include a list of links for various practice areas or subject matters. Another table could include the library's research guides or pathfinders. A third table could house the library's recent acquisitions while a fourth table could contain the databases found in Westlaw or LEXIS. These tables could be related to one another through practice area or subject matter.

Using this data, the library then can develop subject matter pages that organize these various resources on one page. One template page can be created that would include the appropriate data on the subject the user selected. This basic page could be expanded to retrieve from the staff table the name and e-mail address of the librarian who specializes in this subject area. The page could even include a link to the law school catalog and classes on the topic. If the law school also has developed database-driven course pages, these library materials could be linked to the appropriate subject matter course. For example, library reserve items including exams for these courses could be digitized to create "electronic reserves" made available through the course's web page.[42] As the library's online catalog is made accessible to the web, this subject page could display the library's holdings for the subject. A final table accessible only to librarians could contain patrons' e-mail addresses and topic preferences. As new resources are added to the web site, a broadcast e-mail could be sent to all patrons who have expressed an interest in the subject of that resource. Using this technology both LEXIS and Westlaw provide Intranet toolkits in which librarians can develop research sites for their clients.[43]

3. Management Issues

The library administration must decide how to adjust the organizational structure to institutionalize site maintenance. A common solution is to create the position of web site administrator to ensure that the web site is updated and functional. If the web site is very large and involves many departments, responsibility may be allocated to several persons or departments. Even in that scenario an administrator normally acts as a site coordinator. Distributed updating can be done more easily if the site takes advantages of tools such as Cold Fusion. HTML forms would permit the content of the site to be added, modified, and deleted. Staff will need an HTML editor and access to the site's web pages if HTML forms are not used.

As HTML editors have become easier to use, a detailed understanding of HTML is no longer needed. The web site pages can be made available through a file transfer protocol (FTP) server or directly mapped to the user's workstation. Either way, the network administrator will need to ensure that security is not compromised. Security is particularly important if the site takes advantage of broadcast e-mail capabilities in which the staff can send an e-mail message to a list of individuals at one time.

VI. OTHER CLIENT CONSIDERATIONS

A. Security

Security measures protect clients, servers, and their data and configurations from alteration or destruction. The basic weapon in the security arsenal is anti-virus software, which should be on every computer on the network and updated regularly. Updated virus definition files can be downloaded to a shared directory on the server or, if the computers are connected to the Internet, through the program's update feature. Protection is needed for the programs and files on each workstation as well. Users should be prevented from installing unauthorized applications and thereby altering the configuration of the computer which could lead to system failure and downtime.

A number of different tools can be used to secure the computer. Windows Policy Editor is on the Windows CD-ROM or the Microsoft web site.[44] This program permits the library to disable or configure certain aspects of the Windows 95/98 environment. For example, the library can disable all access to the control panel and prevent unauthorized DOS programs from running. A similar commercial tool called Fortres[45] secures the Windows 95/98 environment and offers more options than Policy Editor. TweakUI is available from the Microsoft web site[46] and allows the control of certain features of the Windows 95 user interface. For example, drives can be hidden in Windows Explorer or the documents folder can be automatically purged, among other things. TweakUI also can be used to automatically log the computer onto the network or to log on public workstations with a certain account while hiding the logon screen.

If the client computer is connected to the network, the network administrator should install a firewall between the library's network and the Internet. A firewall monitors and controls the data that flows into and out of the network.[47] The network administrator also should ensure that files and directories are appropriately restricted from users. Passwords should be kept confidential and changed periodically using complex combinations of letters and numbers. One easy method to do this is to create a sentence and then combine the first letter of each word and all the numbers to form the password. For example, the password TDOIWSI1776 is derived from the sentence "The Declaration of Independence was signed in 1776." Lastly, the library should physically lock-down all public computers, using devices that chain or bolt the computer to the table.

B. Printing

Although libraries may be creating virtual environments to house their electronic resources, patrons will still need hard copies of their research. For stand-alone workstations, a printer can be attached to the parallel port. A small, light-duty laser printer can be purchased for a few hundred dollars.[48] Depending on the amount and type of documents, an ink jet printer may be sufficient. If the workstation is connected to the network, printing solutions may become more complicated. As with the stand-alone workstation, a printer can be directly attached to the computer. However, the library can direct that workstation's printing to a networked laser printer that can service multiple computers.

Charges for printing can be handled at the source, such as with a coin or credit card swipe on the printer, or through a software program such as AND Technology's PCounter.[49] PCounter monitors print jobs sent to network printers through a Microsoft Windows NT or Novell Netware server and tracks the cost and pages of each print job as well as keeping a running balance. With PCounter the administrator can either charge users for their print jobs or at least set a ceiling on the amount of free printing given to a user.[50] Another option is to direct jobs to a printer behind the Circulation Desk with patrons paying when they retrieve their print jobs.

VII. CONCLUSION

As libraries continue to expand their electronic collections they will need to continue to develop more sophisticated information delivery systems. The Internet and web technology currently provide the best way to deliver these electronic resources. Patrons now look to the web for a variety of information. Law schools have redesigned their web sites to provide student access to classroom and administrative materials. Libraries are providing feature-rich and useful web sites of electronic resources for their patrons.

Of course, these technologies require learning new skills. For both the development and management of the web site, the library may need technical expertise from the IT staff or may need to outsource development altogether. With either solution, the library may perceive a loss of control over the finished product. Librarians possess the best understanding of available resources and how patrons use them to seek answers to their information needs. Librarians may not want to give up that control to non-librarians who may not share their public services orientation.

Another option is for librarians to develop the needed technological expertise, which becomes more important as the virtual library changes the traditional roles of the librarian. Librarians are acquiring database development skills and learning programming languages such as HTML, JavaScript and perhaps even Cold Fusion or Active Server Pages. For years, technical services librarians have filled a similar role as database administrators of bibliographic records. As the library profession broadens to accommodate new modes of information delivery services, the role of librarians must adapt to new technologies and information industry realities. Librarians should not feel threatened by these changes but should embrace the opportunities they provide to better serve their patrons. As information professionals, librarians have a great deal to offer in this new information age.

NOTES

1. *See* Richard Warner et al., *Teaching Law with Computers,* 24 RUTGERS COMPUTERS & TECH. L.J. 107 (1998).

2. *See* Michael A. Geist, *Where Can You Go Today?: The Computerization of Legal Education from Workbooks to the Web,* 11 HARV. J.L. & TECH. 141 (1997).

3. *See* Bob Rayner, *Preparing for a Wired World,* RICHMOND LAW., Winter 1999, at 5.

4. A search for "virtual library" but not "book review" in the descriptor field of the *Library and Information Science Abstracts* (LISA) database retrieved 268 abstracts as of June 1, 2000.

5. *See* David Barber, *Building a Digital Library: Concepts and Issues,* 32 LIBR. TECH. REP. 573 (1996), *available at* 1996 WL 11214016.

6. *See* Michael Schuyler, *The Virtual Popsicle (Online Libraries Like Popsicles, Are Vulnerable to Power Failures),* COMPUTERS IN LIBR., Feb. 1, 1998, at 28, *available at* 1998 WL 10864206.

7. *See* Cherrie Noble, *Reflecting on Our Future: What Will the Role of the Virtual Librarian Be?,* COMPUTERS IN LIBR., Feb. 1, 1998, at 50, *available at* 1998 WL 10864210.

8. LOIS provides electronic access to federal and state legal materials through CD-ROM or *Loislaw.com* (visited June 5, 2000) <http://www.loislaw.com>.

9. *CD-ROM Format Declining, But Not Dead; DVD to Take Its Place,* ELECTRONIC INFO. REP., Mar. 19, 1999, *available at* 1999 WL 8894806.

10. *Thompson Expects Internet Revenues to Double in 1999,* ELECTRONIC INFO. REP., May 14, 1999, *available at* 1999 WL 8894901.

11. Sharon Machlis, *U.S. to Have 133M Internet Users Next Year,* COMPUTERWORLD, July 7, 1999 <http://www.computerworld.com/home/news.nsf/all/9907073users>.

12. Steven Bonisteel, *Online Retail Revenue Up 300 Percent–Survey,* NEWSBYTES, Dec. 29, 1999, *available at* 1999 WL 29944387.

13. TIM BERNERS-LEE, WEAVING THE WEB: THE ORIGINAL DESIGN AND ULTIMATE DESTINY OF THE WORLD WIDE WEB BY ITS INVENTOR (1999).

14. *Netscape Communicator 4.7 Suite Released,* LIBR. SYS. NEWSL., Nov. 1999, at 89.

15. Netscape is available from Netscape's web site at <http://home.netscape.com/download/index.html>. Explorer can be downloaded from Microsoft's web site at <http://www.microsoft.com/windows/ie/default.htm>. As of June 1, 2000, Internet Explorer is at Version 5.01 and Netscape Navigator is at Version 4.73, but Netscape is readying release of Version 6.

16. <http://www.microsoft.com/windows/ie/offers/default.asp>.

17. An IP address or Internet Address is a unique 32-bit host address defined by the Internet Protocol in STD 5, RFC 791. It permits devices such as computers and printers to access and be accessible on the Internet. An institution's Internet Service Provider usually gives the institution a range of IP addresses. Users who log on to a library computer defined in the IP address range have access to the database. Some libraries prefer this method because library personnel do not have to be responsible for passwords. For example, Gale Group provides access to its InfoTrac and Legal-Trac products with this method.

18. Palm Pilot is a product of Palm Incorporated. Palm, *Handheld Computing Solutions* (visited June 6, 2000) <http://www.palm.com>.

19. *See* Dominique Deckmyn, *Wireless Web Access Will Be Vital,* COMPUTER-WORLD, Jan. 10, 2000, at 1, 81.

20. Richard W. Boss, *Electronic Information Technologies (for Libraries),* 31 LIBR. TECH. REP. 416 (1995), *available at* 1995 WL 14193896.

21. *See CD-ROM Format Declining, But Not Dead; DVD to Take Its Place, supra* note 9.

22. *See* Marshall Breeding, *Does the Web Spell Doom for CD and DVD?,* COM-PUTERS IN LIBR., Nov.-Dec. 1999, at 70, *available at* 1999 WL 11637277.

23. Karen Perone, *Networking CD-ROMs: A Tutorial Introduction,* COMPUTERS IN LIBR., Feb. 1, 1996, at 71, *available at* 1996 WL 8953361.

24. Small Computer System Interface (SCSI) hard drives, the type typically used in servers, can be purchased for about 2.5 cents per megabyte. For example, a 9.1 GB SCSI hard drive sells for $229.95 from MicroWarehouse, *PC Products* (visited June 6, 2000) <http://www.microwarehouse.com>.

25. For more information, see Kintronics, *The Expertists in CD-ROM and DVD-ROM Technology* (visited June 6, 2000) <http://www.kintronics.com>.

26. Deborah Jessop, *DVD Basics for Libraries and Information Centers,* COMPUT-ERS IN LIBR., Feb. 1, 1998, at 62, *available at* 1998 WL 10864229.

27. *See CD-ROM Format Declining, But Not Dead; DVD to Take Its Place, supra* note 9.

28. Dan McIver et al., *OCLC Systems Run on State-of-the-Art Platforms,* OCLC NEWSL., Mar.-Apr. 2000, at 22.

29. *Redundancy and Diversity Help Eliminate Single Points of Communications Failure at OCLC,* OCLC NEWSL., Mar.-Apr. 2000, at 26.

30. Westlaw requires as a minimum Explorer 4.01 or Netscape 4.06. West Group, *New Westlaw.com Minimum Requirements* (visited June 23, 2000) <http://www.westlaw.com/MoreInfo/Newwestlaw/install.wl?nav=n>.

31. For example, the *Library Systems Newsletter* published by TechSourceALA, an imprint of the American Library Association is an excellent resource for keeping

current on new developments. ALA, *American Library Association Periodicals* (last modified May 31, 2000) <http://www.ala.org/library/alaperiodicals.html>.

32. *See* Bernie Sloan, *Service Perspectives for the Digital Library Remote Reference Services,* LIBR. TRENDS, June 22, 1998, *available at* 1998 WL 17144303.

33. *See* Noble, *supra* note 7.

34. *See* Sloan, *supra* note 32.

35. Beginners might consult C|Net's Builder.Com web site at <http://home.cnet. com/web building/0-3880.html> for HTML and web site development instruction.

36. For a listing of the most popular links provided by law school web pages, see Robert C. Vreeland, *Law Libraries in Hyperspace: A Citation Analysis of World Wide Web Sites,* 92 L. LIBR. J. 9, 23-25 (2000).

37. *See, e.g.,* Shirley Duglin Kennedy, *Trapped in a Web of Bad Design,* INFO. TODAY, Apr. 2000, at 32-33 < http://www.infotoday.com/it/apr00/it-cont.htm >; Janet L. Balas, *The "Don'ts" of Web Page Design,* COMPUTERS IN LIBR., Sept. 1999, at 46, *available at* 1999 WL 11637190.

38. Carol Casey, *Accessibility in the Virtual Library: Creating Equal Opportunity Web Sites,* INFO. TECH. & LIBR., Mar. 1999, at 22.

39. *Id.*

40. For more information on Cold Fusion, see Allaire, *Is This How You Imagine the Web?* (visited June 6, 2000) <http://www.allaire.com>.

41. For more information, see Microsoft, *Active Server Pages* (visited June 7, 2000) <http://msdn.microsoft.com/library/psdk/iisref/iiwawelc.htm>.

42. For more information about electronic course reserves, see Electronic Reserves Clearinghouse, *Links and Materials on the Web* (last modified June 19, 2000) <http://www.columbia.edu/~rosedale/>.

43. For more information, see LEXIS-NEXIS, *Intranet Solutions* (visited June 23, 2000) <http://infopro.lexis.com/reference/pdf/intranet.pdf> and West Group, *West Intranet Toolkit* (visited June 23, 2000) <http://www.westlaw.com/WestlawFeatures/toolkit/>.

44. <http://www.microsoft.com/>.

45. Fortres is available from Fortres Grand Corp., *Fortres Grand* (visited June 6, 2000) <http://www.fortres.com/>.

46. The search phrase "tweakui" can be used in the search engine on Microsoft's web site to locate additional information and the file for download. <http:// www.microsoft.com/>.

47. Richard W. Boss, *Security Technologies for Libraries: Policy Concerns and a Survey of Available Products,* 35 LIBR. TECH. REP. 271 (1999), *available at* 1999 WL 31834290.

48. For example, a Hewlett-Packard LaserJet 1100se laser printer can be purchased for about $400 from MicroWarehouse, *PC Products* (visited June 6, 2000) <http://www.microwarehouse.com>.

49. For more information about PCounter, see AND Technologies, *Cross-Platform Printer Management Tools for Windows and NetWare Networks* (visited June 6, 2000) <http://www.andtechnologies.com/>.

50. For additional information on library printing fees, see the article in this volume by Kumar Percy, *User Fees in Academic Law Libraries.* For a list of schools using PCounter, see the site maintained by Joyce Manna Janto, *Law School Printing Survey* (last modified June 5, 2000) <http://law.richmond.edu/general/printsurvey.htm>.

Enhancing Reference Services
Through Technology

Beth Smith

SUMMARY. Technology makes it possible for library users to ask reference questions using e-mail or forms on the web and for librarians to conduct reference interviews using chat or videoconferencing software.

Beth Smith is Assistant Director and Head of Public Services at the Ross-Blakley Law Library, Arizona State University, Tempe, AZ 85287-7806 (E-mail: beth. smith@asu.edu).

[Haworth co-indexing entry note]: "Enhancing Reference Services Through Technology." Smith, Beth. Co-published simultaneously in *Legal Reference Services Quarterly* (The Haworth Information Press, an imprint of The Haworth Press, Inc.) Vol. 19, No. 1/2, 2001, pp. 133-146; and: *Emerging Solutions in Reference Services: Implications for Libraries in the New Millennium* (ed: John D. Edwards) The Haworth Information Press, an imprint of The Haworth Press, Inc., 2001, pp. 133-146. Single or multiple copies of this article are available for a fee from The Haworth Document Delivery Service [1-800-342-9678, 9:00 a.m. - 5:00 p.m. (EST). E-mail address: getinfo@haworthpressinc.com].

This article explores each of these technologies and their current and potential use in reference services. A discussion of how technology has changed the way librarians find answers to reference questions is followed by a review of the tools needed for a well-equipped reference desk. *[Article copies available for a fee from The Haworth Document Delivery Service: 1-800-342-9678. E-mail address: <getinfo@haworthpressinc.com> Website: <http://www.HaworthPress.com> © 2001 by The Haworth Press, Inc. All rights reserved.]*

I. INTRODUCTION

Technology is creating new ways for librarians to provide reference services to remote researchers. Researchers outside the library are no longer limited to using the telephone but may send reference requests via e-mail or forms on the web, depending on the options offered by their library. Librarians can conduct reference interviews with these remote researchers using text-chat, voice-chat, or videoconferencing technology. Application sharing software can further enhance remote reference services. This article discusses each of these technologies.

Technology also is changing the way librarians find answers to reference questions. Librarians now have the assistance of online catalogs, CD-ROMs, the web, e-mail discussion lists and much more. A summary of these electronic resources is in Part V. Part VI discusses the tools reference librarians need to take advantage of these technologies.

II. IMPETUS FOR ELECTRONIC REFERENCE SERVICES

Not long ago researchers with reference questions had two options: ask their questions in person while visiting the library or telephone the librarian at the reference desk. Regardless of the option chosen, the question had to be asked during scheduled reference hours. This traditional reference model was satisfactory when everyone researched in the library, but today many people are using their computers and the Internet to research at home or their office. This type of research certainly will increase as the amount of information available remotely increases and as more people take advantage of distance education. Many libraries already are assisting remote researchers by providing home pages with access to databases, their online catalogs, links to recommended web sites and research guides. Some libraries are expanding this service by providing remote reference assistance, either by accepting reference requests by e-mail or by providing forms on the web for this purpose.

In November 1999, the author conducted an informal survey of 86 academic law libraries throughout the United States. This survey was conducted over e-mail via law-lib,[1] an e-mail discussion list congregated by law librarians. Of the 86 libraries responding, 42 allowed reference questions via e-mail, 6 used forms on the web and 38 had no electronic reference services. Of those that used e-mail or web forms, most received fewer than 5 questions a week, 7 received 10-30 questions a week, and 2 libraries received more than 30 questions a week. In addition, 14 restricted the service to faculty; 6 to faculty and students; 3 to faculty, students and attorneys; and 25 did not restrict the service at all.

III. HOW PATRONS ASK QUESTIONS

A. E-Mail and Web Forms

Many libraries have created special reference e-mail accounts (usually with an address that identifies the department as in *reference@library. edu*), "Ask a Librarian" forms on the web, or both. In the survey noted above, 56% of the responding libraries reported using one or both of these types of electronic reference services.

How do these systems work? With e-mail, typed messages are transmitted over the Internet to a library e-mail account, such as the hypothetical *reference@library.edu*. With web forms, users complete a form on the web and click a "submit" button, which directs the completed forms to a library e-mail account (which can be *reference@library.edu*). Having e-mail requests and the completed forms directed to an e-mail account created specifically for this purpose normally works better than having the requests sent to an individual librarian's account. This way requests are not missed because a librarian is out of the office or otherwise unable to check his or her e-mail account. "Ask a Librarian" web forms may be part of the library's home page and, thus, accessible to the world. They also may be placed on an intranet, which would limit access to certain computers, or placed on an extranet, which would require remote user authentication, such as a password. Access to reference e-mail services may be limited by restricting the groups that are advised of the service's availability, such as only law students and faculty.

Although e-mail accounts are easier to create than "Ask a Librarian" web forms, forms have advantages over simple, unstructured e-mail messages. Forms can prompt users to include information they might otherwise omit. For example, users can be prompted to select their patron type (such as faculty or student) and input their name, e-mail address, daytime phone number and preferred method of reply (such as by phone call or e-mail message). Forms can ask about deadlines, sources already consulted and relevant jurisdictions, as well as give a lengthy space for reference questions. Librarians can use the form to explain the scope of the service, including: which patron groups may participate, the librarians' expected turnaround time for answering electronic questions, the reference desk phone number, and the types of questions accepted (such as short factual questions, questions regarding research strategies and questions about the library's collection and services). The form could have information about the library's document delivery service and a disclaimer that librarians cannot give legal advice.

1. Benefits

One of the primary benefits to remote researchers of submitting requests over e-mail or web forms is that they are not limited to asking questions during scheduled reference hours. Of course, questions cannot be answered immediately if no staff is available.

The asynchronous nature of e-mail and web forms gives librarians time to compose written answers that are clear and complete. Thorough, written responses may be preferable to the "on the spot" oral responses received when questions are asked in person, over the telephone or using videoconferencing or voice-chat. Additionally, written responses are less likely to be misunderstood or forgotten. Because the reference interview is conducted in writing, librarians easily can electronically file e-mail and web form requests and their responses so that the responses can be retrieved later when similar questions are asked or the same person returns. Even though people asking questions using text-chat also receive written answers, chat is synchronous so librarians must reply immediately, which often will not provide the opportunity to craft a well-written response.

2. Problems

Reference interviews conducted via e-mail and web forms do not occur in real time, so answers to these questions will take longer than answers to questions asked in person, by telephone, in chat rooms, or over videoconferencing. Answers to the simplest questions sent over e-mail or the web may take 24 hours, and if the request is complicated or unclear, it could take even longer. Good, efficient e-mail reference interviews should consist of three messages (five if the question is unclear and an additional message and reply are needed), the initial question, a summary by the librarian, and a confirmation of the summary by the requestor. If more exchanges are needed, a telephone call may be warranted.[2]

Librarians can easily misinterpret reference requests sent over e-mail or the web because they will not have the benefit of clues such as the requestor's gestures, facial expressions and tone of voice. To reduce the risk of miscommunication, librarians should restate the reference request as they understand it and ask for feedback or a confirmation that the librarian's interpretation of the request is correct.[3] If the only communication will be in writing, librarians should be especially careful to draft clear responses to make sure that the response will be understood.[4]

Although e-mail and the web have become commonplace, they are not universal, so e-mail and web reference will not be an option for everyone. Some people who have web access and e-mail accounts may not be comfortable using them or may not have fast computers, making the use of web forms frustrating. Librarians may want to respond to reference questions by sending attachments to e-mail messages, but not all e-mail programs can open attachments, and the attachment may require software that the e-mail recipient does not have. Librarians may want to respond by sending e-mail messages imbedded with hotlinks to web pages, but not all e-mail software can handle these links.

B. Chat

Librarians could conduct reference interviews with remote researchers using chat, which is an online, real-time conversation between two or more people using a computer and the Internet.[5] With text-based chat, one party types words on a keyboard and these words instantaneously appear on the other's computer monitor. With voice-chat, users can communicate by speaking or by typing and either their voice or their typed words are transmitted to the recipient's computer. Voice-chat is similar to a telephone call (without the long-distance charges), but the voices are not as clear. Voice-chat experiences can be "as annoying as talking to someone on a cell phone with a bad connection."[6]

An example of how a library could use chat is to have a link labeled "Chat with a Librarian" on the library home page with text surrounding the link telling users the hours chat service is available. When someone clicks on the link, a message would pop up on the reference desk computer saying: "Someone would like to talk to a reference librarian. Are you available? Yes or No." If the librarian clicks on "Yes," a window for web-based chat would open. If the librarian clicks on "No" or does not answer in time, the remote user would be told that no one is available to chat and to try again later.

1. Benefits

The primary benefit of using chat for reference interviews is that chat occurs in real time. As soon as a user types a question, the question appears on the librarian's monitor. The librarian can respond immediately simply by typing. If the question is unclear, the librarian can ask for clarification and receive a quick response. Once the request is clear, the librarian can promptly answer the question or indicate that research is needed.

2. Problems

Chat can be available only when a reference librarian is on duty, so remote researchers would not be able to send reference requests 24 hours a day as they could with e-mail or web form reference services. Unless there is a mechanism alerting librarians that someone has initiated a chat session, such as a beep, librarians would have to monitor their computer screens constantly, which would be inconvenient. Beeps or messages popping up on a computer monitor could be distracting when a librarian is with a patron at the reference desk (although this would be no more distracting than a ringing telephone). Additionally, if text-based chat is used, reference librarians would not have the benefit of clues such as the requestor's tone of voice. However, because chat is a real time conversation, reference librarians would be able to immediately ask for clarification and feedback.

C. Videoconferencing

A few libraries have experimented with using videoconferencing for reference interviews, where video and audio are delivered in real time to and from the library over the Internet.[7] Desktop videoconferencing requires that both locations have a computer, Internet connection, digital camera, microphone, and videoconferencing software, such as CUseeMe[8] or Microsoft's NetMeeting. Headphones are a nice addition if videoconferences will be held at the reference desk. Some videoconferencing software, such as NetMeeting, includes a chat window that allows written communication between participants. NetMeeting is readily available as it comes bundled with Windows 98, Windows 2000 and many digital cameras and can be downloaded for free from Microsoft's web site at http://www.microsoft.com/windows/netmeeting/.[9]

1. Benefits

The only way to conduct remote reference interviews with both audio and video is to use videoconferencing. Conducting reference interviews without seeing or hearing the other party can be very difficult. Because many videoconferencing programs come with chat features, parts of the reference interview could be conducted in writing.

2. Problems

Videoconferencing will not be an option for the average person with a reference question. Although videoconferencing software can be downloaded at no cost, remote users also must have a digital camera and microphone, as well as someone who knows how to use them. This is not as much of a problem when videoconferencing is used to provide reference to certain specific locations where equipment and technical personnel are already established. Many law firm librarians conduct reference interviews of attorneys in branch offices of the firm and law school librarians conduct reference interviews of students and faculty participating in semester abroad programs.

Videoconferencing could be staff-intensive and therefore only be made available for limited hours. Staff may need to be present in the remote location to provide assistance, at least at first. A reference librarian would need to watch the monitor, waiting for questions from the remote location, although the remote reference interviews could be by appointment or remote users could telephone the library in advance.

D. Remote Application Sharing

Libraries should consider using remote application sharing or remote control software as part of a videoconferencing session. Some videoconferencing software, such as CUseeMe or Microsoft's Net-Meeting, include remote application sharing features.[10] Application sharing software would allow remote users to view on their computer monitors what the reference librarian is doing on his or her computer, such as searching the online catalog. Similarly, librarians could view on their computer monitors what remote users are doing on their computers. This could help librarians troubleshoot problems remote users are having with online databases.[11]

IV. ELECTRONIC REFERENCE CONSIDERATIONS

A. Cost-Benefit Analysis

Librarians contemplating the addition of any type of electronic reference service have a number of issues to consider before making a decision. A useful first step is to compare how much the service is likely to be used with the time and expense of creating and maintaining it. Is it cost-effective to add electronic reference services if the library is only going to receive 2 questions a week? What if the number is 5? 20? Of course, how much the service is used will depend on a variety of factors, such as how much the service is publicized, but the experiences of other libraries can offer guidance.

As noted earlier, more than half of the law school libraries surveyed provide some type of electronic reference services, and most receive fewer than five questions a week. In January 1999, 13 Colorado academic libraries that used e-mail or web forms for reference were surveyed. Ten of these libraries reported receiving fewer than 10 electronic reference questions a month and the other libraries reported averages of 20, 20 to 30, and 60 questions a month.[12] In 1996, librarians of the Boston University Alumni Medical Library surveyed 40 academic and health science libraries in the United States that used e-mail for reference, and the libraries reported low usage of their e-mail reference services.[13] The figures from the 1996 survey might be different today in light of the overall growth of web and e-mail usage.

During the 1995-96 academic year, the University of Michigan's Shapiro Library conducted reference interviews with students at the university's residence hall libraries by using desktop videoconferencing with CUseeMe software and inexpensive black-and-white video cameras. Fewer than 20 students used the service.[14]

Once the potential use of the service has been assessed, the time, expertise and cost needed to create and maintain the service must be considered. These factors will vary greatly, depending on whether e-mail, web forms, chat, or videoconferencing is used. In his article *Electronic Reference Services–Some Suggested Guidelines,* Bernie Sloan recommends that libraries not provide electronic reference services "on the cheap."[15] He suggests that libraries considering an extensive electronic reference service create a budget line for it that includes staff time, equipment, software, and supplies.

The Minnesota State Law Library used an interactive television system to provide remote reference services to the Moose Lake Correctional Facility as a way to save staff time.[16] Although the library was committed to providing reference services to the facility, an in-person visit by a librarian would take a full day. Both the library and the prison already had access to interactive television equipment, so the only cost to the library has been the connect charges. Although the library considered reference interviews over telephone instead of interactive television, they chose interactive television because it allows librarians to see the prisoners, making communication easier, and because the system includes a graphics camera, which allows the librarians to transmit an image of a book page to the prison's monitor.

This option may increase in popularity for institutions that have had to deal with inmate escapes during a library visit.[17]

B. Guidelines

Before implementing an electronic reference service, it is a good idea to develop usage guidelines. Answering the following questions may help in that process:

(1) How will the service help meet the library's mission to serve its clientele?
(2) Will the service be restricted to certain groups, such as faculty and students? If the service is restricted to certain groups, how will this restriction be enforced?
(3) Will the service be restricted to certain types of questions, such as short, factual questions? How in-depth will the answers be? Should the amount and type of service provided electronically be more than, less than, or the same as the service provided to people in the building or on the telephone? How will the document delivery service of the library be affected?
(4) If the service is available to everyone, librarians should expect questions from the public asking for legal advice.[18] What will the response to these questions be? Should the response include telephone numbers for legal aid or bar referral services? Should a response be drafted in advance?
(5) Should there be uniformity in the librarians' responses to electronic questions, no matter which librarian answers the question?

The following issues also should be considered for reference services using e-mail and web forms:

(1) Which librarian(s) will be responsible for checking the account? How often will the account be checked? Who will answer the questions?
(2) How soon must questions be answered? Within 24 hours? 48 hours? Will users be informed of this turnaround time? An autoresponder can be used to send a reply to the requestor's e-mail address, giving the anticipated turnaround time and suggesting that users send a follow-up message if they have not received a reply in a couple of days. This information also could be stated on the web form.

(3) Will statistics be kept? Will copies of all requests be retained? Should a copy of librarians' answers be kept? Should the questions and answers be put into a database to benefit the reference staff or made available on the library web page for the benefit of library users?

(4) How will the service be publicized? Will there be links from the library's web site? If so, will this link be on the main page?

(5) Will librarians respond to questions electronically? By telephone?

(6) Will librarians send attachments to e-mail messages? If so, which software will be used?

V. HOW LIBRARIANS ARE FINDING ANSWERS

Once librarians receive reference requests (whether electronically, by telephone, or in person), they can take full advantage of technology to find the answers. They may search for items in their library's collection using an online catalog. Items in the collections of other libraries may be found through several sources, including OCLC's WorldCat database.[19] Librarians may search for journal articles using bibliographic databases such as LegalTrac[20] or full text databases on Westlaw or LEXIS. Articles may be sent and received electronically from libraries using scanners and imaging software, such as Ariel.[21] Librarians can search for court opinions, statutes, and other legal documents using full text databases on Westlaw, LEXIS, CD-ROMs or the web. The Law Library Resource Xchange's Research Guide (<http://www.llrx.com/guide/>) and research guides prepared by other libraries and placed on libraries' home pages may provide assistance as well. Colleagues can provide input by answering questions posted on one of the many e-mail discussion lists congregated by law librarians, such as Law-lib.[22] When librarians are researching issues over a period of time, they can have new documents delivered to their computers using SmartCILP,[23] Westlaw's WestClip or LEXIS' ECLIPSE.

VI. REFERENCE TOOLS NEEDED

What should a well-equipped reference desk have for a librarian to make full use of the basic technologies described above? (This discussion excludes tools needed for chat and videoconferencing.) The reference desk should have a computer that has fast and reliable Internet access, a web browser, e-mail access, Adobe Acrobat Reader[24] software, virus protection software, word processing software, a CD-ROM (or DVD) drive, and a high-speed printer. Access to a scanner should be readily available. Online systems and databases such as Westlaw, LEXIS, WorldCat, and LegalTrac must be retrievable from the desk.

The computer should be networked so reference librarians can access files whether they are using the reference desk computer or their office computer. Frequently used web sites should be bookmarked on the computer's web browser or linked from the library's home page to facilitate quick responses to questions. The reference staff may consider creating a database of frequently asked reference questions, either on the library web site or as a file on the reference desk computer. Manuals for electronic resources should be readily accessible to assist reference librarians as well as patrons.

The reference desk should have a telephone with either a shoulder rest or a head set so librarians can talk on the telephone and use the computer at the same time. Having a cordless telephone that reference librarians can take with them when they leave the desk is a valuable tool. The telephone system should be configured so unanswered calls from the reference desk roll to the circulation desk, another librarian, or voice mail. If the messaging system permits options, the voice mail message could offer the caller a number of different options, such as library hours, reference hours, and e-mail or web addresses.

VII. INTEGRATION OF TECHNOLOGY

How might the tools described in this article work together? In the survey of academic law libraries noted above, 49% allowed reference questions over e-mail. These libraries may consider expanding this service by adding a form on their web site for reference questions. The submitted forms could be directed to the already existing reference e-mail account. If the library wants to provide special reference services to a particular patron group, such as students and faculty on a semester abroad program, the library may consider chat, videoconferencing, and/or application sharing programs.

Once a library decides to implement a new electronic reference service, the library should establish guidelines for its use. The reference desk computer must have the necessary hardware and software, and the library staff must be well trained in the use of the applicable technology. Reference librarians may need different sources for answering remote reference questions than those used for answering the questions of patrons physically present in the library. For example, librarians cannot hand a book to remote patrons.

Patrons may need training on the new technology, which could be accomplished by classes or written guides. The new service should be publicized by an announcement on the library web site, sending e-mail to affected groups, writing an article for the library newsletter, and/or posting signs in the library. The service should be re-publicized from time to time. Statistics should be kept showing how often and by whom the service is used, and the service should be re-evaluated periodically. This re-evaluation may include a patron survey.

VIII. CONCLUSION

Technology is expanding rapidly. In fact, some suggestions in this article could be out of date in the very near future. Librarians should stay abreast of new technology, watching for innovations that would allow them to provide more and better services to library users, especially as the cost for some technology becomes less expensive. As new technologies are introduced, librarians must consider how the innovations might be applied to providing new and better reference services. There is no need to limit reference interviews to in-person and telephone conversations, especially when so many patrons are researching from their home and office computers. In addition, librarians should take full advantage of the web, e-mail, and other computer resources to answer reference questions.

NOTES

1. Law-lib is hosted by the University of California-Davis at *law-lib@ucdavis. edu* with archives at <http://lawlibrary.ucdavis.edu/LAWLIB/lawlib.html/>.

2. Eileen G. Abels, *The E-Mail Reference Interview,* 35 RQ 345, 354 (1996).

3. Laura Staley, *E-Mail Reference: Experiences at City University,* PLNL Q., Summer 1998, at 20.

4. Abels, *supra* note 2, at 348.

5. For a discussion of the use of chat for law firm web sites, see Joshua D. Blackman, *Bull's Eye! Hit the Mark by Targeting Clients Online,* LAW OFFICE COMPUTING, Dec.-Jan. 2000, at 78.

6. Lisa Guernsey, *The Web Discovers Its Voice,* N.Y. TIMES, October 21, 1999, at G1.

7. For insight into what was presented at the 1997 National Conference of the Association of College and Research Libraries, see Kathleen M. Folger, *The Virtual Librarian: Using Desktop Video Conferencing to Provide Interactive Reference Assistance* (visited May 10, 2000) <http://www.ala.org/acrl/paperhtm/a09.html>; Susan Lessick et al., *Interactive Reference Services (IRS) at UC Irvine: Expanding Reference Services Beyond the Reference Desk* (visited May 10, 2000) <http://www.ala.org/acrl/paperhtm/a10.html>.

8. *See CUseeMe Networks* (visited June 26, 2000) <http://www.cuseeme.com/> (formerly White Pine Software).

9. Les Freed, *Now Which Software Should You Use to Manage Your Videoconference?*, PC MAG., April 18, 2000, at 165.

10. *Id.*

11. Robert B. McGeachin, *Videoconferencing and Remote Application Sharing for Distant Reference Service*, 65 REFERENCE LIBR. 51, 52 (1999).

12. Minna Sellers, *Reference Over the Net: New Service or Just a New Line*, COLO. LIBR., Spring 1999, at 6.

13. Katherine Schilling-Eccles & Joseph J. Harzbecker, Jr., *The Use of Electronic Mail at the Reference Desk: Impact of a Computer-Mediated Communication Technology on Librarian-Client Interactions*, MED. REFERENCE SERVICES Q., Winter 1998, at 21.

14. Folger, *supra* note 7.

15. Bernie Sloan, *Electronic Reference Services–Some Suggested Guidelines*, REFERENCE & USER SERVICES Q., Fall 1998, at 77.

16. Karen Westwood, *Lights! Camera! Action!*, AM. LIBR., Jan. 1997, at 143.

17. *See Two Cons Escape While Using PL*, LIBR. J., Nov. 1, 1999, at 18.

18. For a discussion of some of the legal issues in providing reference services, see the article in this volume by Charles J. Condon, *How to Avoid the Unauthorized Practice of Law.*

19. *See* Online Computer Library Center, *WorldCat* (visited June 26, 2000) <http://www.oclc.org/oclc/man/6928fsdb/worldcat.htm>.

20. *See* Gale Group, *Product Information* (visited June 26, 2000) <http://www.galegroup.com/library/index.htm>.

21. *See* Ariel Corp., *Open Remote Access Solutions* (visited June 26, 2000) <http://www.ariel.com>.

22. For information about law-lib and other law-related e-mail discussion lists, see Lyonette Louis-Jacques, *Law Lists Info* (visited June 23, 2000) <http://www.lib.uchicago.edu/~llou/lawlists/info.html>.

23. This service provides citations to articles appearing in the Current Index to Legal Periodicals (CILP) based on the subjects of interest identified by the subscriber. For more information, see Marian Gould Gallagher Law Library, University of Washington Sch. of Law, *SmartCILP* (visited June 23, 2000) <http://lib.law.washington.edu/cilp/scilp.html>.

24. The Adobe Acrobat Reader is software that is needed to retrieve documents in Adobe Portable Document Format (PDF), which is a commonly used format on the web. The software can be downloaded for free at <http://www.adobe.com/products/acrobat/readermain.html>.

"Library Police":
Drafting and Implementing
Enforceable Library Rules

Jessie L. Cranford

Jessie L. Cranford is Circulation Librarian and Assistant Professor of Law Librarianship at the University of Arkansas at Little Rock/Pulaski County Law Library, 1203 McMath Street, Little Rock, AR 72202 (E-mail: jlcranford@ualr.edu).

[Haworth co-indexing entry note]: "Library Police": Drafting and Implementing Enforceable Library Rules." Cranford, Jessie L. Co-published simultaneously in *Legal Reference Services Quarterly* (The Haworth Information Press, an imprint of The Haworth Press, Inc.) Vol. 19, No. 1/2, 2001, pp. 147-163; and: *Emerging Solutions in Reference Services: Implications for Libraries in the New Millennium* (ed: John D. Edwards) The Haworth Information Press, an imprint of The Haworth Press, Inc., 2001, pp. 147-163. Single or multiple copies of this article are available for a fee from The Haworth Document Delivery Service [1-800-342-9678, 9:00 a.m. - 5:00 p.m. (EST). E-mail address: getinfo@haworthpressinc.com].

SUMMARY. Librarians are often faced with the task of enforcing un-popular rules. This can seem like a losing battle with the librarian gaining nothing for his or her trouble except a reputation for being a "Nazi." This article examines rules that currently exist in many law libraries, methods of enforcement, and new rules that are being implemented. Also discussed is what librarians can do about rules from a public relations standpoint. *[Article copies available for a fee from The Haworth Document Delivery Service: 1-800-342-9678. E-mail address: <getinfo@haworthpressinc. com> Website: <http://www.HaworthPress.com> © 2001 by The Haworth Press, Inc. All rights reserved.]*

I. INTRODUCTION

Through the years librarians have been plagued with various stereo-types; perhaps the most prevalent is that of the town spinster, hair in a bun, going around shushing patrons: "Please whisper," "Shhh! Quiet in the library." In academic libraries where students typically spend long hours studying or researching, there is often a great deal of resentment towards librarians and staff over policies, especially those prohibiting food and drink in the library. This leads some students to perceive staff as adversarial "carrel police" or "food Nazis"; they wonder why anyone cares so much if they have a little snack, and they often work hard to circumvent such policies.

Most librarians do not enjoy playing this role of "library police." So why do libraries have so many rules? Libraries have limited re-sources that must be organized, controlled, and preserved. Library personnel must devise methods for fairly allocating these resources, including staff time, to numerous users; in keeping with a given insti-tutional mission, librarians often must devote the majority of their resources to a recognized primary clientele while still assisting other patrons. Facilities must be preserved, and the security of patrons and staff is paramount.

II. METHODOLOGY

This article attempts to identify rules common to most law libraries, discuss methods of enforcement, and explore whether some rules could or should be modified. The majority of the information was gleaned from rules posted on library web pages accessible by following links from FindLaw's Law Schools Full List A-Z.[1] Policies from 139 institutions were reviewed. Information also was gathered from the Arkansas Supreme Court Library, the Law Library of Louisiana, the Little Rock Branch of the Federal Court Library for the Eighth Circuit, and the Robert A. and Vivian Young Law Library at the University of Arkansas-Fayetteville. The objective was to gain a quick sense of what types of rules are expressly stated and widely disseminated, even if the methodology was not comprehensive.

A good description of the spirit of most library rules can be found on the web page of the Norman Adrian Wiggins School of Law library at Campbell University:

> Library policies are not intended as barriers to the use of the collection; rather, they facilitate use by making the collection available to all users without unreasonable delay. Most rules are based on common sense and equitable principles and derive from a commitment to make the Law Library a pleasant environment.[2]

Rules typically fall into four broad categories: (1) Controlling the library's physical environment, (2) Controlling access to facilities and the collection, (3) Ensuring the personal safety (and feelings of safety) of staff and patrons, and (4) Allocating limited staff resources. There is some overlap among these categories; for example, some methods of controlling access to the facilities can also help ensure patron and staff safety.

III. CONTROLLING THE PHYSICAL ENVIRONMENT

Among those libraries with a clearly delineated list of rules, rules governing food and beverages, smoking and use of other tobacco products, and noise restrictions are almost universal. Food and drink is totally prohibited at twenty-eight schools[3] while fifty-three prohibit food but allow beverages, with forty-eight of those specifying that the beverages must be in approved spill-proof containers. Bottled water is the only beverage allowed at three libraries.[4] Food and beverages are permitted at six institutions which prohibit them in the computer labs; two apparently allow food and drink anywhere, and two more have designated areas for eating in the library. The food and drink policies can be summarized as follows:

Food and Drink Restrictions[5]

Food Prohibited	38% (53)
Food and Drink Prohibited	20% (28)
Beverages Permitted in Spill-Proof Containers	35% (48)
Bottled Water *Only* Permitted	2% (3)
Food and Beverages Allowed Except in Computer Labs	4% (6)
No Food or Drink Restrictions	1.5% (2)
Designated Areas for Eating and Drinking in the Library	1.5% (2)

Smoking is prohibited at forty libraries, while thirty-one go further to explicitly prohibit the use of all tobacco products. Two libraries have designated smoking areas. Policies stating that the library is a "quiet area" and urging no unnecessary conversation or noise are in place in thirty-nine libraries. Cellular phone use is totally banned in twenty-four libraries and six more restrict the use of cellular phones to certain areas. Laptop computer use is restricted in eighteen libraries which have "laptop free" zones, presumably to ensure that clicking keyboards do not disturb those wanting a quiet study space. Policies prohibiting all animals other than service animals for disabled individuals are in effect at fourteen libraries.

IV. CONTROLLING ACCESS

A. Controlling Access to Facilities

1. Admission to Building

Libraries have a mission to serve their primary clientele, yet most still allow some degree of access to members of the public; those which are federal depository libraries must allow the public to use government documents to retain their depository status.[6] Policy statements allowing public access are present at seventy-seven institutions, although twenty-three restrict that access to depository patrons using the government documents area; fourteen have a statement to the effect that public patrons must have a "legitimate legal research need." Public access is limited through the use of tickets or passes at seven institutions.[7] Eleven have policies closing the library for all patrons except law students during exam and reading periods.[8]

Those libraries with access limitations enforce them in a variety of ways. A guard at the UCLA library entrance checks identification and signs in patrons.[9] The Edward Bennett Williams Law Library at Georgetown University Law Center has a guard at the entrance to check identification.[10] Southwestern University School of Law in Los Angeles, which is closed to the public except for its government documents, uses a swipe card system to control access.[11]

2. Conference and Group Study Rooms

American Bar Association Standards[12] require that law libraries make group study space available for students. Fifty libraries have rooms which may be reserved while ten make rooms available on a first-come, first-served basis. The overwhelming majority restricts reservation of conference and group study rooms to law student use, although one library states that its conference room is available to all patrons and another promotes a special "Attorney's Room." Most policies limit reservations from two to four hours, and many state that while individuals may use the rooms, they must vacate for groups. For an example of a conduct code specific to group study rooms, see Arizona State University's website at <http://www.lawlib.asu.edu/services/study.html>.

3. Computer Lab Use

In many institutions the computer facilities are located within and controlled by the library. It has fallen to the librarians and library staff to formulate policies and regulate access to these resources. Computer lab use is limited to law faculty, staff, and students in forty-seven libraries. Undergraduates from the main campus can use the labs in three libraries. Two institutions allow alumni to use their labs. An ID is required to enter the lab at four libraries. Two request that students reserve time on the computers, and two state that the equipment in the labs is to be used for "law school purposes only." Students must obtain a password and attend an orientation before accessing the labs at three schools. The most prevalent rule concerns not reconfiguring the operating system or loading software (fourteen policies spell this out).

B. Controlling Access to Collections

1. Reshelving Policies

Due to the nature of legal materials and high demand for certain items, large portions of most library collections do not circulate, and rules govern use of items even within the library. Patrons are asked to reshelve materials at forty-seven libraries, although a few request that classified materials be placed in a designated pre-shelving area. The University of Indiana-Indianapolis Law Library requests that patrons reshelve materials with the spine upward so staff can verify the location.[13]

2. Circulating Materials

While most law libraries do not check out circulating materials to members of the public, thirteen institutions do extend those privileges. Circulation privileges are restricted to faculty, staff, and students at twenty-eight schools; twenty-two extend privileges to alumni; nineteen grant "associate patron" status to students from specified schools; and thirteen offer free access for area attorneys. Memberships with circulation privileges can be purchased at seventeen libraries. Policies requiring patrons to present a current borrower's card to charge out materials are found in forty-nine schools.

3. Unauthorized Removal, Damage to, or Concealing Materials

Rules concerning the unauthorized removal of materials from the library, damage to materials, or concealing of materials are almost universal. Not only must these rules be stated clearly, but the procedures to follow in case of a violation must be part of staff training and be readily accessible in the Circulation Desk Manual.

V. ALLOCATING LIMITED STAFF RESOURCES

A. Paging and Messaging

Because of the long hours students and attorneys typically spend in the library, it is not uncommon for family members or secretaries to call the circulation desk looking for them. Libraries have had to develop policies in response to this influx of calls. Paging is not done in twenty-five libraries and ten will page only in the case of emergencies; one library pages without restrictions. Staff will take messages and post them on a library bulletin board at twenty schools while eight have a stated policy against taking messages.

B. Children

Unsupervised or rowdy children are sometimes a problem in libraries. Students may believe that it is acceptable to allow their children to play on the computers in the lab while the parent goes to class; public patrons permit their kids to ride the elevators and play chase through the stacks while mom or dad researches. The library staff cannot be expected to act as babysitters. Policies addressing this problem include statements that "Children thirteen and under must be supervised by an adult,"[14] and "Authorized patrons who find it necessary to bring minor children with them to the law library may do so as long as the child(ren) respect(s) the academic environment of the facility. Patrons and their children may be asked to leave if their child's deportment is inappropriate."[15] While law libraries may not have the level of problems experienced by public libraries in this area, having a policy in place should the situation arise is a good idea.[16]

VI. ENSURING PERSONAL SAFETY OF STAFF
AND PATRONS

Examples of measures to ensure staff and patron safety (or feelings of safety) include policies requiring photo identification or keycard access for entry into the library.[17] At the University of Missouri-Columbia School of Law Library, access is monitored on weekends and after 5:00 p.m. on weekdays by having patrons sign in at the Circulation Desk.[18] Duke University Law Library is open to the general public from 7:30 a.m. to 5:00 p.m. and restricts access at all other times to current DukeCard holders; a magnetic card system is coded to give extended hours to all cardholders and 24-hour access to Duke law students.[19]

Many policies address rowdiness or disruptive behavior. Most libraries state that they will request patrons who are causing a disturbance to leave the library. Policies also ban firearms or other weapons and prohibit inappropriate sexual behavior, bathing in or other misuse of restrooms, and physically or verbally harassing staff or other users. Many libraries have "Disaster Plans" or "Emergency Plans" in place so that staff members know what to do when challenging situations arise.[20] Every member of the staff should be familiar with the plan and know when it is appropriate to call security personnel.[21]

VII. METHODS OF ENFORCEMENT

Sanctions for violating library rules vary, ranging from confiscation of contraband food and beverages to criminal prosecution for unauthorized removal or damage to materials. Most academic law libraries have recourse against student offenders under their law school's code of student conduct.

Often, it is difficult to enforce rules prohibiting food and beverage in the library because staff coverage is not sufficient to walk around "policing the stacks." When food trash is found in open areas, it is usually impossible to know who has left it there. Some policies state that if a library staff member observes a patron with food or drink, the patron will be asked to leave the library; others state that the offending items will be confiscated. Enforcement is easier in specific areas to which access can be controlled. Hofstra University's Law Library has a rule requiring that all members of a study group leave a valid student I.D. at the Circulation Desk when checking out a room. All members are responsible for the key; abuse of the room will result in the loss of the privilege to use the rooms.[22] The University of Arkansas at Little Rock Law Library issues written warnings to occupants of its closed carrels; repeated violation of carrel policies results in the loss of carrel privileges. (See sample policy in Appendix A.)

The sanctions for violations of rules regarding staff and patron safety are more severe, as might be expected. Patrons causing a disturbance in the library or harassing patrons or staff face the possibility of an escort off the premises by campus security, may be accountable to both civil authorities and to the University, and may be subject to suspension or expulsion. Most policies also state that the library will pursue criminal prosecution of offenders if appropriate.

VIII. NEW RULES

New technologies and a changing library environment have created a need for new rules or have given rise to new solutions for old problems. Laptop, pager and cell phone rules are responses to new problems brought about by new technology. Printing abuse has been a problem for many libraries for some time. Technologies such as vendacards and printer control software now make it possible to hold patrons accountable.[23]

Some institutions circulate laptop computers to law students. The policy created at George Washington University Law Library for this relatively new situation is available at <www.law.gwu.edu/burns/libdepts/laptop.htm>. Rules governing computer use change as technology improves and usage patterns reflect the evolving needs of today's students. For an example of rules regarding use of public workstations, the University of San Francisco's *Reference Workstations Policies* is available at <http://www.usfca.edu/law_library/refwkst.html>.

IX. PUBLIC RELATIONS ASPECTS

Libraries must have rules, and rules are meaningless unless they are enforced. How do libraries communicate and enforce their rules without developing adversarial and antagonistic relationships with their patrons? An important step is to proactively communicate the rules and the reasoning behind them. One library states "to prevent damage to library materials, furniture and carpeting, food and beverages are not allowed in the library."[24] Another library appeals to patrons to

"Please help us keep our new library beautiful. In addition, the pests that are attracted to the library by food also eat our books."[25]

Another important step is to seek input from students or other clientele when promulgating new rules. If library patrons are part of the rule-making process, there may be more support for the rules. An explanation of how the rules will help achieve library goals should be communicated to key members of the patron population. An example of such cooperative efforts can be seen in the conference room policy at Arizona State University, which was developed by a joint committee of the Student Bar Association and the Ross-Blakely Law Library staff.[26] When the University of Arkansas Young Law Library enacted its policy allowing food and drink, Director Glen-Peter Ahlers informed students by memo that such privileges would remain only if they cooperated with the spirit of the policy and self-monitored compliance. (See Appendix B.)

Clear and concise language should be used to state library policy. Rules may be distributed in a library guide, posted prominently near the entrance of the library, posted on the library's web page, or all of the above. Signage in appropriate areas is helpful, as are handouts. Students who apply for a closed carrel at the University of Arkansas at Little Rock Law Library must sign a statement which reads "I have read the attached regulations and agree to comply with them." (See Appendix A.)

Using positive language instead of negative language can make a significant difference in how the message is perceived. For example, the difference between signs stating "No entrance without registration" and "Please sign in at the Circulation Desk" is considerable. Which library seems more patron-friendly? Users might react differently to these two signs: "No Attorneys in Lab" and "Lab Reserved for Law Students." The desired outcome is the same, but the impression on attorney patrons will probably be quite different.

Education and empowerment of front-line staff is crucial in successful enforcement of library rules and in the maintenance of positive public relations. Staff must know the rules and the justifications for them, and must enforce those rules firmly and consistently. At the same time, staff must know when it is appropriate to make a reasonable exception. A student suffering dry mouth and nausea as a result of cancer treatment can be allowed to keep a bottle of Sprite in her carrel;

the staff person doing carrel sweeps should be able to make that call on the spot rather than referring the patron to a supervisor.

In his book *Dealing With Difficult People in the Library,* Mark R. Willis states, "Rules are only necessary to help run a smooth, safe, and efficient library. If a rule doesn't contribute to those causes, banish it."[27] Librarians should be willing to modify or dispense with rules if they are no longer justified. If there is not heavy demand from groups for study rooms, individual students might be allowed to reserve them–perhaps with the caveat that they must yield the room to a requesting group. Some libraries seem to have liberalized their policies regarding food and drink in an effort to meet students halfway. Permitting beverages in spill-proof containers is a common compromise. The *Library Guide* for the Robert A. and Vivian Young Law Library illustrates perhaps one of the more liberal accommodations, stating that "Drinks and non-messy foods are allowed as long as library users clean up after themselves."[28]

Clearly writing out rules and their resultant sanctions is essential. An unwritten policy is difficult, if not impossible, to enforce. Patrons can rightfully say they had no notice. Staff may enforce the policy inconsistently or be unaware the policy exists at all. As the need for new policies arises, an effort should be made to reduce them to writing. If exceptions to an existing policy are becoming the norm, or more restrictions than those stated have become necessary, the policy should be revisited and the changes noted. It is also helpful if all the rules and their resultant sanctions are accessible in one place, such as the Circulation Desk Manual.

X. GUIDELINES FOR DEVELOPING LIBRARY RULES

The following checklist should be helpful in formulating enforceable rules that provide the best environment possible for staff and patrons.

1. *Determine what rules are needed and why.* Problems to be addressed or prevented should be identified. Adopting a proactive approach may be more advantageous than simply reacting to problems as they arise.

2. *Seek patron input in developing new rules.* Cooperative efforts with student or bar groups may result in creative solutions for the problem and a better understanding by users of the need for the rules.

A suggestion box might be used in addition to newsletters, postings, surveys, and other means for input.

3. *Involve the library staff in rulemaking.* Staff members are critically important in the success of library rules. Input is needed especially from those who may be responsible for implementation. Other departments may have insights or be able to offer suggestions.

4. *Develop a plan for monitoring and enforcing the rules.* A rule that is not enforced may be worse than having no rule at all. Depending on the rule, staff may choose to conduct walkthroughs, control access to certain areas, use technology such as printer control software, or consider other measures.

5. *Publicize new rules well in advance of implementation.* Patrons can be notified of rules via announcements, postings, website additions, newsletters, student newspaper, etc. Advance notice gives more opportunity to educate patrons on the justifications for the new policy.

6. *Communicate the reason for the rule.* Patrons and staff need to understand why the rule is necessary. The policy should be stated using positive rather than negative language and relate to the library's mission and goals.

7. *Empower and educate the staff concerning the rules.* Staff should be trained in how the rules will be enforced. Procedure manuals must be updated to include the new policies.

XI. CONCLUSION

While few librarians or library staff enjoy the "library police" persona, rules are necessary for maintaining order in any group environment. Some problems will always be present. New technology requires new policies. Changes in society at large may drive policy changes in libraries with public access. For example, pro se or attorney traffic may increase to the point that primary clientele (whether students and faculty or judges and clerks) are not being well served. The growing self-help law movement has impacted many law libraries to some extent. Equitable methods for controlling, preserving, and allocating resources can help libraries continue to serve their patrons efficiently. Reasonable rules must be established, revisited, and enforced for the greater good.

NOTES

1. Findlaw, *Law Schools: USA A–Z Links to Law School Home Pages* (visited June 8, 2000) <http://lawschools.findlaw.com/schools/fulllist.html>.

2. Norman Adrian Wiggins Sch. of Law Library, *Law Library Handbook* (visited June 8, 2000) <http://webster.campbell.edu/law_library/hb96_1.htm#dd>.

3. When library policies were initially reviewed for this article, the University of Pittsburgh Law Library policy made an exception for law review students with offices in the library. Since then a coffee station has been added in the library commons and patrons can consume food and drink there. Outside of that area, beverages are allowed only if they are contained in spill-proof cups or bottles. Food is not permitted elsewhere and no food or drinks are allowed in the computer labs. University of Pittsburgh School of Law Library, *Policies* (visited Jan. 23, 2001) <http://www.law.pitt.edu/library/using/policies.html>.

4. The S.J. Quinney Law Library at the University of Utah School of Law states a specific exception allowing consumption of food and beverages by students while in their assigned study carrels. S.J. Quinney Law Library Info., *Library Rules* (visited Jan. 23, 2001) <http://www.law.utah.edu/Library/information2.html>.

5. Figures are rounded to the nearest .5 percent and totals may not equal 100%. Not every site visited had clearly posted rules, and there may be some overlap between categories.

6. 44 U.S.C. § 1911 (1994) states: "Depository libraries shall make Government publications available for the free use of the general public. . . . "

7. For an example of a library that uses the access ticket method, see Hugh & Hazel Darling Law Library, UCLA School of Law, *Policy and Procedure on Access to the Library Facility* (visited June 8, 2000) <http://www.law.ucla.edu/library/limitedaccess.html>.

8. One example is Harvard Law School Library; during exam periods, the turnstile card reader is programmed to allow access only to law students. E-mail from Deanna Barmakian, Reference Librarian, Harvard Law School Library (May 18, 2000) (on file with author).

9. Hugh & Hazel Darling Law Library, UCLA School of Law, *General Services and Regulations* (visited June 8, 2000) <http://www.law.ucla.edu/library/information/general.html>. "Identification will be checked at the Library entrance and you will be asked to sign in at the guard desk during all hours the Library is open." *Id.*

10. E.B. Williams Law Library, Georgetown Univ. Law Center, *Law Library Guide: Access Policy* (visited Jan. 23, 2001) <http://www.ll.Georgetown.edu/lb/guide/access.htm>.

11. E-mail from Carole Weiner, Associate Director, Southwestern University School of Law Library (May 16, 2000) (on file with author).

12. ABA, *Standards for Approval of Law Schools* (2000) (visited Jan 23, 2001) <http://www.abanet.org/legaled/standards/standards.html>. ABA Standard 703 on Research and Study Space provides: "A law school shall provide, on site, sufficient quiet study and research seating for its students and faculty. A law school should provide space that is suitable for group study and other forms of collaborative work." ABA, *Chapter 7: Facilities* (visited Jan 23, 2001) <http://www.abanet.org/legaled/standards/chapter7.html>.

13. Indianapolis Law Library, Indiana Univ. Sch. of Law, *Library Handbook* (visited June 8, 2000) <http://www.iulaw.indy.indiana.edu/library/handbook.htm>.

14. University of Hawaii Law Library, *General Information* (visited Oct. 7, 1999) <http://library.law.hawaii.edu/public/lp3.html>.

15. William M. Rains Law Library, Loyola Law Sch.-Los Angeles, *Access Policies* (visited June 8, 2000) <http://www.law.lmu.edu/library/access.htm>.

16. *See, e.g.*, JEANETTE LARSON & HERMAN L. TOTTEN, MODEL POLICIES FOR SMALL AND MEDIUM PUBLIC LIBRARIES 142 (1998).

17. *See supra* Part IV.A.

18. University of Missouri-Columbia Sch. of Law Library, *Library Policies* (visited June 8, 2000) <http://www.law.missouri.edu/library/libpolcy.htm>.

19. Duke Univ. Law Library, *Access and Hours* (visited June 8, 2000) <http://www.law.duke.edu/lib/library.htm>.

20. *See, e.g.*, ROBERT GENOVESE, DISASTER PREPAREDNESS MANUAL (1998); or MIRIAM B. KAHN, DISASTER RESPONSE AND PLANNING FOR LIBRARIES (1998).

21. For more ideas on library security, see *Library Security Guidelines: Draft Document* (last modified April 20, 1999) <http://www.ala.org/lama/committees/bes/sslbguidelines.html>.

22. Deane Law Library, Hofstra Law Sch., *Group Study Rooms* (visited June 8, 2000) <http://www.hofstra.edu/Law/librarygroupstudyrooms.html>.

23. For a list of schools using printer controls, such as PCounter or VendaCards, see the site maintained by Joyce Manna Janto, *Law School Printing Survey* (last modified June 5, 2000) <http://law.richmond.edu/general/printsurvey.htm>.

24. Wake Forest Prof'l Ctr. Library, *Food, Beverages and Tobacco Use in the Professional Center Library* (visited June 8, 2000) <http://www.law.wfu.edu/library/policies/food.htm>.

25. Hugh & Hazel Darling Law Library, *supra* note 9.

26. John J. Ross-William C. Blakely Law Library, Arizona State Univ. College of Law, *Study Room Conduct Code* (visited June 8, 2000) <http://www.lawlib.asu.edu/services/study.html>.

27. MARK R. WILLIS, DEALING WITH DIFFICULT PEOPLE IN THE LIBRARY 114 (1999).

28. Robert A. & Vivian Young Law Library, University of Arkansas-Fayetteville, *Library Guide 1999-2000*, at 4 (on file with author).

APPENDIX A

| Date _____ |
| Time _____ |

UALR/PULASKI COUNTY LAW LIBRARY
CLOSED CARREL APPLICATION

Name: _____

ARE YOU A: LAW STUDENT (IF SO, LIST YEAR AND DIVISION) _____ ;

     JUDGE/ATTORNEY _____ ; OR LAW FACULTY MEMBER _____

     ADDRESS: _____ PHONE NUMBER: _____

     _____ HOME _____

     _____ WORK: _____

PLEASE PROVIDE A BRIEF DESCRIPTION OF THE NATURE OF THE PROJECT THAT YOU WILL BE WORKING ON WHILE USING THE CARREL. **IF YOU ARE A LAW STUDENT, LIST THE CLASS OR ACTIVITY AND THE NAME OF THE SUPERVISING FACULTY MEMBER.**

_____

_____

ANTICIPATED DATE OF COMPLETION OF PROJECT: _____

You will be assigned a carrel partner unless you have a need to keep your work confidential. You may list the names of one or more possible carrel partners.

Names of any preferred carrel partners: _____
_____

Do you have a preference for a specific carrel? _____

I have read the attached regulations and agree to comply with them. I understand that I must vacate my carrel on or before the date listed below and that I will inform the Library of any problems that I might have with my carrel.

_____
(Signature)   (Date)

| Patron may occupy carrel _____ until May 10, 2001. |
| Patron issued key number _____ . |
| Name of carrel partner (if any): _____ |

CLOSED CARREL REGULATIONS

Please read the regulations listed below. Failure to comply with these regulations will result in the loss of your carrel privileges.

1) Carrels may be occupied for only a set length of time. You may not renew your carrel; however, you may apply for a new carrel at the end of your occupancy period. *Promptly return your carrel key on or before the due date.*

2) Listing a person on your carrel application as a carrel mate does not automatically qualify him or her for a carrel; each carrel applicant must qualify in his or her own right. We randomly assign a carrel mate to those who list ineligible carrel mates.

3) The carrel keys that we issue to carrel occupants are library property and should not be lent to another person. Keys must be surrendered on request. The library assesses a charge of *$20.00 for lost keys.*

4) Moot Court participants receive shared carrel assignments and check out shared keys for library use only. We do not issue Moot Court carrel keys without receiving a list from the supervisors.

5) All library books that are to be kept in your carrel *must* be checked out at the Circulation Desk on the first floor. Library books not checked out will be removed. Books checked out to a carrel will be due at the end of the semester.

6) Books may be checked out to carrels with the following exceptions: reserve books, reference books, digests, codes and indexes.

7) The storage or consumption of food, drink and tobacco in carrels is prohibited.

8) Please do not affix anything to the carrel walls, windows or doors. Do not use tape on the furniture, walls or doors.

9) The Library assumes *no* responsibility for personal items left in carrels.

10) The Library reserves the right to modify or add to these regulations.

11) I have read the regulations and I agree to comply.

APPENDIX B

TO: Law Students
FROM: Professor Ahlers
RE: Library Food and Drink Policy
DATE: 10 March 1996

Beginning today, the law library will experiment, for the remainder of the spring 1996 semester, with allowing limited food and drink in the library. We will assess the program in May and determine if we will extend it into the summer. Whether the policy continues is up to you. The library staff and custodians are busy enough; we haven't time to clean up after students.

Beginning today, you have the opportunity to read, study, and relax with a beverage or snack. No food patrol will be out to get you. In order for the new temporary policy to work everyone must be careful, courteous, and clean. The library staff will be closely monitoring the situation. You may want to monitor it also, because one or two inconsiderate students can ruin the privilege for everyone.

I hope this is the start of a new era in the law library. Let's make it work!

ROBERT A. AND VIVIAN YOUNG LAW LIBRARY
LIMITED FOOD AND DRINK POLICY

This policy is in effect on a trial basis from 10 March until 10 May 1996.

THE LAW LIBRARY WILL PERMIT THE CONSUMPTION OF SOME FOOD AND DRINK

1. There remains in effect an absolute ban on all food and beverages in the library computer lab and at every library computer station.
2. There also remains an absolute ban on pizza, soups, hamburgers, french fries, doughnuts, and other "messy" foods likely to spill, splatter, spread and stain books, furniture, and carpet.
3. Food cannot be delivered to the law library by commercial operations.
4. Library users who bring food or drink into the library must clean up after themselves and deposit all waste into appropriate containers.
5. Library users who consume food or drink in the library must do so without disturbing others. Rattling wrappers and biting apples can be quite bothersome in an otherwise quiet location.
6. Library users are asked to use common sense and not work towards stretching the outer limits of the guidelines, for example, when defining "messy" foods.
7. Those who refuse to comply with the Limited Food and Drink Policy will be instructed to leave the library.

Used with permission.

How to Avoid the Unauthorized Practice of Law at the Reference Desk

Charles J. Condon

SUMMARY. A librarian's duty to avoid the unauthorized practice of law limits what reference services can be provided. Traditional approaches to reference services are being influenced by new initiatives in delivering legal services and information. Pro se patrons and the reference librarians

Charles J. Condon is Computer Services/Reference Librarian and Assistant Professor at the Northern Illinois University College of Law, Dekalb, IL 60115-2890.

[Haworth co-indexing entry note]: "How to Avoid the Unauthorized Practice of Law at the Reference Desk." Condon, Charles J. Co-published simultaneously in *Legal Reference Services Quarterly* (The Haworth Information Press, an imprint of The Haworth Press, Inc.) Vol. 19, No. 1/2, 2001, pp. 165-179; and: *Emerging Solutions in Reference Services: Implications for Libraries in the New Millennium* (ed: John D. Edwards) The Haworth Information Press, an imprint of The Haworth Press, Inc., 2001, pp. 165-179. Single or multiple copies of this article are available for a fee from The Haworth Document Delivery Service [1-800-342-9678, 9:00 a.m. - 5:00 p.m. (EST). E-mail address: getinfo@haworthpressinc.com].

who serve them benefit from the web-based resources, authorized non-lawyer assistance programs, and other innovative programs now available. Identifying new resources and using them effectively should enable a librarian to provide excellent reference service while avoiding the unauthorized practice of law. *[Article copies available for a fee from The Haworth Document Delivery Service: 1-800-342-9678. E-mail address: <getinfo@ haworthpressinc.com> Website: <http://www.HaworthPress.com> © 2001 by The Haworth Press, Inc. All rights reserved.]*

I. INTRODUCTION

Reference is a central component of law librarianship. It is the public face of the profession and it defines the law librarian in the public mind. Librarians want to maintain high quality reference service to the public while avoiding the unauthorized practice of law. Understanding the regulation of the legal profession requires a review of its purposes and underlying philosophy. Possible sanctions for the unauthorized practice of law must be considered in determining the boundaries within which reference librarians must work. Analyzing examples of "practicing law" will help illustrate common pitfalls associated with reference work so librarians can avoid those problems. Exploring the implications of these standards on law librarianship should aid in creating or refining a reference philosophy that is best suited for a library's clientele.

The role of law librarians as information providers includes the ethical considerations of providing information within the limits imposed by institutional policies and professional standards. Traditional approaches to reference must be evaluated in light of the librarian's duty to avoid practicing law. This analysis stresses the importance of providing information rather than advice. Recent literature provides examples of the traditional methods law librarians employ to avoid the risks of unauthorized practice.

New programs and initiatives are enabling the public to obtain legal information and legal assistance. Legal reference is influenced by the significant changes in the legal environment which impact law libraries. Better service to patrons should be possible from considering the suggestions below for integrating new programs into legal reference.

II. REGULATING THE PRACTICE OF LAW

The practice of law is regulated through standards of competence and ethical behavior developed by the profession to protect the public from unqualified or unethical attorneys. By controlling admission to practice, each jurisdiction limits practice to those meeting and maintaining the prescribed standards. Once admitted, an attorney is subject to disciplinary rules and can be sanctioned for unprofessional or unethical conduct. This procedure protects the public from non-attorneys and ensures that only licensed attorneys offer legal assistance.

This regulatory framework provides a functional method for monitoring the delivery of legal services to the public. Each state establishes its own set of regulations, but most share the common features found in the Model Rules of Professional Conduct.[1] While enforcement mechanisms vary, all states monitor and enforce unauthorized practice rules to protect the public from violators.

A librarian should first understand how the practice of law is defined to help ensure that reference services comply with legal limitations.[2] The intentionally broad language used in most jurisdictions[3] which provides no precise, working definition remains a problem.[4] Madison Mosley believes the profession should be more concerned with "not performing lawyerly functions" rather than concentrating on the definition of the practice of law.[5] Yvette Brown notes that law librarians dispense information, not advice[6]–a distinction that recognizes the traditional duties of librarians.

III. THE ROLE OF LIBRARIANS
AS INFORMATION PROVIDERS

A. Ethical Considerations

When law librarians provide access to legal information, they are governed by institutional policies and by the profession's ethical standards based on a commitment to "open and effective access to legal and related information."[7] However, the principles establish service limits "imposed by our institutions and by the duty to avoid the unauthorized practice of law."[8] While most law librarians support open and effective access to legal information, the scope of reference services may vary.

B. Traditional Approaches to Reference Service

The level of reference assistance may range from minimum[9] to mid-range[10] to maximum.[11] The minimum service approach is the basic service level for those who are generally cautious in assisting pro se patrons. These patrons may be classified as "secondary" users with either minimum service or, at best, referral service.[12] The librarian is admonished to "err on the side of caution" by limiting service to avoid any risk of the appearance of practicing law.[13] This approach is perhaps most evident in Virginia where librarians are very limited in the assistance they can provide non-lawyers.[14]

Another reason for this cautious attitude is the belief that a pro se patron will monopolize a librarian's time or otherwise disrupt the reference desk. Some believe pro se patrons see the law librarian as the equivalent of a legal adviser, not as an information provider.[15] Even if patrons recognize the distinction, they may nevertheless pursue questions that go beyond seeking information to asking advice. Using the minimum service approach, patrons are quickly dispatched to the resources available with very brief instructions on how to use the materials and a reminder that no legal advice can be given. This approach may alienate the patron and give a poor impression of the profession. Those who wish to provide more comprehensive assistance argue that librarians have an obligation to do more than just point to the books and let patrons fend for themselves.[16]

C. Giving Information, Not Advice

A mid-range approach to reference involves analyzing needs using service as the primary objective. First, the librarian will likely obtain more information from the patron concerning the legal problem. At this stage, Brown cautions that an analysis should be made to determine whether the question requires mere guidance or actual legal advice.[17] If guidance is all that is required, the librarian can provide instruction in the use of resources and answer questions related to the use of the materials, but not interpret the content.[18] The law librarian would then be providing a valuable service while avoiding the pitfalls of legal advice.[19]

The maximum approach to reference risks the possibility of coming close to or engaging in the practice of law. For example, librarians may attempt to explain or interpret statutes or cases to laypersons who do not understand the language of the legislature or courts–a role normally reserved for lawyers. Some writers believe law librarians may only be responding to the acknowledged needs of those who cannot afford legal assistance.[20] Others argue that patrons receive much needed help at the reference desk and librarians are unlikely targets for unauthorized practice actions.[21] In any event, law librarians should be aware of the problems in pro se reference to ensure their conduct complies with legal requirements.

D. Service Limitations

Information access is the foundation of legal reference. Because law librarians serve as gatekeepers of legal information, they should facilitate information dissemination to the public[22] and explain how to use the resources.[23] The pro se patron, however, occupies a different status in the legal system than the person represented by an attorney.

If a pro se patron is preparing for litigation and the librarian offers help by selecting forms, suggesting strategy, making qualitative judgments on the patron's evidence, and providing other sophisticated assistance, the patron has an advantage over litigants who have no assistance. As litigation begins, the judge may routinely accommodate the pro se party since the assumption remains that the pro se is not familiar with the subtleties of the legal system. From the judge's point of view, a certain amount of help is warranted since the proceedings will run smoother without overtly favoring the unrepresented party. In addition, the court is required in some circumstances to apply a less stringent standard to pleadings filed by pro se litigants.[24]

The judicial process may be harmed by too much behind the scenes help from anyone, including a law librarian. The opposing party's attorney may well treat the unrepresented client differently because of the lack of representation. If pro se litigants begin demonstrating a greater understanding of the process, fewer judges and attorneys may be willing to accommodate pro se litigants needing help. The librarian could be doing more harm than good by offering extra suggestions and tips. Another unintended consequence might be that the patron may achieve success in litigation and return for further assistance, even referring friends to the library as a resource.

For lawyer-librarians, an ethical issue may arise with providing too much help. A lawyer occasionally may assist a pro se litigant without formally entering the case as the attorney of record. If the assistance is limited to guidance, the lawyer risks no penalty. However, if an attorney assists in the preparation of pleadings, motions, briefs and other documents filed in a pending case, but without acknowledging that an attorney has been involved in creating the documents, this "ghostwriting" is arguably an ethical violation which results in an unfair advantage if the other litigant is unrepresented.[25]

Preparation of pleadings in a pending case without attaching the attorney's signature violates procedural rules in most jurisdictions and could subject the attorney to sanctions.[26] Lawyer-librarians could risk this penalty if their assistance goes too far. Could a librarian's assistance in completing forms for court submission be considered ghostwriting? Although no reported cases indicate that librarians have been charged with unauthorized practice,[27] reference librarians still are governed by ethical principles[28] and assistance must be carefully limited. In resolving the service vs. unauthorized practice dilemma, law librarians must appreciate that their perception of legal reference and that of the patron may be quite different.

IV. STRATEGIES FOR AVOIDING THE UNAUTHORIZED PRACTICE OF LAW

When a patron arrives at the reference desk, the librarian expects to provide information while the patron expects answers and solutions to legal problems. The inability of many communities to respond to the legal needs of those with limited resources has resulted in growing numbers of pro se patrons. The law library is often a pro se's primary resource for legal assistance. Because the profession has a reputation for helping others, librarians offer what help they can within the constraints of their particular situation.[29] The following guidelines should assist in formulating a reference policy.

1. Avoid Lengthy and Detailed Interviews of the Patron

Although some discussion is necessary to determine the issues presented by the patron's question, the librarian should discourage lengthy conversations. The reference librarian normally has limited time to devote to a single patron; skillful questioning usually brings the problem in focus rather quickly. Directing the conversation to broad subject areas allows the librarian to suggest resources for the patron's review. Introducing the patron to the materials as soon as possible allows the research process to begin and reinforces the librarian's role as one who helps by showing, not doing.[30]

2. Use Signage to Inform the Patrons

A sign tactfully stating that librarians provide access to information, not legal advice, serves as a good reminder for patrons and librarians. Almost all law libraries follow this policy whether signs are posted or not. Signs reinforce the information vs. advice distinction and make it clear that reference is limited to providing information access.[31] Signs should be worded in a positive manner, indicating the willingness of librarians to help find needed information.

3. Offer Referral Lists for Legal Services

If a patron loses interest in the research process or has not yet identified any legal referral resources, reference desk staff can provide alternatives for seeking help. Most experienced reference librarians have developed a list of options, perhaps beginning with the American Bar Association's Lawyer Referral Service[32] which identifies national, state, and local programs. For example, the Chicago Bar Association maintains a list of legal assistance programs ranging from Asian Legal Services to Equipped for Equality (Disability Rights) to Lawyers for the Creative Arts.[33] As attorneys increasingly embrace the pro bono publico philosophy, more programs for underserved groups are being developed.[34]

4. Establish a Collection of Legal Information Brochures

Bar associations and public interest groups offer brochures to outline services available to the public. A central file of brochures and a collection policy will strengthen these resources. Developing and maintaining the collection enables the reference staff to stay current with available services and provides valuable information to patrons. In addition, staff members can add items to the collection as newly developed resources or programs are discovered.

5. Prepare Research Handouts for Common Research Techniques

The fundamentals of legal information can be reduced to a series of short handouts indicating the assistance available to library patrons. These research tools save time and give the patron a framework from which the research process can begin. In addition, these documents reinforce the role of the librarian in supplying tools and some limited guidance so the patron can perform the research. In drafting research aids the librarian should assume that the pro se patron will be one of the primary users and indicate what assistance patrons can expect. The guides also provide the patron with a useful tool for future trips to the library.[35]

6. Identify and List Federal, State, and Local Agencies for Referral of Patrons

Governmental agencies often have programs designed specifically for a patron's legal dilemma. Having a list of contact numbers can help direct patrons to needed expertise at little or no cost. For example, the State Attorney General's Office frequently handles consumer complaints and is equipped to conduct the necessary investigations to resolve citizen complaints at no cost to the patron. Since programs are constantly changing, frequent contact with these agencies will improve the resources the librarian can give the patron.[36]

7. Conduct In-House Staff Training Seminars

Sharing information among staff members is a key ingredient in providing dependable reference service. Periodic meetings and seminars encourage the exchange of ideas and allow staff members to discuss problems and solutions which can enhance reference services. Training is especially useful to newer staff but also will benefit experienced librarians who function as mentors.

8. Initiate a Collection Development Policy for Pro Se Materials

Development of self-help collections reflects the growing need to accommodate patrons who are handling their own legal problems. Several publishers such as Nolo Press[37] and Oceana[38] provide many self-help titles so law libraries can easily collect materials for lay patrons. An annotated bibliography of self-help books compiled by Southern Illinois University Law Library personnel can facilitate that process.[39] SIU also maintains the Self Help Legal Center web page to assist pro se patrons.[40]

9. Provide Directions to Access Free Internet Resources

Librarians should develop a sheet showing patrons how to access free legal websites. The handout should list the URLs for the key federal and state government sites[41] as well as sites that provide easy access to legal information.[42] A short disclaimer may be added to indicate that the library does not endorse any of the websites listed. Libraries also must consider how to address the access and printing needs of the public in using the Internet. Some government depository libraries may designate a particular computer for accessing those electronic materials.

V. NEW PROGRAMS AND INITIATIVES FOR SERVING THE PRO SE PATRON

Librarians have provided assistance to the pro se population when others seemed unable to help. Public libraries continue to assist pro se patrons, although materials and expertise may be limited. Law libraries are the logical choice to provide assistance in legal research and information. In some communities cross referrals involving law libraries, courts, law schools, and public libraries are quite common.[43]

Economics and political action fueled the development of legal assistance programs to help those with problems in criminal law, landlord tenant law, consumer law, and other legal areas. However, many are still unrepresented and this unmet need triggered the development of innovative programs to make the system more user-friendly for the non-lawyer.[44]

A. Court Assistance

As courts adapt to greater participation by unrepresented litigants, the "no legal advice" signs which once greeted courthouse visitors may become a relic of the past.[45] New approaches recognize the needs of pro se litigants and plan for their participation by training court personnel to provide assistance.[46] Although a few programs involve the law librarian in the process,[47] most provide staff attorneys or non-lawyer support personnel in public contact positions.[48]

Idaho's addition of courthouse assistance offices now provides skilled help to those using the justice system.[49] Self-help centers or similar programs have been meeting the needs of pro se litigants in Arizona, Colorado, and other states for several years.[50] The common goal of these programs is the delivery of detailed legal assistance and instruction. Even with this progress, some jurisdictions are not addressing pro se concerns.[51] Alabama, for example, apparently is taking a wait-and-see approach to their state's unrepresented litigants after reviewing other programs.[52]

B. Electronic Options

Electronic assistance from legal software and websites provides another resource for pro se researchers that may raise the unusual information vs. advice question. Although objections to self-help books were resolved years ago in the controversy surrounding Norman Dacey's book *How to Avoid Probate,*[53] the availability of legal software covering the same topics resulted in new concerns.[54] In Texas, the Unauthorized Practice of Law (UPL) Committee argued that "Quicken Family Lawyer," a software program designed to assist in the preparation of probate forms among other legal documents, was actually a "cyberlawyer" practicing law without a Texas license.[55] Although the federal district court agreed with the UPL committee, the Texas legislature amended the statute to exclude software from the definition of unauthorized practice.[56]

The public also can seek assistance online using any of the many websites devoted to law.[57] The range of online services may include simple information, answers to legal questions, or law firm advertisements with fee quotes. Websites even offer legal services via auction.[58] These developments generate the same questions faced by reference librarians and prompted this analysis by Professor Geoffrey Hazard, "The question of whether they are offering information or legal advice obviously at some point becomes a question of intensity and detail."[59] Also relevant are the comparisons to medical information and advice,[60] which are repeated when legal websites are discussed.[61] Distinguishing information from legal advice on the Internet may be no easier than doing so in the library.

C. Role of Non-Lawyers

Using specially trained non-lawyers to perform limited legal functions is one option suggested to address the growing need for legal assistance.[62] Proposals involving lay assistance address the high cost of legal services by assigning less complex tasks to less costly personnel. As these methods become more accepted, the character and scope of law practice may drastically change.[63]

Even though the practice of law changes slowly, the old model of lawyer-client representation is being aggressively challenged. Not only are non-lawyers beginning to perform some of the simpler legal tasks, but attorneys are parsing their representation packages into discrete tasks and pricing them per piece. This "unbundling" of legal services is a response to the public's resistance to high-cost representation in favor of limited help on complex legal issues.[64] If clients assume more responsibility for basic legal issues, the law librarian's role may increase as the client's need for research assistance increases as the lawyer's responsibilities are redefined. The client then must resolve the legal issues not handled by the lawyer, probably by using a law library.

VI. CONCLUSION

The role of law librarians in the delivery of legal services is changing as the legal profession reacts to new attitudes and approaches to the law. Law libraries initially were designed to serve judges, lawyers, professors, and students. As the legal profession changed and legal fees increased, more laypersons began using law libraries. Reference librarians found themselves helping more and more unrepresented patrons, which increased the concerns about the unauthorized practice of law.

At the same time, public libraries, courts, governmental agencies, and other institutions were dealing with restrictions on helping the pro se population. As the problems became acute, the need for guidance was met by self-help books, legal assistance programs, and other initiatives. Law librarians provided what help was allowed, supported the efforts of others to resolve the problem, and encouraged the distribution of legal information and assistance. However, the direct delivery of legal advice was uniformly discouraged except in limited circumstances. Law librarians continued to advocate free and open access to legal information. This support role is as important as ever with the changes in how people choose their legal resources and information.

The Internet provides a myriad of options from "ask a lawyer" websites to legal information repositories, legal advertisements, and self help centers. Patrons who earlier visited the law library as their only option now have many choices. The legal assistance centers operated by state and local agencies have pre-empted law libraries in some cities and legal software may be selected over law libraries by others. The legal profession now offers pro bono help and unbundled services to lower the costs of legal representation.

Law libraries may see fewer pro se patrons as participation in these new programs increases. Law librarians must still be vigilant to avoid the unauthorized practice of law, but the information access function is even more important as the legal resources expand and legal research methods evolve. Some patrons will still come to the library seeking "free legal advice" and librarians must respond with help that stops short of practicing law.

NOTES

1. *See* STEPHEN GILLERS & ROY D. SIMON, REGULATION OF LAWYERS, STATUTES AND STANDARDS (2000) (includes the MODEL RULES OF PROFESSIONAL CONDUCT (1983)). Rule 5.5 covers the unauthorized practice of law.

2. *See, e.g.,* Yvette Brown, *From the Reference Desk to the Jail House: Unauthorized Practice of Law and Librarians,* 13(4) LEGAL REFERENCE SERVICES Q. 31 (1994); Paul D. Healey, *In Search of the Delicate Balance: Legal and Ethical Questions in Assisting the Pro Se Patron,* 90 L. LIBR. J. 129, 134 (1998); Robin K. Mills, *Reference Service vs. Legal Advice: Duties vs. Liabilities,* 72 L. LIBR. J. 180 (1979).

3. *See* JUSTINE FISCHER, UNAUTHORIZED PRACTICE HANDBOOK: A COMPILATION OF STATUTES, CASES AND COMMENTARY ON THE UNAUTHORIZED PRACTICE OF LAW (Justine Fischer & Dorothy H. Lachmann eds., 1972).

4. Madison Mosley, Jr., *The Authorized Practice of Legal Reference Service,* 87 L. LIBR. J. 203, 204 (1995).

5. *Id.* at 205.

6. Brown, *supra* note 3, at 34.

7. AALL Code of Ethics, *in* AALL Directory and Handbook, 1999-2000, at 379 (1999).

8. *Id.*

9. Robert T. Begg, *The Reference Librarian and the Pro Se Patron*, 69 L. Libr. J. 26 (1976).

10. Mosley, *supra* note 4, at 209.

11. Moses Aspan, *Note, Assisting the Pro Se Litigant: Unauthorized Practice or the Fulfillment of a Public Need?*, 28 N.Y.L. Sch. L. Rev. 691 (1983).

12. *See* Cameron Allen, *Whom Shall We Serve: Secondary Patrons of the University Law School Library*, 66 L. Libr. J. 160 (1973); Brown, *supra* note 6, at 32-33; Carleton Kenyon, *The Mission of the Legal Reference Librarian*, 58 L. Libr. J. 123 (1965).

13. *See* Brown, *supra* note 3, at 33 (quoting Peter C. Schanck, *Unauthorized Practice of Law and the Legal Reference Librarian*, 72 L. Libr. J. 57, 62 (1979).

14. *See* Va. State Bar Ass'n UPL Op. 152 (1991); *see also* Va. State Bar Ass'n UPL Op. 161 (1994).

15. Brown, *supra* note 3, at 32.

16. Mosley, *supra* note 4, at 207.

17. Brown, *supra* note 3, at 33.

18. *See* Healey, *supra* note 3, at 146; Paul D. Healey, *Chicken Little at the Reference Desk: The Myth of Librarian Liability*, 87 L. Libr. J. 515 (1995); Mosley, *supra* note 4, at 209.

19. *See, e.g.*, C.C. Kirkwood & Tim Watts, *Legal Reference Service: Duties v. Liabilities*, Legal Reference Services Q., Summer 1983, at 67; Gerome Leone, *Malpractice Liability of a Law Librarian?*, 73 L. Libr. J. 44 (1980); Maria E. Protti, *Dispensing Law at the Front Lines: Ethical Dilemmas in Law Librarianship*, 40 Libr. Trends 234 (1991).

20. Sally K. Hilander, *Unauthorized Practice Linked to Unmet Pro Bono Need*, Mont. Law., Dec. 23, 1997, at 1.

21. Healey, *supra* note 18; Mills, *supra* note 3, at 192.

22. AALL Code of Ethics, *supra* note 7.

23. *See* Mosley, *supra* note 4, at 205.

24. White v. White, 886 F.2d 721, 725 (4th Cir. 1989).

25. *See* Laremont-Lopez v. Southeastern Tidewater Opportunity Ctr., 968 F. Supp. 1074 (E.D. Va. 1997); Johnson v. Board of County Comm'rs, 868 F. Supp. 1226, 1231 (D. Colo. 1994).

26. *Id.* Johnson, 868 F. Supp. at 1231.

27. *See* Healey, *supra* note 21, at 520.

28. AALL Code of Ethics, *supra* note 7.

29. *See supra* note 3.

30. Peter C. Schanck, *Unauthorized Practice of Law and the Legal Reference Librarian*, 72 L. Libr. J. 57, 62 (1995).

31. Brown, *supra* note 3, at 41.

32. ABA, *Lawyer Referral Services* (visited June 16, 2000) <http://www.abanet.org/referral/home.html>.

33. This information is posted on the CBA website along with numerous other helpful community contacts. Chicago Bar Ass'n, *Where to Go for Legal Assistance in Chicago* (visited June 16, 2000) <http://www.chicagobar.org/public/whereto.html>.

34. Brown, *supra* note 3, at 41; Mills, *supra* note 3, at 192; Schanck, *supra* note 30, at 64.

35. Brown, *supra* note 3, at 42; Mills *supra* note 3, at 192.

36. Mills, *supra* note 3, at 193.

37. *See* Nolo.com, *Law for All* (visited June 16, 2000) <http://www.nolopress.com>.

38. The Legal Almanac Series by Oceana Publications provides 50 "Law for the Layperson" titles edited by Margaret Jasper. Oceana Publications, *Oceana Online Direct* (visited June 16, 2000) <http://www.oceanalaw.com/>.

39. *See* FRANK G. HOUDEK, LAW FOR THE LAYMAN: AN ANNOTATED BIBLIOGRAPHY OF SELF-HELP LAW BOOKS (1991); JEAN M. MCKNIGHT, LAW FOR THE LAYPERSON: AN ANNOTATED BIBLIOGRAPHY OF SELF-HELP LAW BOOKS (2d ed. 1997).

40. Southern Illinois Univ. Sch. of Law, *Self Help Legal Center* (visited June 16, 2000) <http://www.law.siu.edu/selfhelp/>. The center was selected as a recipient of the 2000 Louis M. Brown Award for Legal Access given by the American Bar Association Standing Committee on the Delivery of Legal Services. *Id.*

41. *See, e.g.*, Superintendent of Documents, U.S. Government Printing Office, *GPO Access* (visited June 16, 2000) <http://www.access.gpo.gov/su_docs>; Library of Congress, *Thomas: Legislative Information on the Internet* (visited June 16, 2000) <http://thomas.loc.gov>.

42. The following sites and others offer comprehensive information on legal subjects. *See* Americounsel, *Quality Legal Services. Flat Fees* (visited June 12, 2000) <http://www.americounsel.com>; Findlaw, *Ignorance of the Law Is No Excuse* (visited June 12, 2000) <http://www.findlaw.com>; *TheLaw.com* (visited June 12, 2000) <http://www.thelaw.com>; *USLaw.com* (visited June 12, 2000) <http://www.uslaw.com>. For a listing of additional Internet resources, see the article in this volume by W. David Gay and Jim Jackson, *Creating and Using Web Resources to Train Attorneys: An Experience with the State Bar.*

43. Begg, *supra* note 9, at 32.

44. *See* Hilander, *supra* note 20; Deborah L. Rhode, *Too Much Law, Too Little Justice: Too Much Rhetoric, Too Little Reform*, 11 GEO. J. LEGAL ETHICS 989 (1991); JONA GOLDSCHMIDT, MEETING THE CHALLENGE OF PRO SE LITIGATION: A REPORT AND GUIDEBOOK FOR JUDGES AND COURT MANAGERS (1998).

45. John M. Greasen, *"No Legal Advice From Court Personnel" What Does That Mean?*, JUDGES' J., Winter 1995, at 10.

46. *See, e. g.*, John M. Greacen, *How Fair, Fast and Cheap Should Courts Be? Instead of Letting Lawyers and Judges Decide, New Mexico Asked Its Customers*, 82 JUDICATURE 287 (1999); J. Thomas Greene, *A Kinder, Gentler Justice System*, JUDGES' J., Summer 1999, at 22; David Reichert, *Video Aids Pro Se Litigants*, 83 JUDICATURE 210 (2000); GOLDSCHMIDT, *supra* note 44.

47. The Montana State Law Library is directly involved with the 1st Judicial District Court in the State Law Library Advice Clinic. *See* Beth Lynch Murphy, *Results of a National Survey of Pro Se Assistance Programs: A Preliminary Report in* NA-

TIONAL CONFERENCE ON PRO SE LITIGATION: COURSE MATERIALS (American Judicature Society & ABA Standing Committee on the Delivery of Legal Services eds., 1999) (materials from the meeting in Scottsdale, Ariz. held Nov. 18-21, 1999).

48. GOLDSCHMIDT, *supra* note 44.

49. Patrick D. Costello, *Courthouse Assistance Offices*, ADVOC. (Idaho), June 1999, at 13.

50. GOLDSCHMIDT, *supra* note 44, at 72-73, 84.

51. John Gibeaut, *Turning Pro Se: The Number of Unrepresented Clients is Growing, but Few Courts Have Developed Policies in Response*, A.B.A. J., Jan. 1999, at 28.

52. Wade Baxley, *Please Mr. Custer, I Don't Wanna Go*, 61 ALA. LAW. 6, 8 (2000).

53. New York County Lawyers' Ass'n v. Dacey, 234 N.E.2d 459 (N.Y. 1967) (discussing NORMAN F. DACEY, HOW TO AVOID PROBATE (1965)).

54. *See* William H. Brown, Comment, *Legal Software and the Unauthorized Practice of Law: Protection or Protectionaism*, 36 CAL. W. L. REV. 157 (1999).

55. *See* Pat Newcombe, *Web Regulation Battle Heats Up*, AM. LIBR., Nov. 1999, at 50 (discussing Unauthorized Practice of Law Comm. v. Parsons Technology, Inc., No. 3:97-CV-2859-H, 1999 WL 47235 (N.D. Tex. Jan. 22, 1999), *vacated and remanded*, 179 F.3d 956 (5th Cir. 1999)).

56. *Id.* at 51. The Texas Legislature enacted an amendment to TEX. GOV'T CODE ANN. § 81.101(a) providing that "the 'practice of law' does not include the design, creation, publication, distribution, display, or sale . . . [of] computer software, or similar products if the products clearly and conspicuously state that the products are not a substitute for the advice of an attorney," by H.B. 1507, 76th Leg., Reg. Sess. (Tex. 1999). Unauthorized Practice of Law Comm. v. Parsons Technology, Inc., 179 F.3d 956, 956 (5th Cir. 1999).

57. *See supra* note 42.

58. *See* Mark Voorhees, *Legal Services on the Cyberauction Block*, LEGAL TIMES, May 29, 2000, at 24.

59. Terry Carter, *Checkbook Credibility?*, A.B.A. J., June 2000, at 50, 52 (quoting Geoffrey Hazard).

60. *See* Mosley, *supra* note 4, at 207.

61. Carter, *supra* note 58, at 50.

62. *See* Deborah L. Rhode, *Meet Needs with Nonlawyers: It Is Time to Accept Lay Practitioners–and Regulate Them*, A.B.A. J., Jan. 1996, at 104.

63. *See* Charles L. Brieant, *Is It the End of the Legal World as We Know It?*, 1999 PACE L. REV. 21; *Defining and Redefining Professionalism: Assessing the Roles and Regulation of Lawyers in the Twenty-First Century*, 27 FLA. ST. U. L. REV. 205 (1999); Robert W. Minto, Jr., *The Future of the Legal Profession and the Organized Bar*, 43 ADVOC. (IDAHO), Feb. 2000, at 21.

64. *See* Forest S. Mosten, *Unbundling Legal Services*, OR. ST. B. BULL, Jan. 1997, at 9.

User Fees in Academic Law Libraries

Kumar Percy

SUMMARY. Fees for services in 58 academic law libraries are reviewed using results from a national questionnaire and interviews with law library staff. Five fee-based services were investigated: printing, document delivery, reference services, unaffiliated borrowing, and library

Kumar Percy is Reserve and Media Services Librarian at Jamail Center for Legal Research, Tarlton Law Library, University of Texas School of Law, 727 East Dean Keeton Street, Austin, TX 78705 (E-mail: kpercy@mail.law.utexas.edu).

The author would like to acknowledge the support of Roy M. Mersky, John Edwards, Jill Duffy, Eric Glass, Melinda Johnson, Keith Stiverson, Tobe Liebert, and Betsy Springgate.

[Haworth co-indexing entry note]: "User Fees in Academic Law Libraries." Percy, Kumar. Co-published simultaneously in *Legal Reference Services Quarterly* (The Haworth Information Press, an imprint of The Haworth Press, Inc.) Vol. 19, No. 1/2, 2001, pp. 181-205; and: *Emerging Solutions in Reference Services: Implications for Libraries in the New Millennium* (ed: John D. Edwards) The Haworth Information Press, an imprint of The Haworth Press, Inc., 2001, pp. 181-205. Single or multiple copies of this article are available for a fee from The Haworth Document Delivery Service [1-800-342-9678, 9:00 a.m.-5:00 p.m. (EST). E-mail address: getinfo@haworthpressinc.com].

access. The primary factors influencing fees include: the reason for the fee, the type of services, geographic location, and whether the law school is private or public. Additional factors include the receptiveness of the student body to the fees and the impact the fee may have on fund-raising. Libraries should consider reevaluating fee policies based on the data presented. *[Article copies available for a fee from The Haworth Document Delivery Service: 1-800-342-9678. E-mail address: <getinfo@haworthpressinc. com> Website: <http://www.HaworthPress.com>* © *2001 by The Haworth Press, Inc. All rights reserved.]*

I. INTRODUCTION

The success of Internet-based companies is forcing every organization to rethink "business as usual." For law libraries this may mean that it is time to reevaluate fee-based services. The Internet economy is largely founded upon a "follow the free" principle. The idea is to give away basic services or products and charge for enhancements and extra services.[1] This is similar to the model that many libraries are using: provide basic access for free, but charge for extra services such as laser printing or document delivery. However, while Internet based services are booming, libraries have seen a dramatic drop in usage.

One study of academic libraries found a 10% decline in reference questions from 1994 to 1996.[2] Although data for academic law libraries is limited, Association of Research Libraries' statistics indicate that this is a national trend.[3] Between 1997 and 1998, for example, the University of Michigan reported a 71% decrease in reference transactions while the University of Oklahoma had a 60% decrease in circulation.[4] In law libraries much of that traffic may be going to commercial online companies such as Westlaw and LEXIS as well as free web-based reference services such as Ask Jeeves[5] or Webhelp.[6] Ask Jeeves reports that usage typically grows by 46% each quarter.[7] In the year ending April 1, 2000, researchers "Asked Jeeves" 697.3 million queries.[8] This figure is almost two and one-half times the number of reference transactions in all U.S. public libraries combined during 1996.[9]

Because identifying current practices is the first step in a reevaluation, this article describes what academic law libraries charge for various services and why.[10] This study is primarily based on responses to a questionnaire sent to law library directors and staff through two electronic mailing lists: law-lib,[11] a list for law librarians, and law libdir-l, the law library directors' listserv. The survey is reprinted in Appendix A. Additionally, the research is supplemented through interviews and correspondence with academic law librarians. In order to better focus the results, the analysis is limited to five common types of fee-based services: computer printing, document delivery, reference services, borrowing privileges, and library access.

II. LIBRARY FEES

A. Types of Fees

Libraries charge a variety of fees and each accomplishes a different goal. Before setting a fee, a library must identify the goals behind the charge and then select the type of fee that will best achieve those objectives. A specific fee can fall into one or more of the following categories:[12]

- *Compliance Fees:* charged in an effort to force good behavior, e.g., overdue fees;
- *Cost Recovery, Partial:* used to collect only out-of-pocket or direct costs of materials;
- *Cost Recovery, Total:* charged to recoup the indirect labor and administrative costs as well as direct costs;
- *External Fees:* levied only on outside patrons for specific service;
- *Internal Fees:* collected from the library's primary clientele;
- *Generalized User Fees:* levied on the outside public for use of the library;
- *Restrictive Charges:* used to restrict usage when patron demand for a service is greater than the library can afford to provide;
- *Uniform Transaction Fees:* assessed for all transactions of a particular type, e.g., interlibrary loan fees.

The purpose behind a service fee also has implications on the method of calculating the price charged. If cost recovery is the only issue, identifying the direct and indirect expenses of the services is all that need be done.[13] If the library is interested in supplementing its budget, a market survey as well as a cost analysis may be appropriate.[14] A library can only make a profit if it knows what customers will pay and what the competition is charging. Similarly, setting a fee that will limit library usage requires knowledge of what patrons will pay, and then establishing a fee slightly higher than that figure.

B. Policy Considerations

1. Arguments Against Library User Fees

The primary argument against charging fees is that information is a public good that should be free to every citizen in a democracy. Citizens cannot effectively participate in representative government without access to information, especially the law. Charging for extra services limits the poor's access to the law and to government. Just as police and fire departments do not have tiered services, neither should libraries.[15] Fees pose a similar problem in academic law libraries when some students cannot afford access to the same library services as others.

Library fees also may be seen as a double taxation or charge.[16] Students who pay thousands of dollars for tuition do not want to pay extra for library services. Similarly, the public does not want to pay for services in a library funded by tax dollars. This is especially true for public law schools, where it may be politically difficult to charge taxpayers fees for basic services.

Organizations that rely on fees to finance the library may be tempted to divert too many resources to the paying customer instead of fully sustaining the free basic services to faculty and students.[17] In this way fees can undermine the library's primary mission of supporting the law school's clientele.

Fees also pose a morale and marketing problem for academic law libraries. Students can become resentful about paying library fees in addition to already expensive tuition. Additionally, fees can alienate the people most likely to make donations to the law school: alumni and members of the bar. They may be less likely to donate if fees make it difficult for them to use library services.[18]

A practical argument against charging fees is that the cost of administration can be greater than the revenues generated.[19] For example, in some libraries the direct and indirect expenses of charging for laser printing may be more than the costs to subsidize the printing. Systems to control printing can be expensive and difficult to administer. A library then has to decide if there are other intangible benefits of the fees that outweigh the administrative costs. In this example the value of avoiding wasted printouts may be greater than the fee collection costs.

The American Library Association opposes all economic barriers to information in libraries primarily funded by the public. An ALA Interpretation of the Library Bill of Rights calls for libraries to "resist the temptation to impose user fees to alleviate financial pressures, at long term cost to institutional integrity and public confidence in libraries."[20] The ALA's Intellectual Freedom Committee has stated that libraries should not provide any services that they cannot afford to provide for free.[21]

The American Association of Law Libraries does not specifically address library fees as part of its own Ethical Principles. However, the Principles do call for libraries to "promote open and effective access to legal and related information."[22] Some fees could be seen as violating the spirit of this tenet of open access.

2. Arguments Supporting Library User Fees

In academic law libraries the strongest argument for charging a fee is to protect the interests of the primary patrons: students, faculty and law school staff. A problem many academic law libraries face is that services to outside patrons diminish their ability to serve primary patrons. A library cannot afford to provide all requested services for free, since doing so could devastate most budgets.[23] It is possible to control patron demands by providing basic services for free while charging for enhanced services.

The AALL Ethical Principles require that libraries "provide zealous services using the most appropriate resources and implementing programs consistent with our institution's mission and goals."[24] If the demands of unaffiliated patrons are depleting the library's budget to the detriment of the student body and faculty, it may be appropriate to charge outside patrons for some services. Fees could limit the toll the service takes on the library's resources and could supplement the school's budget.

At one time, for example, students could not study at the Golden Gate University Law Library because of the large number of outside patrons. In response, the library began to charge for admission, primarily as a cost-recovery method of limiting usage by unaffiliated patrons but also to preserve library resources for the primary clientele.[25]

Although information is a public good, Americans always have paid for some public goods such as toll roads and national parks.[26] Now that the country is moving towards an information-based economy, patrons seem more comfortable with paying for information services than ever before.[27] Another argument for fees is that entrepreneurial programs will bring the efficiencies of the marketplace into the library.[28] By charging fees the library will effectively become part of the new economy. A collateral benefit is that it may increase the value society places on libraries and librarians.[29]

Pay services can be effective advertising. By assisting patrons outside of the law school, the library is marketing its available resources.[30] Lawyers might rather pay for enhanced services such as document delivery or reference than not have access to them at all. Additionally, those who are aided by the library would logically be more likely to become supporters.[31]

Service fees can provide an additional revenue stream. The extra money can help enhance the library's free services.[32] Academic law libraries can use the funds in other ways as well, such as purchasing practitioner-oriented materials or databases they could not otherwise afford or hiring staff to provide support for outside patrons.[33]

III. SURVEY RESULTS AND RESEARCH FINDINGS

Survey responses from 58 academic law libraries provided data from throughout the United States between November 1999 and January 2000 (as listed in Appendix B).[34] The majority of these responses, 36, came from private schools while 22 came from public schools. A wide range of libraries responded from varying academic tiers with vastly different budgets and user bases. The average tuition of the respondents was $14,830, with an average student body of 692.[35]

A. Printing Fees

1. Policy Considerations for Printing Fees

Laser printing fees are used for various purposes: recover the cost of printing, restrict wasteful printing, or even to teach proper research techniques. Implementing printing charges involves considerations about free access to library materials, student receptivity, the types of items printed, and the way patrons are printing.

A frequent argument against print charges is that patrons prefer to read articles on paper rather than on a computer screen. Printing costs are a barrier to information because only patrons who can afford to print documents will be able to comfortably read them. Printing can be a hot-button issue with law students who pay thousands of dollars and do not want to spend more. Several schools have privately decided that the easiest way to maintain student morale is to give them free printing.

Computer resources were supposed to create a paperless society; instead, printing levels in libraries have risen rather than declined.[36] Printing takes far less effort for a patron than photocopying. With unlimited free printing rights, patrons are inclined to print an item before determining if it is necessary or useful. In some libraries with free printing, hundreds of unclaimed printouts are discarded each day. Besides being destructive to the environment, this behavior is not an effective use of resources. Charging students for this service should cause most to evaluate the research value of each document before printing it.

Another argument for charging printing fees is that libraries should not pay for private copies of information. While librarians are concerned about providing more access to online services, users are in effect creating personal copies that will not be shared. Additionally, patrons using computers designated for research often print non-legal information such as stock quotes, sports scores, or e-mail. It may not be appropriate for libraries to cover those expenses.

Printing charges also can be an effective way to teach thoughtful and cost-effective legal research skills. Outside of academia, legal online databases may charge clients for each printed page. No one can afford the luxury of wasting money on hundreds of unwanted pages. Some survey respondents believe that if libraries subsidize this poor research behavior, they squander the opportunity to teach students effective research methods.

A unique aspect of academic law libraries is that Westlaw and LEXIS have given many schools laser printers so students can print Westlaw or LEXIS documents at no charge.[37] A few libraries have denied students access to these printers because free printing hampers the school's interest in teaching good research skills. Others disagree, arguing that laser printing charges are only a cost recovery fee and not a teaching tool; they provide free printing so students can save money.

2. Survey Results for Printing Fees

Although every school in this study charges for photocopies, only 59% of the responding libraries charge students for printing (34 libraries) (see Table 1). Of those schools, 20 were private and 14 were public, representing 56% of the private libraries responding and 64% of the public libraries. Many schools that charge for printing (59%) provide no free access to Westlaw and LEXIS stand-alone printers.[38]

Libraries primarily charge printing fees in order to recoup expenses (82%), which is also the main reason given for photocopy charges. Slightly more than one-half of the libraries charge the same price for printing as for photocopies, an average of 10 cents a page. However, nearly one-third charge less for printing:

- Libraries with Same Price to Print and Photocopy–53% (18)
- Libraries where it is Cheaper to Print than Photocopy –32% (11)
- Libraries where it is More Expensive to Print than Photocopy – 15% (5)

The reasons given by libraries for printing and photocopying fees include:

Fee Justification	Printing	Photocopying
Recoup Expenses	65% (22)	76% (26)
Recoup Expenses and Limit Usage	17% (6)	0
Controlled by University or Other Organization	12% (4)	9% (3)
Limit Usage	6% (2)	0
Supplement Budget	0	9% (3)
Recoup Expenses and Supplement Budget	0	6% (2)

TABLE 1. Prices Charged for Printing

Name of School	Price per Page	Free Pages
American University	$0.10	250 / semester
Boston University	$0.10 (Discounted to $0.05)	500 / year
Drake University	$0.10	300 / year
Florida State University	$0.18 (Discounted to $0.075)	
Georgia State University	$0.05	200 / semester
Harvard University	$0.05	100 / semester
Marquette University	$0.05	200 / year
Mercer University	$0.05	400 / semester
North Carolina Central University	$0.05	200 / year
Northwestern University	$0.05	100 / semester
Pace University	$0.10	50 / semester
Roger Williams University	$0.10	
Southern Illinois University	$0.08	
Southern Methodist University	$0.09	1000 / year
St. John's University	$0.08	250
Stetson University	$0.05	50 / 1st year; 40 / 2nd year, 30 / 3rd year
Touro College	$0.10 (Discounted to $0.05)	250 at beginning of law school
University of Florida	$0.10	
University of California–Boalt Hall	$0.10	1,000 / year
University of Chicago	$0.05	1,000 / year
University of Connecticut	$0.05	
University of Georgia	$0.10	
University of Idaho	$0.05	500 / semester
University of LaVerne	$0.15 (Discounted to $0.10)	
University of Mississippi	$0.12	
University of Richmond	$0.10	300 / semester
University of San Diego	$0.10	
University of Texas	$0.10	
University of Washington	$0.04 ($0.08 for 2 sided page)	750 / year LEXIS & 750 / year Westlaw
University of Wisconsin	$0.07	
Valparaiso University	$0.05	400 / year
Washburn University	$0.10 for non-students after 10 free pages	Free for students
Washington and Lee University	$0.10 (subsidized groups pay $.05)	800 at beginning of law school
Yale University	$0.07	1,000 at beginning of law school

A regularly updated source for information on printing charges can be found at the site maintained by Joyce Manna Janto at the University of Richmond Law Library.[39] The Richmond site includes information from more than 80 schools on print charges, the number of free pages provided, and the tracking system used, such as PCounter and Venda-Card.

B. Document Delivery Fees

1. Policy Considerations for Document Delivery Fees

Document delivery charges are created to finance a service that the library could not otherwise afford to provide to unaffiliated patrons. The service closely resembles the "follow the free" Internet business model. Those who enter the law library can research the law for free. However, the libraries also provide the extra service of delivering a specific item for a fee.

Some libraries maintain lower prices to encourage usage, while others charge a higher fee to discourage excessive requests. Information always has a price, either the expense of personal time researching free information, or the financial cost of having someone deliver it. As society becomes more comfortable with paying for information services, entire industries are growing around information retrieval.[40] Document delivery services in academic law libraries are supplying the needs of patrons who do not have the time to retrieve needed information. The clients of law firms may benefit the most, since document delivery charges are often much lower than an attorney's hourly fee.[41]

Although document delivery services may be new to some law libraries, a study of business patrons in academic libraries found the users often were not able to go to the library to conduct research. The study revealed that charging for document delivery services was an effective research tool for secondary patrons who could not go to the library.[42]

Document delivery also has other benefits. Alumni and local attorneys who take advantage of the service may be more likely to be supporters of the law school, either financially or in other ways.[43] Additionally, fees may provide funds to purchase items the library could not otherwise afford.[44]

Another consideration is who should administer the delivery service. Document delivery requests provide information about patrons' needs, and some librarians believe the reference staff should be involved in this program at least enough to know what is being requested. Reference librarians are an integral part of collection development because they answer reference questions and know the trends in legal scholarship. However, most document delivery services at the libraries surveyed do not involve the reference staff. Only five of the libraries utilize the reference staff in document delivery. Two of the libraries have the entire public services department work on requests. Two others have the reference staff answer the questions in conjunction with the circulation staff. Only one library has the reference staff alone work on document delivery. Document delivery information can be useful in collection development decisions if those filling the delivery requests also help select items for purchase.

2. Survey Results for Document Delivery Fees

Document delivery services are found in 43% of the libraries included in the survey (25 libraries) (see Table 2). Those programs tend to be at public schools (59% or 13 of responding public schools as opposed to 33% or 12 of the private schools).

The majority of the libraries stated that they levy fees primarily to recoup expenses.[45] Some indicate that limiting library usage by unaffiliated patrons is a concern. Others use fees to supplement the library's budget. Market research studies were conducted by 48% of the libraries to determine pricing, which may indicate an interest in more than cost recovery. Fees based on market studies are usually intended to make a profit or limit the demands on the services.[46]

Document delivery charges normally are based upon a set per-document price with an additional charge per page. The per-page prices increase if the document is faxed, and an added charge applies if there is a long distance fax number or a rush request. [47] Three libraries varied from this format with two charging an hourly fee for labor and a third charging a membership fee for document delivery services and library access privileges.

Only two schools mentioned copyright charges as part of the expenses. A large portion of the requests involved government documents which are free of copyright. For most academic journals it is difficult to identify who will collect copyright fees and how much they charge to authorize copies. The process is easier if the journal is represented by a copyright clearinghouse service that can collect reprint fees for several publications at once. Two such services are Copyright Clearance Center[48] and the new company iCopyright.[49] However, these organizations do not currently represent most law journals. Because of the difficulty of paying copyright royalties, libraries may not be collecting them and instead may be relying on the patron to pay them directly to the copyright holder.

C. Reference Services Fees

1. Policy Considerations for Fee-Based Reference Services

Fee-based reference services involve many of the same considerations as document delivery fees. Services are usually created to support the needs of unaffiliated patrons who are willing to pay someone to research a legal question. These services are usually not intended to generate a profit but can help cover staff costs and fund the purchase of materials needed to provide the service.[50]

Reference fees also can be used to limit the resources allocated to unaffiliated patrons. Some academic law libraries are at risk of being overwhelmed by reference questions from the local bar, especially if the library is located in an urban area with a large legal community.

2. Survey Results for Fee-Based Reference Services

Fee-based reference services are very rare; only two responding libraries had them–one public and one private.[51] Both schools have large enrollments and are located near large populations of lawyers, one in New York City and the other in the San Francisco Bay Area.

In order to establish the fee, one library used market surveys and the other used cost calculations. The University of California–Boalt Hall charges $25 per 15 minutes to answer reference questions. Pace University provides reference for $60 per hour to unaffiliated members who pay annual fees ranging from $100 to $600.[52] Both libraries charge the fees primarily to recoup their expenses. By charging an annual membership fee, Pace also is trying to limit the impact that unaffiliated patrons will have on the library's ability to serve its primary patrons.

TABLE 2. Fees Charged for Document Delivery

Name of School	Document Charge Mail	Page Charge Mail	Document Charge Fax	Page Charge Fax
Boston University	$20		$20	
Golden Gate University	$5; $15 Rush	$0.20	$15 for same day	$0.20
Lewis and Clark College	$30 / hour for labor [Courier delivery downtown: $10 checkout charge + $7.50 first book delivered + $5 each additional book]	$0.15	$30 / hour for labor	$0.15–Local Call $0.30–Long Distance
Louisiana State	$8.50	$0.25	$8.50	$0.25
Marquette University	$10	$0.30	$10	$0.50–Local Call $1–Long Distance
Mercer University	$2	$0.25	$2	$1.75
Michigan State	Online Articles only: 50% of Fee Charged by Online Vendor (Available Only to Alumni Ass'n Members)		Same as Mail	
Mississippi College	$10	$0.20	$10	$0.50
Pace University	$5; $10 Rush–Available only with annual fee: $100–Alumni; $150–Without access; $600–Access, Document Delivery, & Borrowing; $1800–Corporations	$5 for up to 5 pages; $1 for each additional page	Same as Mail	
Southern Illinois	$5	$0.30	$10	$1
Southern Methodist University	$10; $7.50	$0.25	$10	$0.25–Local Call $1–Long Distance
Stetson University	$3 + Postage	$0.50		
University of California-Boalt Hall	$25 / 15 minutes–Research	$0.75 overnight or pickup ($15 min.)	$25 / 15 minutes Research	$1.50-4 hour fax ($15 min.) 2.50–1 hour fax ($25 minimum)
University of Florida	$3 + Postage	$0.15	$10–up to 10 pages	
University of Georgia	$5	$0.25	$5	$1
University of Idaho	$7.50 (Attorneys only)	$0.25	$10	$0.50
University of Louisville			$5–(only for law firms outside the Louisville area)	$1.50
University of Michigan	$10; $20-rush		$10; $20-rush	
University of Mississippi	$2	$0.25	$2	$1.75
University of Oklahoma	$10 + Copyright Charges	$0.15 (first 30 pages free)	$15 + Copyright Charges	$0.20 (first 30 are free)
University of Texas	$30	$0.50	$40	$0.50
University of Washington	$15–Mail; $20–Overnight + Shipping $30–Rush (Plus $15 research fee to correct citations)	$0.10 (first 30 pages are free)	$20 $30–Rush (Plus $15 research fee to correct citations)	$0.10 (first 30 pages are free)
University of Wisconsin	$15–Standard + Tax $8–Wisconsin Non-Profit or tax exempt + tax if applicable $25–Out of State ($25–Extra for Rush) ($8–$100 + cost of search for documents from online databases)	$0.20	$15–Standard + Tax $8–Wisconsin Non-Profit or tax exempt + Tax if applicable $25–Out of State ($25–Extra for Rush)	$0.50
Washington and Lee		Cost of copies		Cost of Copies
Widener University	$5.00 (fee waived for alumni; service available for attorneys only)	$0.50	$5.00 (fee waived for; alumni; service avail-able for attorneys only)	$1

D. Borrowing Fees

1. Considerations for Borrowing Fees

Unaffiliated patrons may be charged fees for the privilege of borrowing library materials. Often administered as a compliance fee, the amount charged is intended to insure that books are returned or can be replaced if lost. In a few cases the figure is a restrictive cost recovery fee charged to limit the impact of outside patrons. Each primary patron, as a member of the student body, faculty, or staff, has a connection to the library through the law school. By definition, unaffiliated patrons have no such link to the library. Borrowing fees may be used as a deposit against the risk that the item will not be returned.

2. Survey Results for Borrowing Fees

Borrowing fees are not common in academic law libraries with only 22% of the responding libraries imposing fees. Of the 13 libraries that charge for unaffiliated library borrowing privileges, 8 are private and 5 are public (see Table 3). The primary reason given for the fee is to recoup expenses (46%).[53] Accordingly, one library charges only a refundable damage deposit. Most libraries charge an inexpensive annual membership fee, usually less than $100.[54] Only two libraries charge a per-item fee for borrowing materials. In almost every case the charge is high enough to reimburse the library for a lost law book, but not high enough to stop patrons from using the service.

Only one library used a market research study to set the borrowing fee.[55] Most calculated the cost of providing the service or guessed at a reasonable amount, indicating that the primary purpose is to recoup expenses, not to make a profit.

E. Library Access Fees

1. Considerations for Access Fees

Library access charges may be the most controversial type of fees in academic law libraries because of the significant economic barrier they impose. Fees may be, however, an effective way of limiting the amount of resources needed to support secondary patrons, while still giving them an option for using the library.

TABLE 3. Fees Charged for Borrowing Privileges

Name of School	Annual Membership	Per Item Charge
Harvard University		$25–ILL only
Lewis and Clark College	$40–Attorneys only	Document delivery downtown: $10–checkout charge + $7.50–first item borrowed +$5– each additional item per visit
Marquette University	$50–Members of the Bar, Paralegals, Librarians at Law Firms; $30–Alumni	
Mississippi College	$10	
Pace University	$100 for alumni; $150 without access; $600 for Access, Document Delivery, & & Borrowing; $1800 for Corporations	
Santa Clara University	Included in unaffiliated users' fees: $50–Recent alumni bar member; $100–Alumni bar member more than 5 years; $150–all others	
University of California– Boalt Hall		$30–2 week loan $15–2 week renewal
University of California– Hastings		[Deposit Required: $200–State Bar Member; $100–Alumni, $400–Firms]
University of Florida	$40/semester if unaffiliated with University $100 / year if unaffiliated with University	
University of Mississippi		$5 (MS attorneys oniy)
University of Richmond	Varies based on status of borrower	
University of Texas	$75–Individuals; $250–Corporations	
Valparaiso University	$15	

The main consideration is whether unaffiliated patrons are hindering the library's ability to support its primary clientele. In some urban law schools, near very large legal communities, unaffiliated usage can be so extensive that members of the law school cannot comfortably use the library. In those cases it is in the library's best interest to either close the library to outside patrons entirely or charge a fee for access. Charging fees forces the patrons to decide whether the cost of using that particular library is worth the admission fee. It also gives the library a cost recovery program to help provide services for secondary patrons. In addition, restricting access to legal information may not be as sensitive an issue in urban areas with public law libraries.[56]

A fee that restricts access to the library can alienate those who cannot or will not pay. It may adversely impact fund-raising efforts and public relations for the school. Alumni reactions were a factor considered in Golden Gate University Law Library's decision to charge access fees. Before the fees were implemented the library was unconnected to fundraising.[57] Once the fees were charged, library access became a part of alumni fundraising efforts. The development office was careful to insure that the fees did not offend potential sponsors. However, since library access was a benefit of alumni giving, several donations were the direct result of the library fees.[58] Additionally, restrictive access fees can improve the morale of a student body that would otherwise be unable to use its own library. Students at Golden Gate University were much happier once the access fee protected their ability to use the library.[59]

The library staff often may be uncomfortable with access fees.[60] Golden Gate found that its staff became more supportive of the charge once they understood that the fee was designed to protect the ability of students and faculty to use the library.[61]

Access fees are a particular problem for libraries that are also government depositories. The Government Printing Office requires that all depositories provide the public with free access to depository materials.[62] However, they still may impose access fees as long as they do not charge patrons who want to use government documents.[63] Unfortunately, many patrons may not know this rule. *The Federal Depository Library Manual* calls for depositories to publicize the availability of the collection, stating that the "most important group to target for public awareness is the general public" not just the library's primary clientele.[64] One study found that only 10-25% of private academic (not specifically law related) libraries marketed services to unaffiliated patrons. In the remaining 75-90% of libraries, only the most sophisticated patron who knew to say, "I want to use government documents" had access to the collection.[65]

2. Survey Results for Access Fees

Access fees are very rare with only seven responding libraries imposing charges. All seven are part of larger private schools with an average student body of 928 students located in urban areas with large legal communities, such as the San Francisco Bay Area, New York City, and Cambridge, Massachusetts (see Table 4).

Most libraries with access fees charge an annual membership fee and offer a daily rate. They often subsidize the fees for targeted groups, such as non-profit organizations or alumni. Most of these

TABLE 4. Fees Charged for Library Access

Name of School	Daily Usage	Annual Membership
Golden Gate University	$10–Day; $45–Week pass	$1000–Corporate; $450–Individual $250–Non-Profit
Harvard University	$5–$20	
New York University	$20 (non-profits free)	$1000–Individuals; $1500–Corporations
Pace University	$25	$100–Alumni; $450–Access Only; $600–Access, Document Delivery, & Borrowing $1800–Coporations
Santa Clara University		$50–Recent alumni bar member; $100–Alumni bar member more than 5 years; $150–all others
St. John's University		Varies
University of LaVerne	$10 (first time free)	$60

libraries do not allow unaffiliated patrons to borrow items even though they pay to use the collection.

The libraries were divided between wanting to limit usage by unaffiliated users and the goal of using the fee to supplement the budget. The reasons libraries stated for imposing access fees were: limit usage–43% (3), supplement the library budget–43% (3), and recoup expenses as well as limit usage and supplement the budget–14% (1).

The primary tool used to set the library access fees was market surveys, which were used by three libraries (43%). Most libraries mentioned that the goal was simply to discover how much the patrons would pay and set the price high enough to insure that the demands from secondary patrons did not overwhelm the library.[66] Other means used to establish access fees included: following past practice–29% (2), estimating–14% (1), and combining several tools–14% (1).

IV. CONCLUSION

Donald Riggs notes that changes in technology are forcing each library to reevaluate services to allow better planning for the future needs and expectations of the users.[67] In light of the growing information-based economy, it may be time for every academic law library to consider fee-based service.

Many of the fees studied for this article are restrictive cost-recovery charges intended to limit unaffiliated library usage. However, traffic is already decreasing in many academic law libraries.[68] Some libraries may consider reducing the price of printing, borrowing, and access fees because problems with overuse may no longer be as acute. Additionally, document delivery and reference charges can be lowered to transform them into services that can publicize the resources of the law library and the law school.

This study has not reviewed every academic law library, nor has it covered every type of user fee charged by the schools. Instead, it has identified major trends in user fees and the factors that were considered in setting them. The most important ones overall are for the library to:

1. Determine the purpose behind the fee before setting the price. Each type of fee requires different considerations. Restrictive fees, for example, should be much higher than cost-recovery fees.
2. Assess whether the value of imposing the fee is greater than the expense of collecting the fee. The value of a fee can include intangible benefits such as avoiding wasteful printing.
3. Consider the geographic location of the library. Some fees are more appropriate in urban settings with larger populations.
4. Anticipate the impact of fees on the mood of primary patrons. Students may not like to pay for some services, but may enjoy the benefits of other fees that prevent secondary patrons from depleting library assets.
5. Explore the implications of fees on the law school's ability to conduct fundraising efforts. Some could improve alumni development and others might hinder the process.
6. Review the historical basis for free or fee services, taking into account the public relations concerns in a public or private institution. Some fees are not feasible in a public library.

NOTES

1. Bernard Vavrek, *The Best Things in Life Have Fees*, AM. LIBR., May 2000, at 75.

2. *See* Steve Coffman & Susan McGlamery, *The Librarian and Mr. Jeeves*, AM. LIBR., May 2000, at 66 (noting that several libraries reported declines in usage ranging from 6% to 15% in one year).

3. The Association of Research Libraries maintains user statistics from academic law libraries. Many of the schools have reported decreases in either circulation or reference transactions. The survey results are archived on the ARL web site. Association of Research Libraries, *ARL Academic Law and Medical Library Statistics* (last modified May 1, 2000) <http://www.arl.org/stats/lawmed/>.

4. *Id.* The University of Michigan reported that between 1997 and 1998 reference transactions decreased from 14,044 transactions to 4,080. During the same period the University of Oklahoma circulation statistics (excluding renewals) decreased from 6,883 to 2,754.

5. *Ask Jeeves* (visited May 31, 2000) <http://www.askjeeves.com>.

6. *Webhelp* (visited May 31, 2000) <http://www.webhelp.com>.

7. Ask Jeeves, *Press Releases* (visited May 31, 2000) <http://www.corporateir. net/ireye/ir_site.zhtml?ticker=askj&script=400> (publishing the quarterly reports for the period April 1, 1999 through March 31, 2000). *See also* Coffman & McGlamery, *supra* note 2.

8. *See* Ask Jeeves, *supra* note 7 (publishing quarterly reports for the period April 1, 1999 through March 31, 2000: July 28, 1999 (92.3 million questions), Oct. 25, 1999 (134 million questions), Jan. 19, 2000 (196 million questions), and Apr. 19, 2000 (275 million questions)). *See also* Coffman & McGlamery, *supra* note 2.

9. NATIONAL CENTER FOR EDUCATION STATISTICS, PUBLIC LIBRARIES IN THE UNITED STATES: FY 1996 at 40 (1999) <http://nces.ed.gov/pubs99/1999306.pdf> (reporting that during 1996 the U.S. public libraries conducted 284.513 million reference transactions).

10. The author could find no methodical studies on the topic although libraries have charged fees for some time. For example, in 1984, Golden Gate University set a fee for library access. Nancy Carol Carter & Scott B. Pagel, *Fees for Service: The Golden Gate University Law Library Membership Plan*, 77 L. LIBR. J. 243 (1984-1985). In a study of non-law related urban libraries, two-thirds of the libraries studied did not have a rationale or policy for setting their fees. Evan St. Lifer & Michael Rogers, *ULC Reports Most Members Without Fee-Charging Policies*, LIBR. J., May 1, 1993 at 14.

11. Kumar Percy, *Academic Law Library Fees* (last modified Nov. 23, 1999) <http://lawlibrary.ucdavis.edu/LAWLIB/Nov99/0556.html>.

12. *See* MURRAY S. MARTIN & BETSY PARK, CHARGING AND COLLECTING FEES AND FINES: A HANDBOOK FOR LIBRARIES 8-9 (1998).

13. HERBERT SNYDER & ELISABETH DAVENPORT, COSTING AND PRICING IN THE DIGITAL AGE: A PRACTICAL GUIDE FOR INFORMATION SERVICES 119 (1997).

14. *Id.*

15. *See* Peter R. Young, *Charging Information Access Economics: New Roles for Libraries & Librarians*, 13 INFO. TECH. & LIBR. 102, 106-08 (1994).

16. *Id.*

17. *Id.*

18. *See* Carter & Pagel, *supra* note 10, at 252 (noting that the development office was concerned that access fees may offend potential donors).

19. *Id.*

20. American Library Ass'n, *Economic Barriers to Information Access: An Interpretation of the Library Bill of Rights* (last modified Oct. 10, 2000) <http://www.ala. org/alaorg/oif/econ_bar.html>.

21. American Library Ass'n, *Questions and Answers: Access to Electronic Information, Services, and Networks: An Interpretation of the Library Bill of Rights* (last modified Jan. 9, 2001) <www.ala.org/alaorg/oif/oif_q&a.html>.

22. American Ass'n of Law Libraries, *AALL Ethical Principles* (last modified Apr. 5, 1999) <http://www.aallnet.org/about/policy_ethics.asp>.

23. John A. Dunn, Jr. & Murray S. Martin, *The Whole Cost of Libraries*, 42 LIBR. TRENDS 564, 571 (1994) (stating that photocopies were originally provided for free until the libraries could no longer afford the free service).

24. American Ass'n of Law Libraries, *supra* note 22.

25. Carter & Pagel, *supra* note 10, at 245.

26. *See* Young, *supra* note 15.

27. *See* Stephen Coffman, *Fee-Based Services and the Future of Libraries*, 20 J. LIBR. ADMIN. 167, 177 (1995).

28. *Id.*

29. *See* Mark Alan Folmsbee et al., *A Primer Concerning the Imposition of Fees for Reference and Other Services in Academic Law Libraries*, 10 LEGAL REFERENCE SERVICES Q. 11, 22 (1990) (stating that fees could lead to the increased status of librarianship).

30. Vavrek, *supra* note 1, at 76.

31. *See* Carter & Pagel, *supra* note 10, at 252 (noting that because alumni giving included the benefit of library membership privileges the Golden Gate University Law Library fees were instrumental in increasing alumni donations).

32. *Id.*

33. *See* Boalt Express, *Library Services and Guides* (last modified Dec. 14, 2000) <http://www.law.berkeley.edu/library/services/bex.html> (noting that fees generated from the reference services cover the cost of staff, and other expenses); *see also* Steve Coffman & Helen Josephine, *Doing It for Money*, Libr. J., Oct. 15, 1991, at 32, 33 (noting that most fee-based reference services are not intended to be a profit-making operation, but work on a fully cost recovery basis, specifically recovering the cost of their own employees).

34. The University of Melbourne in Australia also responded. Its responses are not discussed with the others because of difference between U.S. and Australian currencies and educational systems; however, it will be mentioned in the endnotes where relevant.

35. Private school tuition averaged $19,848 with a student body of 717 compared to public schools with average tuition of $6,618 and 651 students. Tuition and enrollment are based upon entries in PRINCETON REVIEW, THE BEST LAW SCHOOLS (1999) or through direct contact with the law school administration. Enrollment figures are the combined number of full-time and part-time students. Tuition figures reflect tuition and student fees for full-time in-state students.

36. *See* Martin & Park, *supra* note 12, at 42 (reporting on PROVISIONS OF COMPUTER PRINTING CAPABILITIES TO LIBRARY PATRONS (SPEC Kit 183) (Suzanne Taylor & C. Brigid Welch eds., 1992)).

37. Although students may consider LEXIS and Westlaw access and printing as free services, law schools pay thousands of dollars annually to provide that privilege.

38. It is difficult to identify which libraries declined a free printer and which ones were never offered one. At least one school declined a student printer to avoid promoting poor research habits and stacks of uncollected printing.

39. Joyce Manna Janto, *Law School Printing Survey* (last modified June 5, 2000) <http://law.richmond.edu/general/printsurvey.htm>.

40. Katherine S. Mangan, *In Revamped Library Schools, Information Trumps Books*, CHRON. of HIGHER EDUC., April 7, 2000, at A43 (reporting that information is so valued that graduates from library schools are being recruited to Internet companies for starting salaries as high as $90,000).

41. *See, e.g., A Firm-by-Firm Sampling of Billing Rates Nationwide*, NAT'L L.J., Dec. 27, 1999, at B12.

42. Douglas J. Ernst, *Academic Libraries, Fee-Based Information Services, and the Business Community*, 32 RQ 393, 400 (1993).

43. *See* Carter & Pagel, *supra* note 10, at 255.

44. Ernst, *supra* note 42.

45. While 64% listed recouping expenses as a primary reason, 72% listed it as at least one reason for the document delivery fee. The reasons libraries gave for creating a document delivery service were to: recoup expenses-64% (16), limit usage-12% (3), supplement budget-12% (3), recoup expenses and limit usage-4% (1), recoup expenses, limit usage, and supplement budget-4% (1), and unknown-4% (1).

46. SNYDER & DAVENPORT, *supra* note 13. Libraries indicate that the following tools were used to create and set prices for a document delivery service: market research-32% (8), cost calculations-16% (4), market research and cost calculations-16% (4), cost plus to limit usage-4%(1). The fee was already set at one institution (4%) while 20% (5) did not know how it was set and 8% (2) believed it was arbitrary.

47. Australian libraries have similar fees, with the University of Melbourne charging in Australian dollars $20 per mailed item, with a $2 per page charge. Fees for a two-hour fax are $30 per item with a $3 per page charge. A request faxed within four hours costs $25 with a $2.50 per page charge. The first 10 pages are always free from per page charges.

48. For updated information, see *Copyright Clearance Center* (visited May 31, 2000) <http://www.copyright.com/>.

49. For updated information, see *iCopyright.com* (visited May 31 2000) < http://www.icopyright.com/>; *see also* Paula J. Hane, *IT Interview: iCopyright CEO Discusses a New Model for Rights and Permissions*, INFO. TODAY, Nov. 1999, at 1.

50. *See supra* note 33 and accompanying text.

51. Although not included in the compilation, the University of Melbourne charges $95 (Aus.) an hour or a flat fee for certain reference services.

52. The annual fees at Pace for unaffiliated members are: $100 for law school alumni; $150 for individuals with no library access; $600 for access, document delivery, and borrowing privileges; or $1800 for corporations.

53. The reasons libraries gave for charging borrowers fees were to: recoup expenses-46% (6), supplement the budget-23% (3), supplement the budget and limit usage-15% (2), limit usage-8% (1), insure book return-8% (1), and unknown-8% (1).

54. The University of Melbourne charges $110 (Aus.) for an annual membership for borrowing privileges.

55. Libraries indicate that the following tools were used to set borrowers fees: cost calculations-23% (3), guessing-15% (2), market research-8% (1). At 53% (7) of the libraries the reason was unknown and at 8% (1) it was believed to be arbitrary.

56. Carter & Pagel, *supra* note 10, at 246.

57. *Id.* at 248.

58. *Id.* at 252.

59. *See id.* at 247. Student evaluations indicated that before access fees were implemented at Golden Gate University Law Library law students were unhappy due to overcrowding.

60. Golden Gate had an initial problem convincing the library staff to charge the established access fees. *See* Carter & Pagel, *supra* note 10, at 264.

61. *Id.*

62. 44 U.S.C. § 1911 (1994); GOVERNMENT PRINTING OFFICE, FEDERAL DEPOSITORY LIBRARY MANUAL 170 (1993) [hereinafter GOVERNMENT PRINTING OFFICE 1]; GOVERNMENT PRINTING OFFICE, FEDERAL DEPOSITORY LIBRARY MANUAL: SUPPLEMENT 2: GUIDELINES FOR THE FEDERAL DEPOSITORY LIBRARY 1 (1996).

63. *See* Carter & Pagel, *supra* note 10, at 254.

64. GOVERNMENT PRINTING OFFICE 1, *supra* note 62, at 112.

65. Daniel Blazek, *Private Academe and Public Depositories: Access and Promotion*, 24 J. GOV. INFO. 285, 306 (1997).

66. *See* Carter & Pagel, *supra* note 10.

67. Donald E. Riggs, *Editorial: A Closer Look at User Services*, 61 C. & RES. LIBR. 188, 189 (2000).

68. *See supra* notes 3 and 4 and accompanying text.

APPENDIX A

PRICE FEES SURVEY

1. Is the law library part of a publicly funded law school? Public _____ Private ___
2. What does your library charge per **photocopy**? _____
   What is the primary purpose behind the photocopy charges?
   Recoup expenses _____ Supplement library budget _____
   Limit usage _____ Other _____
3. Does your library charge for **computer printouts**? Yes _____ No _____
   If no, please skip ahead to question 8.
4. What does your library charge per computer printout? (Please indicate if the school gives students a set number of printouts for free.) _____
5. What is the primary purpose behind the computer printout charges?
   Recoup expenses _____ Supplement library budget _____
   Limit usage _____ Other _____
6. Does your library provide free printing on a Lexis stand–alone printer?
   Yes _____ No _____
7. Does your library provide free printing on a Westlaw stand–alone printer?
   Yes _____ No _____
8. Does your library provide a **for-fee document delivery service**?
   Yes _____ No _____
   If no, please skip ahead to question #14.
9. If so, how much do you charge for the document delivery service? Please explain if there is a base fee for the service and/or a per page fee.
10. If so, which department fills the document delivery request?
    Circulation _____ Reference _____ Special document delivery _____
    Other _____
11. If you do have a for-fee document delivery service, do you negotiate the charges before the service or after the service?
    Before _____ After _____
12. How did you determine the price to charge for the document delivery service? Market survey, cost calculations, or other. Please describe.
13. What is the primary purpose behind this charge?
    Recoup expenses _____ Supplement library budget ____ Limit usage _____
    Other _____
14. Do you have a **for-fee reference service**? Yes _____ No _____
    If no, please skip ahead to question #19.
15. If so, what do you charge for the reference service? Please explain if there is a flat fee for certain services and/or a per hour charge.
16. If you do charge for reference services do you negotiate the charges before the service, or after? Before_____ After _____
17. How did you determine the price to charge for the reference services? Market survey, cost calculations, or other. Please describe.
18. What is the primary purpose behind this charge?
    Recoup expenses ____ Supplement library budget _____ Limit usage _____
    Other _____
19. Does your **law school** charge students a **fee for library services**?
    Yes _____ No _____
    If no, please skip ahead to question #24.
20. If so, how much is the library fee? _____
21. If so, how was this fee calculated? Market survey, cost calculations, or other.
22. Are there any restrictions to the usage of this fee? _____
23. What is the primary purpose behind this charge?
    Recoup expenses _____ Supplement library budget _____
    Limit usage _____ Other_____

APPENDIX A (continued)

24. Does your parent university charge students a **fee for library services**?
Yes _____ No _____
If no, please skip ahead to question #30.
25. If so, how much is the library fee? _____
26. If so, how was this fee calculated? Market survey, cost calculations, or other.
_____.
27. How much of this university fee goes to the law library? _____
28. Are there any restrictions to the usage of this fee? _____
29. What is the primary purpose behind this charge?
Recoup expenses _____ Supplement library budget _____
Limit usage _____ Other _____
30. Does your **law school** charge a **computer fee**? Yes _____ No _____
If no, please skip ahead to question #35.
31. If so, how much is the computer fee? _____
32. If so, how was this fee calculated? Market survey, cost calculations, or other.
_____
33. Are there any restrictions on how the fee can be used? _____
34. What is the primary purpose behind this charge?
Recoup expenses _____ Supplement library budget _____
Limit usage _____ Other _____
35. Does your **parent university** charge a **computer fee**? Yes _____ No _____
If no, please skip ahead to question #41.
36. If so, how much is the university computer fee? _____
37. If so, how much of the university computer fee goes to the law library? _____
38. Are there any restrictions to the usage of this fee? _____
39. How was the fee calculated? Market survey, cost calculations, or other. Please
describe.
40. What is the primary purpose behind this charge?
Recoup expenses _____ Supplement library budget _____ Limit usage _____
Other _____
41. Is there an **unaffiliated borrowers' fee to borrow materials**?
Yes _____ No _____
If no, please skip ahead to question #45.
42. If so, how much is the fee? Please explain if the fee is a refundable deposit or
a charge for the service.
43. If so, how was the fee calculated? Market survey, cost calculations, or other.
Please describe.
44. What is the primary purpose behind this charge?
Recoup expenses _____ Supplement library budget _____
Limit usage _____ Other _____
45. Is there a **charge for unaffiliated borrowers to use the library collection**
(besides the government depository collection)? Yes ___ No ___
If no, please skip the next three questions.
46. If so, how much is the charge and how often is it charged? _____
47. If so, how was it calculated? Market survey, cost calculations, or other. Please
describe.
48. What is the primary purpose behind this charge?
Recoup expenses _____ Supplement library budget _____
Limit usage _____ Other_____

APPENDIX B
Law Schools Included in the Study

American University
Boston College
Boston University
California Western
Cleveland Marshall
Drake University
Florida State University
Georgia State University
Golden Gate University
Harvard University
Hofstra University
Lewis and Clark
Louisiana State University
Marquette University
Mercer University
Michigan State University
Mississippi College
New York University
North Carolina Central University
Northwestern University
Nova Southeastern University
Pace University
Roger Williams University
San Joaquin College of Law
Santa Clara University
Southern Illinois University
Southern Methodist University
St. John's University
St. Mary's University

St. Thomas University
Stetson University
Thomas Jefferson School of Law
Touro College
University of California–Boalt Hall
University of California–Hastings
University of Chicago
University of Connecticut
University of Florida
University of Georgia
University of Hawaii
University of Idaho
University of LaVerne
University of Louisville
University of Michigan
University of Mississippi
University of Oklahoma
University of Richmond
University of San Diego
University of Texas
University of the District of Columbia
University of Washington
University of Wisconsin
Valparaiso University
Washburn University
Washington and Lee University
Western New England College
Widener University
Yale Law School

Staffing the Reference Desk:
Improving Service Through Cross-Training
and Other Programs

Margaret McDermott

SUMMARY. Reference librarians use various methods to deal with the demands of staffing the reference desk. As online catalogs become the norm, the lines between technical services and public services become

Margaret McDermott is Head of Public Services at St. Louis University Law Library, St. Louis, MO 63108 (E-mail: mcdermmh@slu.edu).

[Haworth co-indexing entry note]: "Staffing the Reference Desk: Improving Service Through Cross-Training and Other Programs." McDermott, Margaret. Co-published simultaneously in *Legal Reference Services Quarterly* (The Haworth Information Press, an imprint of The Haworth Press, Inc.) Vol. 19, No. 1/2, 2001, pp. 207-219; and: *Emerging Solutions in Reference Services: Implications for Libraries in the New Millennium* (ed: John D. Edwards) The Haworth Information Press, an imprint of The Haworth Press, Inc., 2001, pp. 207-219. Single or multiple copies of this article are available for a fee from The Haworth Document Delivery Service [1-800-342-9678, 9:00 a.m. - 5:00 p.m. (EST). E-mail address: getinfo@haworthpressinc.com].

blurred and personnel serve dual roles. Cross-training provides librarians with a better understanding of the entire research process and helps expand reference coverage. Some libraries use support staff as the initial patron contact to relieve reference librarians from answering routine and directional questions. A library must determine if the benefits of reference training for technical service librarians and support staff are worth the time required. With the advent of remote reference service, traditional ideas of reference must be reevaluated as libraries consider whether the conventional reference desk could go the way of the card catalog. *[Article copies available for a fee from The Haworth Document Delivery Service: 1-800-342-9678. E-mail address: <getinfo@haworthpressinc. com> Website: <http://www.HaworthPress.com> © 2001 by The Haworth Press, Inc. All rights reserved.]*

I. INTRODUCTION

The convergence of computer labs and public service areas increasingly requires libraries to reassess user needs and their organizational structure to better serve the patron. The traditional model is a highly visible service point or reference desk which handles everything from directional questions to highly complex research requests. As technology and user needs change, alternatives are needed to the traditional model of the reference desk being all things to all people.[1]

One response to the increased demands on the reference desk is tiered service. In this model directional and basic informational questions are fielded at an information desk near the circulation area and more difficult inquires are referred to a reference desk or reference office.

The demands presented by the growth of the digital library result in reference service via e-mail and computerized training programs that require little or no face-to-face contact.[2] Related to this response are web page links that enable the user to access electronic resources without having to come to the library. Some librarians anticipate that "many of the traditional reference inquiries will be handled by improved interfaces and help systems that librarians will pay a primary role in developing."[3]

All of these models require answering the same questions. Where should the reference service point be? What staffing configuration should be used? What services and activities should be given priority? Some librarians believe that the reference desk may be replaced by the combination of an information desk and an office consultation with a professional librarian who works away from a hectic reference desk. An office consultation often is more conducive to one-on-one contact and provides more time for the librarian to develop user aids and teaching materials.

II. STAFFING A REFERENCE SERVICE POINT

A. The Reference Desk: To Have or Not to Have–
That Is the Question

Reassessing reference service in the light of the electronic age was the topic of a Professional Development listserv sponsored by the American Association of Law Libraries in fall 1999.[4] Much of the discussion concerned whether a reference desk was necessary, and if a librarian's time could be spent more productively on other tasks. Some listserv participants believed that a large academic library with a diverse clientele should have personnel staffing the desk. Mary Whisner preferred having questions go to a reference office rather than to "whatever reference librarian the patron hunts down."[5] The advantages she pointed out were uninterrupted time to work on projects and better distribution of the workload.[6] A participant from a library that began reference desk service only five years earlier noted that the five reference librarians who staff the desk would never go back to being without one.[7]

Several threads evolved during the listserv discussion.[8] The model of no reference desk is more prominent in the law firm setting where attorneys are more likely to know who to contact for a particular service. Patrons in the academic setting are undergraduates, local attorneys, and pro se patrons who may not ask for a librarian unless they see a reference desk.

A second thread was the need to distinguish between directional or simple informational questions and more involved research questions. Libraries that eliminated the reference desk noted a sharp increase in the number of patrons asking reference questions at the circulation desk, even though a reference librarian was in a visible office with a reference sign in the window. Patrons probably were reluctant to disturb someone working in an office and therefore hesitated to enter unless specifically directed.

All participants agreed on the need to analyze their clientele to determine who is using the reference desk. This analysis helps determine if the library's primary clientele is being served, or if the majority of reference traffic consists of secondary clientele. A reassessment also can assist in scheduling adequate reference coverage during peak periods.

B. Technical Service Professionals as Reference Librarians

Technology is a major catalyst in uniting public and technical services with some libraries combining these departments into a new Access Services unit. Librarians involved in cataloging and acquisitions often have served at the reference desk. With their expertise in online catalog design and use, however, they are now even more valuable to public services. Integrated library systems and online catalogs place technical service staff in a unique position to serve library patrons.

The blurring of divisional lines between technical and public services was observed a decade ago by Sara Evans Davenport.[9] She described a technical services staff becoming involved in reference activities, and a reference staff increasing their understanding of technical services operations. This cross-training is even more essential today.

Using technical services librarians at the reference desk benefits the staff member and library patrons. The technical services librarian can provide online catalog training for public services staff as well as patrons. In turn they are able to obtain a different perspective on how the online catalog and collection are being used. Good communication between the two departments and regular training are needed to succeed. At St. Louis University Law Library, several technical service librarians took the legal research and writing class and attended in-house lectures on legal resources and research. As a result of that training they welcome the opportunity to provide reference assistance.

A major concern in using technical service librarians at the reference desk is coverage of their other responsibilities. For example, they may wonder how they can keep up with cataloging if they are at the reference desk. Adequate technology, planning and organization can overcome these worries. Equally as important is support from the library administration and a culture which fosters professional development. The model in which librarians are on-call at their desks during specific hours eliminates much of the tension technical service librarians may feel from adding some reference duties.

C. Using Reference Assistants at the Reference Desk

The two major problems in staffing reference desks are the uneven workload and the number of the questions that do not require a professional librarian.[10] Two separate studies found that librarians at the reference desk spend a great deal of their time not engaged in reference service, and that nearly three-quarters of the questions do not require a professional librarian.[11]

Most law librarians recognize that a significant number of reference questions could be handled by well-trained paraprofessionals. Some libraries address this problem by directing routine questions to a paraprofessional while more difficult requests are referred to a librarian. Even this model presents problems when questions which should be handled by librarians are not referred to the professional staff. Referrals may not occur for various reasons, such as when the reference assistant is reluctant to bother the librarian or fails to realize a referral is needed. At other times the librarian may just appear too busy.

With careful training and supervision support staff can handle most basic questions concerning holdings and use of materials. However, adequate monitoring of reference assistants may be difficult when the information/reference service point is not near the reference librarians. When librarians are nearby, the reference assistants are under less pressure to perform and are more likely to refer questions they are not equipped to handle. A readily accessible librarian also can easily show the staff member how a seemingly simple question may be complicated.

As librarians redefine reference service in the digital age they may become more appreciative of the role paraprofessionals can fill and recognize that training them to assist in reference is well worth the effort. Involving paraprofessionals not only provides much needed assistance, but it also provides them with greater job satisfaction.

D. Using Part-Time Professional Librarians

A good source for expanded reference coverage is the part-time librarian. They may be lawyer-librarians who are practicing law but want to remain in librarianship, librarians with young children who are able to cover a night or weekend afternoon, or librarians who may or may not have other jobs. Part-time librarians benefit from maintaining or sharpening their reference skills while full-time librarians are free to work on other responsibilities away from the reference desk.

One challenge with part-time librarians is ensuring that they feel part of the team. If they work evenings or weekends they may have very little contact with the rest of the staff. Maintaining connections with someone who does not work weekday hours can be achieved through e-mail, in-house distribution lists, and routing the minutes of staff meetings. Part-time staff should be encouraged to take advantage of all training sessions and workshops the library provides, and be included either electronically or in person in all library instruction activities. Their insights into the needs of evening students and adjunct faculty other staff may never see can be especially valuable. They also can answer reference questions submitted by e-mail and assist in faculty research projects during slower times at the reference desk.

E. Using Student Assistants at the Reference Desk

Libraries often use law students to handle directional and ready reference questions. Although some libraries may be reluctant to have a law student as the first point of contact or even as a reference backup, others have great success. The law student who is closely monitored and well-trained can be extremely helpful in filtering and fielding questions, particularly during peak periods when backup is essential.

Training is essential to ensure that a law student knows the expectations for reference work. If law students understand that improved research skills will be a benefit of the position, they may appreciate having the experience on their resume and keep the job throughout law school. A conscientious law student who is well-trained and closely monitored can be an especially valuable employee. Training and supervision can address the occasional problems, such as the overconfident student who fails to refer appropriate questions to the librarian.

F. Reference Hours

Reference services at most law school libraries must comply with the rules of the American Bar Association and the Association of American Law Schools. AALS Regulation 8.2 requires that "A member school shall have at least one professional librarian in attendance at all times when there is substantial use of the library."[12] ABA Standard 605 states, "A law library shall provide the appropriate range and depth of reference, bibliographic, and other services to meet the needs of the law school's teaching, research, and service programs."[13] The interpretation for Standard 605 requires "adequate reference services."[14] Each library should analyze reference coverage to ensure that a librarian is available when there is substantial use and that adequate reference services are provided.

Libraries normally attempt to identify their primary clientele and determine when they seek reference assistance.[15] Most libraries track the number of questions by hour, day of the week, and category of question, including: telephone requests for information on holdings, simple telephone requests (ready reference), moderately difficult reference requests (five to ten minutes), difficult telephone requests (ten minutes or more), simple in-person requests (directional or ready reference), moderately difficult in-person requests (five to ten minutes), difficult in-person requests (ten minutes or more).[16]

Researchers using a similar breakdown at Winona State University discovered the main times of heavy usage were not always the 1 to 3 p.m. weekday periods discussed in the literature.[17] Although greater reference usage occurred during early afternoons on Monday through Wednesday, higher use also occurred on Tuesday night and Sunday afternoon. With this data the library determined when the reference desk should be double-staffed.

Further analysis on difficulty of the questions helped in deciding when reference could be staffed by paraprofessionals with more difficult questions being referred to an on-call reference librarian. This flexibility provided the on-call reference librarian with more privacy and time to work on other projects.[18] Combining hourly use statistics with patron type (law student, undergraduate/graduate, pro se, attorney) should help determine reference desk patterns so schedules can better meet patron needs.

III. THE PHYSICAL LAYOUT AND REFERENCE SERVICE

A highly visible service area in close proximity to the circulation desk is the key requirement in the traditional reference desk model. This arrangement makes it easier for circulation personnel to direct questions to the reference staff. Changes to this model have resulted in some libraries eliminating the reference desk in favor of on-call reference service or a research consultation service.[19] Under each model, however, reference staff must be visible and accessible, preferably within sight of the circulation area. Patrons may become impatient if the librarian on-call must be paged from a remote office on another floor of the library.

Unfortunately, the physical layout in some libraries makes physical proximity impossible. Older libraries, such as St. Louis University Law Library, may be housed in the original building and several additions. Because space for reference offices near the circulation area is not available, on-call librarians must come from remote locations to provide reference service.

Some larger academic law libraries depend on other library units to provide reference assistance in specialized areas. Foreign and international reference service may be located by those materials; government documents personnel may be near that collection. Easy communication between the two service areas and good directional signs are essential.

IV. TRAINING AIDS

Today's students have different library needs than past generations.[20] They have grown up in a media age and want information packaged in a concise, laser-printed format they can take with them to view at their convenience.[21] These preferences must be considered in designing pathfinders, bibliographies, and other library materials. Handouts for this audience should be limited in length and avoid long narrative descriptions.[22]

Students have an affinity for technology and need instruction at their convenience. A number of libraries, such as the University of Missouri in St. Louis, have individual online instructional programs describing how to search bibliographic and full-text databases.[23] These interactive programs may be accessed from remote locations or used in-group training sessions. A librarian can refer users to these online training programs and follow-up when the program is completed. Users receive a score indicating how well they formulated queries and searched the database while the librarian reviews the same results.

Web-based information poses some challenges, especially for searchers who are not trained in evaluating Internet sources.[24] Users may be overconfident of their abilities to formulate queries and perform effective web searches. This overconfidence may keep users from coming to the library and seeking guidance from reference librarians. A well-designed website with links to research materials can advertise the library's expertise in electronic research and encourage the researcher to visit the library for assistance in handling more difficult questions.[25]

Research links are often the most heavily used web resource a library provides.[26] The University of Alabama Law Library discovered that combining the use of pathfinders, guides, and online tutorials not only portrays the librarian as Internet savvy, but also improves the transmission of traditional reference information.[27] Web resources also may help free librarians for classroom instruction, training seminars, and informal one-on-one consultation.[28]

V. EVALUATING REFERENCE SERVICES

Evaluation of reference service may produce more scholarship than any other facet of librarianship.[29] Unfortunately, the literature provides limited guidance in assessing the overall quality of reference. Evaluating individual performance seems to receive more attention than whether the reference staff's work is satisfying the library's primary clientele.

A common technique for soliciting patron input is a user satisfaction survey. Many libraries post their surveys on the Web so an Internet search can provide examples that can be adapted to a library's needs.[30] One of the first steps in constructing the evaluation form is establishing general categories for feedback and the areas questions should address. Some of the categories and questions suggested by F.W. Lancaster[31] include:

Patron Motivation Factors

- Is the patron aware the library provides this service?
- Is the library perceived as an appropriate and convenient resource?
- Has the patron had good or bad experiences with the library?

- Is the library open at the time the answer is needed?

Collection Factors

- Does the library own sources that contain the answers to the patron's questions?
- How accessible are these sources?

Those categories could be expanded to include additional questions related to the technology patrons often use:

- Does the patron look to the reference staff for assistance in using electronic sources and formulating research queries?
- Is the patron able to access electronic sources easily and effectively from remote locations?
- If the patron encounters difficulty, is assistance easily accessible by phone or e-mail?

Patron feedback is essential to determine if reference services are fulfilling patrons' needs. User surveys should be easy to complete, perhaps with most questions requiring only that boxes be checked, and widely distributed. Web forms can be used to reach patrons who frequent the library's website. The library may want to encourage patron input throughout the year, even if the means is as basic as a suggestion box. In addition to user satisfaction surveys, staff can gain input about reference services from meetings of the student bar association or other forums, such as library and faculty committee meetings.

VI. REFERENCE STAFFING GUIDELINES

An evaluation of current reference services will help tailor reference staffing to meet the needs of the library and the patron. The following suggestions should be considered in conducting a review of staffing needs.

1. Understand the expectations of the library's primary clientele.
2. Know when the primary users are most likely to require assistance.
3. Explore methods other than the standard reference desk to reach library patrons. Service can be provided through formal and in-

formal classes, electronic and traditional research guides, and e-mail reference service.

4. Evaluate whether the conventional reference desk or the reference office model best serves the library.

5. When using an on call or reference office model ensure that paraprofessionals are able to quickly and easily locate the librarian on duty.

6. Extensively train all paraprofessional staff who will handle directional and ready reference questions.

7. Determine if technical service librarians may be effectively utilized at the reference service point.

8. If part-time professional librarians provide reference assistance, an effective communication exchange must be provided.

9. Analyze the positives and negatives of the physical facility from the reference perspective before determining which service model will be most effective.

10. Evaluate library signs and handouts to determine if they could be improved to reduce directional questions at the reference service area.

VII. CONCLUSION

Reference librarians have assumed a number of additional duties over the past few years. While reference service still consists of providing personal assistance, more emphasis is being placed on classroom teaching and preparing guides which direct users to needed information regardless of whether they are at the reference desk or searching the Internet from home. As websites with numerous research links become the predominant reference tools for patrons and staff, librarians may need to reassess how their time is utilized to ensure patron needs are being met and professional skills are being effectively utilized.

Suggestions for scheduling optimal reference coverage and ensuring appropriate utilization of the librarian's expertise include: cross-training technical services personnel in reference, hiring reference assistants to handle directional and less difficult questions, recruiting part-time librarians to cover some evenings and weekends, and training law students to assist at the reference desk.

Each library should assess the level of satisfaction with current services and consider how they could be improved. Keeping detailed reference statistics can help in determining what coverage may be needed. A user satisfaction survey can provide direction for expanding or adjusting services. Changing clientele and technology require librarians to adapt to the increased expectations for reference assistance, even if that service may not be provided at a traditional reference desk.

NOTES

1. William L. Whitson, *Differentiated Service: A New Reference Model*, 21 J. ACAD. LIBR. 104 (1995).

2. Eileen G. Abels, *The E-mail Reference Interview*, 35 RQ 345 (1996). For more information on e-mail reference, see the article in this volume by Beth Smith, *Enhancing Reference Services Through Technology*.

3. Kerry A. Brandt et al., *Reflections on Reference Services*, 47 J. AM. SOC'y FOR INFO. SCI. 212 (1996).

4. *See* Washburn Univ. Sch. of Law, WashLaw Web, *Mail Thread Index: Reassessing Reference* (last modified Sept. 29, 1999) <http://www.washlaw.edu/pro_dev/threads.html>.

5. Mary Whisner, *RE: Reassessing Ref–The Desk!* (last modified Sept. 27, 1999) <http://www.washlaw.edu/pro_dev/msg00019.html>.

6. *Id.*

7. Sally Curtis Askew, *Reference Desk* (last modified Sept. 27, 1999) <http://www.washlaw.edu/pro_dev/msg00007.html>.

8. *See supra* note 4.

9. Sara Evans Davenport, *The Blurring of Divisional Lines Between Technical and Public Services: An Emphasis on Access*, in ACCESS SERVICES: THE CONVERGENCE OF REFERENCE AND TECHNICAL SERVICES 47 (Gillian M. McCombs ed., 1991).

10. Steve Coffman & Matthew L. Saxton, *Staffing the Reference Desk in the Largely-Digital Library*, 66 REFERENCE LIBR. 141 (1999).

11. Edward Jestes & David Laird, *A Time Study of General Reference Work in a University Library*, 2 RES. IN LIBR. 9 (1968) (conducted at the University of California-Davis); Jeffrey W. St. Clair & Rao Aluri, *Staffing the Reference Desk: Professional or Nonprofessionals*, 3 J. ACAD. LIBR. 149 (1977). For a discussion of how support personnel can assist with reference, see Joan Pedzich, *Paraprofessionals at the Reference Desk: Training and Documentation*, 18(2) LEGAL REFERENCE SERVICES Q. 91 (2000).

12. Association of Amer. Law Sch., *Executive Committee Regulations: Chapter 8 Library* (visited June 20, 2000) <http://www.aals.org/chapter8.html>.

13. ABA, *Standards for Approval of Law Schools: Chapter 6 Library* (visited June 20, 2000) <http://www.abanet.org/legaled/standards/chapter6.html>.

14. *Id.*

15. Donald J. Dunn, *Service Strategies for Non-primary Patrons in Academic Law Libraries*, LEGAL REFERENCE SERVICES Q., Summer 1982, at 5.

16. Russell F. Dennison, *Usage-Based Staffing of the Reference Desk*, 39 REFERENCE & USER SERVICES Q. 158, 160 (1999).

17. *Id.*

18. *Id.* at 165.

19. Inga H. Barnello, *The Changing Face of Reference: A History of the Future*, in THE CHANGING FACE OF REFERENCE 3 (Lynne M. Stuart & Dena Holiman Hutto eds., 1996).

20. Catherine A. Lee, *The Changing Face of the College Student: The Impact of Generation X on Reference and Instructional Services*, in THE CHANGING FACE OF REFERENCE, *supra* note 19, at 107.

21. *Id.* at 114.

22. *Id.*

23. University of Missouri-St. Louis, *Library Instruction* (visited June 21, 2000) <http://www.umsl.edu/services/library/>.

24. Ann Scholz-Crane, *Evaluating the Future: A Preliminary Study of the Process of How Undergraduate Students Evaluate Web Sources*, 26 REFERENCE SERVICES REV. 53 (1998).

25. Creighton J. Miller, Jr., *RE: Reassessing Ref* (last modified Sept. 29, 1999) <http://washlaw.edu/pro_dev/msg00048.html>.

26. For a list of the most popular links from law school web pages, see Robert C. Vreeland, *Law Libraries in Hyperspace: A Citation Analysis of World Wide Web Sites*, 92 L. LIBR. J. 9, 23-25 (2000).

27. Miller, *supra* note 25.

28. For additional information on web resources, see the article in this volume by Robert Linz, *Making Electronic Resources Available to Patrons*.

29. A search of the index *Library Literature* from 1984 to the present on June 22, 2000 retrieved 518 citations to articles and books under the subject Reference Services' Evaluation.

30. *See, e.g.*, Kansas State University Libraries, *KSU Libraries User Satisfaction Survey* (visited June 22, 2000) <http://www.libksu.edu/>. An Internet search using terms such as library, user, and satisfaction retrieve a number of websites with library survey information.

31. F.W. Lancaster, *Factors Influencing the Effectiveness of Question-Answering Services in Libraries*, in EVALUATION OF REFERENCE SERVICES 95 (Bill Katz & Ruth A. Fraley eds., 1984).

Index

Kreimer v. *Bureau of Police*, 28

Laptop computers, library policies for
    use of, 150,155
Laser printing fees. *See* Printing fees
Law, changes in, effect on legal
    reference librarianship, 43-44
Law clerks, library instruction for, 87
Law firm partners, reference
    interviews with, 78
Law firms, legal instruction in, 86-87
law libdir-1 (electronic mailing list),
    182-183
law-lib (electronic mailing list), 52,
    135,182-183
Law Library of Louisiana, 149
Law Library Resource Xchange,
    Research Guide of, 143
Law practice, regulation of, 167
Laws, updating of, 82-83
Law students
    legal research instruction for, 78-79
    reference interviews with, 77-78
Lay legal practitioners, legal services
    provided by, 175
Legal assistance programs, 171,172,
    173-174
Legal List, The (Botluck), 59-60
Legal practice, changes in, effect on
    legal reference librarianship,
    43-44
Legal research information brochures,
    171
Legal research instruction, during
    reference interview, 75-98
    as basic instruction, 84
    as computer-assisted legal research,
      88-89,93-94
    determination of level and type of
      instruction needed, 81-85
    determination of patrons'
      informational needs, 77-80
    determination of patrons'
      receptiveness to instruction,
      80-81

directional responses in, 84-85,88
in electronic searching, 93
in fact finding, 82,91
front-end systems in, 89-90,91-92
guidelines for, 94-95
impact of technology on, 93-94
Internet research and writing web
    courses and resources in, 90,
    98
intranet use in, 86-87
in law firms, 86-87
as one-on-one instruction, 86,92
"one-time" type of, 83-84
online tutorials in, 87
in primary legal resource updating, 92
research guides and handouts in,
    87,88
in subject searching, 91-92
techniques and tools for, 85-93
techniques for specific requests in,
    90-93
in upper-division courses, 87-88
Legal research services,
    computer-assisted, 8,9
Legal system, changes in, effect on
    legal reference librarianship,
    43-44
LegalTrac, 101,143,144
Lewis and Clark College Library
    borrowing privileges fees of, 195
    document delivery fees of, 193
LEXIS, 9,44,143,144,182,187-188
    Intranet toolkit of, 127
    library instruction in use of, 105,
      108
    vendor-provided instruction in use
      of, 85-86
Lexpert, 89
Liability, for patrons' safety, 28-29
Librarians. *See also* Reference
    librarians
    information provider role of,
      167-170
    as "library police," 148
    stereotypes of, 148
    teaching role of, 9